BURN
THE
HAYSTACK

BURN THE HAYSTACK

Decode Dating, Torch the Duds, and Make Room for Men Who Matter

Jennie Young, PhD

WM
WILLIAM MORROW
An Imprint of HarperCollins*Publishers*

Burned Haystack Dating Method® is a registered trademark of Jennifer Jill Young. Used by permission.

The introduction and chapter 1 include some material previously published on *HuffPost*.

Chapter 2 includes some material previously published on *Medium*.

Without limiting the exclusive rights of any author, contributor or the publisher of this publication, any unauthorized use of this publication to train generative artificial intelligence (AI) technologies is expressly prohibited. HarperCollins also exercise their rights under Article 4(3) of the Digital Single Market Directive 2019/790 and expressly reserve this publication from the text and data mining exception.

BURN THE HAYSTACK. Copyright © 2026 by Jennie Young. All rights reserved. Printed in the United States of America. No part of this book may be used or reproduced in any manner whatsoever without written permission except in the case of brief quotations embodied in critical articles and reviews. For information, address HarperCollins Publishers, 195 Broadway, New York, NY 10007. In Europe, HarperCollins Publishers, Macken House, 39/40 Mayor Street Upper, Dublin 1, D01 C9W8, Ireland.

HarperCollins books may be purchased for educational, business, or sales promotional use. For information, please email the Special Markets Department at SPsales@harpercollins.com.

hc.com

FIRST EDITION

Designed by Nancy Singer

Needle: ©OMIA/stock.adobe.com; Shrug emoji: ©Cali6ro/stock.adobe.com; Fire icon: ©Comauthor/stock.adobe.com; Fire border: ©Aletheia Shade/stock.adobe.com; Messaging pyramid: ©Nancy Singer

Library of Congress Cataloging-in-Publication Data has been applied for.

ISBN 978-0-06-344757-8

26 27 28 29 30 LBC 6 5 4 3 2

For Gray and Mom and Dad. And Jolene, of course.

IMPORTANT DISCLAIMERS

1. No hay was harmed in the making of this book.
2. Actually, hay was harmed, but only as a result of its own bad decisions.
3. Grammar was *badly* harmed, but only by hay (toxic men). We have left the errors intact, which was harmful to both author and editors but necessary to faithful transcription.
4. All hays' names have been changed.
5. Women's real names are used with permission and pseudonyms are used upon request.

CONTENTS

INTRODUCTION
The Burned Haystack Origin Story (or, "Single Woman Desperately Googles Things Late at Night")   xi

1
SO MANY BADASS WOMEN
The Feminist Dating Revolution Begins . . .   1

2
SMILING DEVILS AND BITCHY PROFILES
The Early Seeds of Burned Haystack   18

3
COURSE SYLLABUS
Feminism and Rhetorical Theory in Contemporary Dating Culture
(AKA Critical Discourse Analysis Is Sexy)   32

4
THE BURNED HAYSTACK METHOD RULES   58
Frequently Asked Questions   77

5
RED-FLAG RHETORICAL PATTERNS
Run!   90

CONTENTS

6
TOXIC DATING COACHES
How to Spot Them and When to Block Them 160

7
MORE TACTICS AND TRICKS TO GAME THE APPS
(So They Can't Game You!) 178

8
DATING APP PROFILES THAT LED TO NEEDLES
What Made Them Work? 206

9
BURNED HAYSTACK BEYOND THE APPS
Date-Me Docs, Speed Dating, and Meeting in the Wild (AKA "Haystack Hacks") 239

10
BURNED HAYSTACK BEYOND DATING
Rhetoric in Real Life 268

About the Success Stories 283

A Love Letter from Me 285

Acknowledgments 287

APPENDIX
The Toxic Rhetorical Patterns 291

HAYSTACK BOOKSTACK
Recommendations for Further Reading 293

Index 295

INTRODUCTION

THE BURNED HAYSTACK ORIGIN STORY

(or, "Single Woman Desperately Googles Things Late at Night")

Just before I sat down to write the introduction to this book, I scrolled through *The New York Times* 100 Notable Books of 2024 and compiled my "to read" collection for the holiday semester break. As I browsed titles, I sighed internally and thought, *My book will never make this list because it's only about women and dating.*

And then I sucked a big gulp of oxygen and thought, *Oh, internalized misogyny.* (We'll talk more about this later; we'll specifically talk about how detrimental it is in the dating arena.)

To be fair, the *Times* had at that point already featured Burned Haystack in "The Sunday Read" episode of *The Daily* podcast and dedicated a full eleven paragraphs to it in the print and online editions of the yearly "Modern Love" issue of *The New York Times Magazine*, and that happened before a book deal was even in the works. The dating method had also been covered in *Newsweek, Business Insider, Rolling Stone, HuffPost, The Independent, The Wall Street Journal,* and a whole bunch of other places.

So why was I assuming failure, that this book wouldn't be taken seriously? I'm sure it's because of the massive amount of sociocultural messaging that tells us "women's issues"—particularly women's issues related to romantic relationships—are fluffy, inconsequential things unworthy of serious public consideration, the stuff of old-school women's magazines and current-day Instagram influencer feeds. Here's why this messaging is bullshit.

Every single element of society is predicated upon the conditions of women's romantic relationships. Romantic partnership is the initiating point of every couple, family, community, and government from the level of village to nation; this also means that every institution (educational, industrial, spiritual, medical, and financial) is also at some embryonic point derived from a woman's relationship. Romantic pairing is the foundational element of human life. This is partly straight-up evolution; the conditions in which humans are conceived and reared dictates their future viability or inadequacy as citizens, workers, leaders, teachers, parents, and friends. But we can even take that part out of it: successful long-term partnership outside the context of procreation is related to positive economic outcomes and better physical and mental health; loneliness and/or unhealthy partnership can result in poverty, poor health, abuse, violence, and death.

Viewed through this lens, it becomes more difficult to discount the quest for love as something trifling or "extra." Viewed through this lens, it seems clear that *everyone* should be invested in finding healthier, safer, and more effective ways to broker human partnership. That is exactly what Burned Haystack is designed to do, and I'm so glad you're holding this book, whether you're interested in trying it or just learning more about it for whatever reason. There's a lot about Burned Haystack online now, in platforms I have contributed to (Facebook, Instagram, TikTok, Substack) and in reputable publications featuring interviews and verified journalistic coverage of the method. There are also a lot of podcasts, interviews, and Reddit forums, not to mention "men's rights" groups, that are getting Burned Haystack extremely wrong, intentionally or unintentionally.

This book is now the official document. It contains the origin stories, the academic background and methodologies (presented in layperson's terms), the evolution of the revolution, the success stories, and all the tools you need to successfully employ the method. It's a handbook, but it's also a manifesto for a different way to approach not only the world of dating, but the world in general. I hope it will function as a manual and reference book, but also as a trusted place to go for reassurance, inspiration, and comfort, not to mention a lot of humor. Thank you for picking it up.

I want to start by sharing my Burned Haystack origin story.

MY STORY

When I first got on the dating apps, several years postdivorce and well into middle age, I was horrified. Night after night I grew more demoralized, flipping through my "matches" and seeing all the clichéd nonsense I hadn't really believed was real prior to experiencing it myself: fish pics and leering bathroom mirror selfies and married men who wanted to "ethically explore." Was this really all there was? I wanted to have an actual partner, not just to be someone's "partner in crime" from the back seat of his Harley so we could "keep it casual and see what happens."

Still, though: there had to be a *few* out there, right? There had to be a few decent, desirable, monogamous men who wanted the same things I did, and who wanted them with a woman in their own age group. I was convinced I was missing something about how to make these apps work in my favor. None of the advice I read online made any difference in helping me find decent dates, let alone a suitable partner. The few dates I did go on ranged from boring to annoying to bizarre. One guy showed up for our coffee date wearing swim trunks and a stained tank-style undershirt—the kind those of us who grew up in the '80s horrifyingly called a "wifebeater"—snugly tucked into the waistband of the trunks. I forced myself to stay for forty minutes, the entirety of which was spent listening to musings about his son's heroin addiction. Another man lectured me for ninety minutes straight about the merits of his pet corn snake and the band Tool.

I'd set up dating apps and then rage-quit them more times than I could remember, and the more women I talked to the more I realized how common this experience is. I called it the "dating app cycle of doom," and this is what it looks like: You decide you're going to give the dating apps a try, so you download a couple of them, and you spend a ton of time setting up a killer profile with thoughtfully curated photos and insightful bio text and engaging responses to prompts. And then maybe a week or a month or six months down the road, you feel so frustrated and demoralized and depressed that you shut down all your apps, swear off the mission forever, and decide you'd rather die alone. And then three months later you do it all over again. I decided there had to be a way out of this horrible vortex; there had to be a way to online date *and* live an enjoyable life simultaneously, regardless of what was happening on the apps.

Late one night a few weeks into one of my doom cycles, bleary-eyed from scrolling and swiping, I asked Google, "How do you find a needle in a haystack?" I was really just fooling around, but when I saw the answer, I got chills. The answer—the way you find an actual needle in an actual haystack—is to burn the haystack to the ground. What you'll be left with are the needles, because metal doesn't burn.

I knew immediately that this had to be the key. All this picking through pieces of hay to find one needle was too tedious and time-consuming. I understood that some people use Tinder almost like a sport or as a kind of video game, that they weren't always using it to find "the one," but I wasn't interested in that kind of sport or game; I wanted a real partner, and I didn't want to waste a lot of time looking for him. I decided that I needed to burn the whole haystack to the ground so that I could snap up a needle and be on my way.

I went back to the apps and started applying a few simple rules—and it changed everything. I got so strict about what and whom I was willing to engage with that nearly 100 percent of my effort was spent on men whose values and goals aligned with mine. It felt like I'd stumbled upon a cheat code or a magic spell: Had these stable and decent men been hiding in the apps all along? I was suddenly chatting with articulate men who were capable of interacting within the realm of conversational norms (if you're a woman who's spent any time on a dating app, you already know how rare this is); these newly unearthed men would ask me questions, and then discussion based upon my responses to those questions would ensue. I would ask them questions, and their responses were interesting and funny and refreshing. It was *normal.* It was a miracle.

Out of several promising options, I began seeing someone who turned out to be a needle, and we stayed together for a little over two years. It ultimately didn't work out, but he's still a friend, and I wouldn't trade the experience; he's still a clear "needle," just not mine.

But I still wanted a partner. When it felt like time for me to try again, I decided I was going to formalize my haystack-burning method and share it with others.

I'm a university professor, and I'd been joking with my students for years that someday I was going to start some kind of feminist revolution. This suddenly felt like "it"—my own (decidedly less lofty) version of the mantra to "Be the change you want to see in the world." Plus, my academic credentials had prepared me well for this project. I have a PhD in rhetoric and discourse studies with specialization in applied rhetoric and primary metaphor analysis (in other words, I could see through their bullshit). I had the metaphor now: the burning haystack. I just had to figure out how to translate the discipline of applied rhetoric into something everyone could understand and use. Applied rhetoric sounds like a fancy academic term, but it just refers to the fact that an academic knowledge of rhetoric, which is the study of language and persuasion, can be applied to everyday life. That's what I needed to teach people, and I needed to teach them exactly how.

It wasn't very hard. People have far more rhetorical skills and intuition than they give themselves credit for. When I teach undergraduate courses in rhetoric, I frequently begin by asking my students to tell me what they know about applied rhetoric and rhetorical analysis, and initially they stare silently like cattle. Then I ask if anyone is willing to share a text conversation in which they're arguing with someone (this generation was raised in the era of emotional sharing; someone is always willing). We never get past the first few exchanges before someone interjects "Wait, what did he mean by *that*?!" or "That's gaslighting!" and then I calmly say, "Okay, great. You're all already practicing a form of applied rhetoric. You're taking your innate and experiential knowledge and using it to analyze someone's words. That's what this whole class is going to be about."

I decided that I could "teach" this method online in the public sphere of social media by applying the same methods I use to teach my students at the university. Moreover, I have been personally and professionally committed to public scholarship and public intellectualism—purposely bringing the work of the academy beyond the academy's walls—for many years now; here was an opportunity to put my money where my mouth was.

And because I'm an academic who'd been a single parent for a decade by that time, I had no extra money to throw at this endeavor. I had no following and knew nothing about marketing or social media when I started Burned Haystack, nor did I have the financial resources to hire help or to promote posts. I knew that the only way I could circulate this idea was if I could offer content people found helpful and worthwhile enough that they started sharing it on their own. I decided to just see what would happen, and began by creating a Facebook group called the Burned Haystack Dating Method.

I embarked upon my mission with two foundational inspirations, one idealistic and one selfish. The idealistic reason, the public scholarship component, meant that the work must be accessible—intellectually, logistically, and financially—to everyone. In order to be intellectually accessible, it would have to be presented in ways that anyone could understand without any prior academic background in the relevant methodologies. To be logistically accessible, I had to place it where people already are and where it's quick and easy to take in new information, so social media was the obvious answer. And finally, for my work to be financially accessible it had to be free—totally free. There could be none of the bait-and-switch tactics used by so many self-proclaimed "dating coaches" who lure people in by offering a tidbit of clever advice and the promise of unlocking the real secrets if you just buy the PDF/pay the subscription/sign up for a few consultations/join the exclusive community, and so on. (I'm not saying no one could ever benefit from such things; I'm just saying that's not how I wanted to do it.)

The selfish reason I embarked on this mission was that I decided there was no way I could tolerate the epic disaster that is dating apps unless I justified it by turning it into an academic project. If I could make this thing do double duty—find me a partner *and* feed my scholarly interests—then maybe it would feel worth it. I even built a class around it (The Rhetoric of Dating and Intimacy), and teaching it has been one of the most rewarding experiences of my career.

At the beginning, I didn't think much beyond those two reasons; I just dove in. What happened next is where the story really begins.

1

SO MANY BADASS WOMEN

The Feminist Dating Revolution Begins...

To fully understand the ethos of Burned Haystack, you need to understand something about the women who built the community around the method. In the beginning—the *very* beginning—I can't honestly claim to have envisioned anything resembling what's happened. Intellectually, I was interested in the rhetorical possibilities of using critical discourse analysis (CDA), my academic specialty, to game the dating apps and find myself a partner. Sharing it with other women would help me justify the amount of time it was going to take to flesh out the method, recruit others to test and refine its rules, and see if it would work beyond me. I thought maybe I'd gather enough data to get a publication or two out of it, and that appealed as well, since part of my job is to produce scholarship. I was a complete novice at creating social media content, but like all single working moms, I am a professional multitasker.

Because I'm a middle-aged Midwestern woman, I decided I would use Facebook; that's what we do. I told a couple of colleagues that I was starting a social media project by building a private, women-only Facebook group, and they looked at me sideways, as if to indicate "I'm not sure you really know how social media works in 2023," which was 100 percent true. And I'm *glad* I didn't know, because in retrospect, building a private and safe space for women without the presence of men turned out to be exactly what we all needed.

Here's the truth I've learned. If you provide something actually useful to women, you don't have to know anything about marketing or advertising or finances or social media, because of this one crucial fact: Women help other women. It's something we're wired to do. So what happened was that, yes, the Facebook group was private, and no, I had no resources to promote it, but in the end none of that mattered because women began sharing it on their own. It went viral in the most authentic way possible. It went viral because women are generous and insightful and community-oriented and experts at drawing people together. It's why we're the matriarchs of families and the organizers of office birthday parties and the leaders of Girl Scout groups (and also because someone has to do these things, and one thing men are supercompetent at is weaponized incompetence, but we'll get to that later).

There have been many surprises since the inception of Burned Haystack, and one was that the method is apparently ageless. Initially, I focused only on the dating scene for women over forty, as this was my personal reality and my primary concern. It had also occurred to me that even though people are finally realizing that older women are on the rise everywhere from corporate America to Hollywood, nobody had recruited us yet to work on the disaster that is the dating apps. Gen X women were *made* for this disaster. We're a generation characterized by resourcefulness, self-sufficiency, and creativity. We're tech savvy but not tech dependent, which means that we're perfectly capable of navigating the apps but generationally less likely to scroll ourselves into spirals of depression. We bring a stick-to-itiveness honed by spending our latchkey years figuring out how to do things without the benefit of YouTube. We've also, at our age, developed incredibly sharp bullshit detectors and are in possession of a hormonal balance that renders us unwilling to suffer fools and unable to feel too bad about it. All these attributes align perfectly with the process of burning dating app haystacks.

I started the Facebook group with a small number of friends and colleagues and a handful of women who came over from an online women's writers group I shared it with.

Initially, the membership was predominantly middle-aged women, and over the first four months it grew to about six hundred. This struck me as a lot. Being in the group was fun and entertaining. We'd all get in there and share dating horror stories, snippets from serial-killeresque profiles, and wacky solutions to thorny dating problems. One woman shared that she always suggested Indian food for Date #1 even though she didn't really care for Indian food. Why? "Because toxic American men hate Indian food. Or they think they do, but either way, it gets them to reveal themselves fast; it weeds them out." I realized women have had their own little ways of burning the haystack all along, and together we could refine the rules, crowdsource, troubleshoot, and support each other along the way.

We collectively experimented with various ways of burning the haystack, making tweaks here and there to account for the mechanisms of different apps. For example, we decided to interact only with individual messages that are well written, reference our profiles, and do something to extend the conversation—no more entertaining "hey gorgeous" messages or men whose profiles contain only their cell phone numbers because they're not actually paying to use the app.

We refused to be pen pals—texting endlessly with no endgame (e.g., a concrete plan to meet in real life)—and we refused to fight with men or to waste any of our time and energy putting them in their place, even if they deserved it; we just blocked them. If a conversation was decent but not moving toward meeting in real life within a week or two, we blocked without further interaction. (We'll go over all the rules and how to apply them in chapter 4.)

Employing these tricks and others began paying off: the women in the group (me included) were suddenly meeting men who were respectful and relationship minded, and we were actually going out on good dates.

And if something wasn't working—if someone was following all the rules and not experiencing success—the group members would join in to investigate. Was there confusion about how algorithms work? The data scientists in the group would weigh in. Was dating tanking our mental health? Let's consult with the psychologists. When there were questions about legal or ethical matters, the attorneys could speak from their respective areas of expertise.

Rule 4, Block to burn, quickly caught fire and has now become somewhat synonymous with Burned Haystack in social media circles. It refers to the fact that at the point you realize you're not interested in someone, you should block him immediately, even if he's not behaving badly. If you just swipe left or pick the X, the app will recycle that guy to you again, which not only wastes your time but could preclude the app from sending you a different profile who might be a better fit. If you block, the app has no choice but to show you new matches. I termed it "block to burn" because I'm an English professor and appreciate alliteration and because I thought it was snappy and memorable (and in keeping with the haystack metaphor, of course, because I would *never* mix metaphors!!!). I had no idea that my little phrase was about to become famous.

The women in the Facebook group initially signified it "B/b," and then that morphed into "B2B," and now it's become part of the vernacular in dating app discourses in general and can be found all over social media. A lot of people refer to Burned Haystack as the "block-to-burn" method, which is totally fine with me.

And then things just kind of... bloomed. Fast. The thirty-five- to fifty-five-year-old cohort of heterosexual, monogamous women remains the significant portion of the method's followers, but every week the categorical lines are dissolving. The method now spans generational and other divisions. The first official "Burned Haystack Couple" was two women. Group members started sharing the method in other

Facebook groups, and with their daughters and sisters and mothers and coworkers and friends, on TikTok and Instagram and beyond. The Reddit forums materialized.

I started a new position as associate dean at my university at the end of August 2023, on the same day that a *HuffPost* article I wrote about Burned Haystack was published. By that evening, people were joining the Facebook group faster than I could click "admit" (literally—for several hours that day I simply sat in front of my laptop and clicked "admit" until my eyes blurred, at which point I surrendered and just hit "admit all," knowing I'd have to go back later and root out all the men, which I did). After that mini explosion in followers, it began to spike and swell in less predictable patterns.

The community would pay off in unexpected ways. For example, during the initial expansion, I was vacillating between being delighted and totally overwhelmed and freaked out (because in addition to the increased workload of moderating social media, I was getting calls for interviews and podcasts and angry emails from men on Instagram). In the middle of the madness I received a message from a woman on Facebook whose name I didn't recognize. She said, "Listen, you need to trademark this thing, like, yesterday. I'm an attorney, and if you want, I can call you on my commute home and talk you through the registration process." She included a link to the New York City law firm she worked for, and I verified her identity. She called me on her way home from work that Friday night and explained the entire application process on the .gov site. For free. I also got messages from graphic designers, translators, therapists, and other academics, all offering their services for free. I took some of them up on it. Nobody shows up for single women like other single women; we are a sisterhood.

That support and camaraderie is exemplified in online exchanges like this one on Facebook, in which Commenter #1 says, "Jesus, this is the best fucking thing on Facebook," and Commenter #2 says, "Isn't it? I'm running out of popcorn. And am learning things!" In a less lighthearted example, an IG follower commented, "Someone's gotta say it: You're literally saving women's lives." I was wholly unprepared for this kind of feedback, but as it continued to roll in, I became more and more invested in the project myself. It's fair to say I became obsessed. So obsessed, in fact, that in a truly ironic move, I decided to remove myself from the dating apps and from the dating pool entirely. I became the proverbial "cobbler whose children have no shoes." Shortly after the membership began to expand rapidly, I posted this message to the group:

> So . . . (this post is overdue), people frequently ask me, "What about you? Have YOU met anyone?" Totally legit question, I'd want to know that too. [Sidenote: My parents ask this frequently.] I did meet my last partner using Burned Haystack dating method—that's what inspired this whole thing. We didn't end up staying together but remain good friends. I also met LOTS of datable men in that go-round prior to meeting my former partner; everything changed for me when I began using Burned Haystack principles.
>
> I started this project in late February 2023, published a few articles about it, and started this group, which stabilized around a thousand members for several months.
>
> The *HuffPost* article that brought many of you here came out on August 29, and I shut my own dating apps down on August 30 or September 1, as this group's membership began to explode (yay!) and as it became apparent that something was going to have to give. I couldn't do my job, manage this group, teach my classes, and continue to write and publish if I were *also* dating and managing a dating app, and yes, I did decide to sacrifice my own love life for the sake of academic research, but don't feel bad for me because to be completely transparent I love rhetoric more than I love men.
>
> I will get back out there someday, my friends, and I apologize for my hypocrisy in conducting this project while not dating, but I *promise promise promise* I've tested it, I've got skin in this game, and I wouldn't be doing this if I didn't believe in it 100 percent.

Because of the feminist and women-supporting-women tone of the movement, Burned Haystack social media comments tend to be encouraging and supportive and empathetic. One woman remarks, "I'm one of the featured success stories and want to encourage everyone not to lose hope. The method works! Don't lose hope, use the tools Jennie offers. Your needle may be out there, and if you don't meet them sooner rather than later, you'll still feel more confident and have better results overall while you search for the right person for you." Another shares that "in a few days since joining and starting using your method, my matches on the app improved so much, I cannot believe it!! This method works, ladies."

We all celebrated (and laughed) when an IG follower posted this: "I overheard two guys (I would put them in their late twenties) talking about Burned Haystack on the crosstown bus today! I live in NYC. One of them said . . . and I quote . . . 'If this is how women are screening us on apps now, getting laid just got harder.'"

Humor has been an important component of Burned Haystack from the beginning. For one thing, a sense of humor, a very dark one at times, feels absolutely necessary to surviving dating in the current climate. Additionally, and specific to me: I am unable to contain or corral my own snark, so I figured that embracing my gallows humor from the get-go could entertain my audience.

I've definitely received my fair share of hate mail two years into this project, mostly from conservative men (though some from conservative women as well), but the overarching response has been one of camaraderie and gratitude, not just to me but to other members of the community. A group member who found her needle comments, "Thank you, Jennie, for your gift of tireless labor. Your method was the key to my finding love. Thank you to the community members who support each other on this wild ride. It's been a lifesaver to feel that I'm not alone." In all the notes people share with me there's a tone of collective relief, of finally understanding that our individual experiences have not been isolated incidents, have not been personal failures. A commenter on Instagram says, "Honestly, out of all the dating podcasts and all the information out there around dating, this is the advice, data, and information that actually WORKS." Another says, "You are the only one who tells the truth and doesn't blame women." Women-blaming is an enormous problem in the public discourse surrounding contemporary dating. Women are constantly accused of "having a scarcity mindset" and "taking ourselves too seriously" and "being too demanding" and a whole bunch of other misogynistic myths that we will dismantle in this book.

. . .

When I talk about women showing up for other women, I don't mean only emotionally. When my university had a one-day fundraising drive in 2024, I put up a brief post in the Facebook group explaining what it was and linking to the donation site, emphasizing that I was only posting it since so many group members had expressed willingness to financially support this work, that there was zero expectation, and that I only wanted people who were in a comfortable position to donate to do so.

    I didn't think too much about it and went downstairs to the gym in my apartment building for a quick workout. When I came upstairs twenty-five minutes later, my phone had exploded. The first message was from my dean, and it said, "Jennie . . . You created something really extraordinary with Burned Haystack. Look at this." It contained a link to a spreadsheet that made no sense to me because I am a moron about data. The next message, from another administrator, said, "Are you watching these metrics?" I've never watched metrics a day in my life, and I had no idea that "watching metrics" was even something that could be done in conjunction with the fundraising drive. The next message was from our dean's assistant, and it said, "Damn, lady. Your people are BLOWING UP our donation page. So amazing to see and read." Eventually, I was made to understand that the university tracks the origin of every donation and even gives people an option to leave little notes with those donations (duh). Later that day, the dean texted me again and said, "You need to write the book."

So here I am, writing the book. My boss told me to.

I can't separate Burned Haystack or this book from my day job anyway. The signature line in my email says, "Professor of English, Rhetoric, and Women/Gender Studies and Associate Dean of the College of Arts, Humanities, and Social Sciences," but my core identity is simply "teacher," and I don't mean that in any kind of reductive way. I was raised by two educators, and I believe teachers are the heroes of the world. I mean it in the way that being a teacher is the lens through which I approach most things in life, and that "teaching" is at the core of who I am. It's also my number one excuse for being so bossy.

The first time I made an Instagram reel about Burned Haystack, I panicked and told a friend, "I have no business doing this. I don't know how to film this thing or how to be this person who thinks she gets to talk to the World." He said, "Just be yourself. Be the teacher." That I understood, and it gave me a framework for how I wanted to share academic methodology and applications in the social media sphere.

A crucially important parallel between classroom teaching and developing the Burned Haystack community online relates to the intragroup dynamics. When I teach a course, I pay close attention to my students' interactions with me—how they communicate or not, how they do or do not listen, whether they seem engaged in ways that transcend what they must do to achieve a good grade. And I pay even more attention to how students interact with one another than how they interact with me. I believe that, as the professor, it is my responsibility to model a tone of kindness, acceptance, interdependence, and mutual support, and when I see students extending those qualities toward each other I feel the classroom is vibing in a way that will support true learning and growth. In that vein, and because this chapter is dedicated to the development of the community, I want to share some comments from Burned Haystack social media platforms that exemplify the ways in which community members support each other:

> I love everything about this group. There's not a single comment I've read since I've been in the group that hasn't made me either nod in agreement, look something up, think, reconsider, or redirect my actions. This group is such a positive force in my single journey. I count myself fortunate to learn from all your stories, posts, and wisdom. Thank you to everyone here who shares.
>
> Thank you ladies! I posted a question and am so grateful for all your comments! Where have you all been my whole life! Canceled the date . . . feeling empowered by being true to myself and not ego. This group is fully upping our EQ and IQ. #girlpower!
>
> I am so content with all of your company. I am finding out how to love myself better than ever before.
>
> As Audre Lorde so humbly reminds us, there is no such thing as one-way liberation. As for the feminist perspective and how that evolved in the Burned Haystack method, I see it as a beautiful development of wisdom dispensed as guidelines. Like bumper rails for bowling. Sometimes we need a solid, alternative structure to the patriarchy we so deeply inhale and hold up as a society. Sisterhood is the antidote.

I agree that sisterhood is the antidote. And for those of us in the Burned Haystack community, it hasn't just been the antidote to the woes of online dating. It's been the antidote to loneliness and isolation and self-doubt and internalized misogyny that even snuck up on me as I began to write this book. It's the antidote to being gaslighted by the dating apps, by men, by ourselves. It's the antidote to being driven to madness by the very, very real challenges of trying to date in the digital era. Which brings me to a couple of important messages I want to share with you at the outset of this book.

It's not you; you are not the problem. If you're anything like me, you may be thinking it's you. You may be concerned that you're the problem, that you "don't get it," that you're doing something wrong, that you're too sensitive or too demanding or too old-fashioned or too liberal or too feminist or too independent or too . . . whatever. I don't even have to know you to assure you that you are not the problem; I know what the problems are, and they're not you.

The things you want—a life partner, a best friend, someone who shows you kindness and respect and honesty—these are not unreasonable things. They're also not impossible to find. Throughout this book you're going to read a lot of success stories about women who've used this method to find their needle in the haystack. I'm writing this book to help you do the same.

BEFORE WE REALLY DIVE INTO THINGS, SOME IMPORTANT NOTES

Burned Haystack was created to help women find long-term, monogamous partners, and all its tactics and tools are aimed toward that goal. This is not because I believe long-term monogamy is the best or only relationship structure, and it's definitely not because I find it to be morally superior or "right"; it's because it's the hardest structure to find right now, and therefore the most in need of a feminist correction and of a rules-governed, academic method.

The method seeks to combat problems that are rooted in toxic masculinity and that are most frequently experienced by hetero women dating hetero men, so the language I use throughout the book reflects that. However, I do believe the rules and values of the method are useful and applicable to anyone and everyone of any gender and orientation.

And finally: This book makes no promises that following Burned Haystack will result in finding true love. No method can make that promise. What it *can* promise, though—and this is now substantiated by hundreds of thousands of women—is a more peaceful and empowered life.

SUCCESS STORY!

Throughout the book, I'll share Burned Haystack success stories about women who used the method to find their needles. But what follows here is a different kind of success story, one that speaks to the larger mission, and that's why I want to start with this one. I'm thrilled anytime anyone uses this method to go on a single fun date, make a new friend, or find their lifelong partner. But I also believe that the work this community is doing transcends any individual success.

I want Burned Haystack to change the culture of dating in a way that's protective and empowering of women; that's the ultimate goal. I believe we reach that goal by introducing people to the ideals of feminism and gender equity, by equipping them with a mindset of deep strength and inner self-respect, and by explicitly teaching a set of rules and tools that can facilitate a healthier date/life balance. Here's what I mean by that: I want you to actively date and nurture the rest of your life; to actively date and cultivate positive mental health; to actively date and be happy in a way that's independent of how the dating is going.

Burned Haystack doesn't aim to simply decenter men; it aims to decenter the whole idea that partnership is a requirement of happiness and security; it aims to decenter the notion of looking for love as some kind of all-consuming "quest" and instead frames it as a set of attitudes, behaviors, and guidelines for living so that you can work toward the dream of love while moving the search quietly out of your way. You might not put it on the furthest of the back burners, but you can definitely set it over to the side and turn it down to simmer so that you can focus on other things.

In some ways, women of younger generations know and do this more intuitively than those of us who are a bit older. They have been raised in a world in which they have greater access to higher education and high-paying careers than women of previous generations, so they have not been as programmed to see partnership or marriage as a necessary component of life success and security; they have had the benefit of growing up immersed in discourses of "boundary protection" and "self-care" and "#MeToo." Many young women do quite naturally what my generation has had to teach itself to do—yet they do this while watching and learning from us as well.

The following success story was emailed to me by a Burned Haystack community member, and it beautifully blends this two-way channel of learning in a way that speaks to the best aspects of the Burned Haystack movement: women sharing with, emulating, and holding up other women.

> So I wanted to send this to you. It isn't a happy ending story for me personally, but it kind of is.
>
> I've been single for quite a while, gave up bothering with dating really. I just didn't feel like the juice was worth the squeeze anymore. I have an amazing career, my own home, a grown son who is happily married, and a daughter in college.
>
> My daughter is my Burned Haystack success story. She dated a boy off and on in high school and early college. He was nice. Our families were friendly. But she found him to be disrespectful. He was following sexually explicit stuff on IG and she caught him playing around on dating apps—which he tried to explain away.

She told him, "My mom left her partner for treating her badly—I'm not afraid of being alone."

I didn't even know she paid attention.

She has high demands of any potential date. She met a boy in college who has consistently met and overshoots the bar. She is unwavering in her expectations. So much that it would be scary for me to have been that bold and confident.

I don't know if this boy will be "the one," but I am in awe of how she has set her boundaries and expectations so firmly and refuses to back down and has found someone who is so happy to be all the things she demands.

I wish I had her strength and confidence when I was her age, but I am so happy she has it now. She is living Burned Haystack and she doesn't even know it!

HUMOR BREAK

When people ask me what Burned Haystack is all about, I say something like this: "Feminism, dating dynamics, applied rhetoric, and humor."

The first three items are self-explanatory. The humor is partly because I'm a humor writer, partly because I believe humor is a necessary component of surviving the dating apps, and mostly because I believe humor in general and satire in particular are effective tools of combating toxic patriarchy. I believe that toxic behavior deserves to be mocked, that mocking it effectively contextualizes it as the unimportant drivel it actually is. It can also be employed as a megaphone for calling some of this stuff out in a way that captures people's attention in mainstream media and in the public sphere.

Satire has, of course, always been highly rhetorical, rooted in the work of Jonathan Swift, Mark Twain, Dorothy Parker, and others. Rhetoric only matters if it connects to the masses, and satire tends to connect to the masses in ways that strictly serious works do not. In today's digital world, written satire intersects with the political process, it critiques inequities, it exposes exploitation, and it brings light to issues that might otherwise remain beneath people's radar. I'm happy if people think I'm funny, but I take funny writing incredibly seriously, and I knew from the beginning of Burned Haystack that humor would have to be an important component of the movement.

I now frequently get comments that say things like "I'm not even dating [or I already found my needle, or I'm already married], but I just keep coming back to this group for the humor." This delights me, and the Burned Haystack community is a collectively hilarious (and sometimes scathing) bunch. Since it's been such a big part of the culture in social media, I include "Humor Breaks" like this one throughout the book.

Every Male Profile, Written by a Woman
by Burned Haystack Facebook group member Leah Haydock

You're as comfortable in a tuxedo as you are in baggy cargo shorts on a way-too-cold spring day. You catch fish, all the fish, big fish, little fish, all the time, and you know how to hold them. Your bathroom selfie game is killer, and sometimes you leave the seat up to be more edgy. You have a number of small children and dogs in your life that may or may not belong to you; they may or may not have their faces scribbled over to protect their anonymity. You're looking for long-term commitment and a meaningful soul connection but are also open to one-night stands, threesomes, and butt stuff as long as the only other participants are women. You're a man of mystery, hence "Just Ask," or else you're looking for a partner in crime who has a little black dress stashed in the pocket of her blue jeans. Every relationship has involved screaming matches and maybe the police have been called, but you're totally looking for "no drama" this time around. You're a simple guy who's just looking for an emotionally mature woman who's roughly half your age, so they don't challenge you or hold you accountable for anything.

2

SMILING DEVILS AND BITCHY PROFILES

The Early Seeds of Burned Haystack

A couple of years before I started the Facebook group that bloomed into the Burned Haystack community, I was experimenting for my own purposes on the dating apps. During that time, I wrote and published two articles about my experiences, one in which I analyzed a bunch of men's profiles (including one man who was obsessed with the devil, hence the name of this chapter, and another in which I shared the strategy and text of my own ["bitchy"] profile, also hence the name of this chapter). The reader response to these pieces was my first clue that I wasn't alone and that what I was doing academically might be helpful to lots of women, although I was still primarily interested in finding a partner for myself.

The first academic mission I embarked upon was inspired by a man I matched with who was dressed as the devil in his profile picture. He was dressed as the actual devil—not a funny, costumey sort of devil. The photo was an extreme close-up of his face, and in it, he was wearing plastic fangs and red contacts in his eyes; there was something that looked like blood (or perhaps actual blood) dripping from his fangs and drooling down his chin. His profile text was unusually articulate and genuinely appealing and funny. In it, he even *apologized* for the frightening nature of his pics and explained that he was just a normal guy who was really into Halloween. He also had other appealing attributes: He was highly educated, gainfully employed, and good-looking, if one were to remove his makeup and devil costumes (he owned multiple devil costumes, I discovered when I clicked through his other pics).

I had this internal dialogue with myself that sounded like this: "The pickings are pretty slim. This guy is good-looking and articulate and seems to be gainfully employed. Is the fact that he likes to dress up like the devil *really* a deal-breaker?" My gut feeling was that it *was* a deal-breaker for me, but I was unclear on why. I decided to use two academic lenses to bring things into closer focus for myself, to see if I could effect some sort of figurative magnifying glass or microscope that would reveal the virus or malignancy I sensed but couldn't actually see with the naked eye.

The names of those lenses are **thin-slicing** and **critical discourse analysis**. Let's talk about thin-slicing first. It's a psychological concept featured, among other places, in Malcolm Gladwell's second book, *Blink: The Power of Thinking Without Thinking*. Thin-slicing refers to the idea that we can accurately make quick judgments about people based upon very "thin slices" of experience. It's been applied to dating before (think: speed dating), as well as to the detection of personality disorders such as psychopathy.

We take the "thin slice"—his decision to pose as the devil in his online dating profile—and draw reasonable conclusions based upon only that slice. For example, here's a list from worst-case to best-case scenarios for Devil Guy:

- He may actually be dangerous; all the pictures he posted were overtly aggressive and threatening. In addition to the devil costumes, he also appeared dressed up as the psychopath from *A Clockwork Orange* and as a very sinister-looking rabbit.

- He may not be dangerous at all, but he gets some sort of thrill out of scaring women.
- He may not be dangerous or even trying to scare women, but he's so *completely* clueless and tone-deaf that he doesn't recognize that dressing as the devil is a bad choice for an online dating profile.

The third option is the best-case scenario, and even that didn't seem promising in terms of relationship potential. If he couldn't figure out that posing as the devil was frightening to women, then what *else* couldn't this guy figure out about women (or about anything, really)? Once I broke it down for myself this way, I realized it would be a total waste of time, if not dangerous, to start dating Devil Guy, so I blocked him. Maybe more important, I didn't second-guess or regret that decision. I knew why I didn't want to meet him, because I'd used my academic methods to make a rational and defensible decision.

In most cases, I believe women can simply trust their own intuition, because it's inherently trustworthy. However, there are so many voices ready to call women's intuition into question, to gaslight us into acting against our own best interests, that we too frequently disregard our gut feelings and start unconsciously gaslighting ourselves. I was already doing that with this guy: *It's not really that bad to dress up like the devil!!! It's all good fun!!!* After doing the thin-slicing exercise, I also asked myself, *Think of all the men you know who* are *(or could be if they were single) datable—friends, friends' husbands, colleagues, and so on. Would any of them build a dating app profile comprised entirely of devil costume pics?* Of course they wouldn't. It sounds insane when posed this way.

As I write this now, years later, I wonder, *How could I not have blocked this guy immediately? The red contacts in his eyes? The fake or real blood dripping from his lips?* I know why it didn't seem obvious, though. First, the guy had some positive attributes in a field where that was unusual. Second, online dating is just a weird world. Nothing within its realm operates like things do in the real world. Third, there are a lot of loud voices encouraging women to "withhold judgment" or "grant grace" or "give people the benefit of the doubt." I'll make the case for why these voices are wrong—but we should also discuss who's benefiting from such messaging, because it's not you.

The business of excusing bad male behavior is both easy and lucrative. It's easy because there's so much of it, so many opportunities for women to grant grace and give everyone the benefit of the doubt. It's lucrative for dating app companies and dating coaches because permitting bad actors to remain in the dating pool creates more interactions, and more interactions create more opportunities for dating coaches to "coach" and more matches for the apps. Tinder and Bumble and Hinge, despite what they say, don't benefit from people falling in love and canceling their accounts. They benefit from having as many people as possible matching and interacting with as many other people as possible, and they benefit more when this goes on forever.

After I realized how much time thin-slicing could save me on the apps, I realized there was a set of words and phrases that I could effectively "code" so that any profiles that featured them would be automatic noes without any further consideration. It was the guys who screamed "NO DRAMA" in all caps, the men demanding that women "not take themselves too seriously," the guys who "just want to take it easy and see what happens," the ones who are in the market for women who are "loyal" and "generous" and "open-minded" and "fit." I added words like "traditional," which right now in America almost always actually means "conservative," because I knew that wouldn't be a good fit for me.

Below is a sampling of the texts I was getting from men I'd matched with on the dating apps that I decoded in an article I published pre–Burned Haystack:

> I'm looking for a woman who is trustworthy, honest, and able to get along with others.

This guy is looking for a golden retriever. Move along . . .

> You should be positive, open-minded, and willing to try new things. You should enjoy staying fit, staying sharp, and truly believing that the best things are still ahead! You should be well-read but not take yourself too seriously, responsible but still fun!, and take good care of yourself but still be able to enjoy good food and a few drinks now and then! If this sounds like you and you're ready to jump wholeheartedly into love, send me a message!

This one is tricky. The content of what he's saying, while clichéd and overly exclamation-pointed (!!!), is not the real problem here. The real problem is that he wrote this text in response to the question "A Little Bit About Me." And also that he's written in the second person ("you" should be this, "you" should be that). If he'd written it in the first person ("I'm positive, open-minded, and willing to try new things..."), we wouldn't be analyzing this text. But this guy took a question about him and co-opted it to tell *you* exactly what qualities you need to have in order to be worthy of his attention. This guy is mansplaining to you *in his dating profile*. Imagine what it would be like to live with him.

> I'm looking for an open-minded woman who is giving and generous and passionate, who understands that there is more joy in giving than receiving.

This guy is not only telling you that he's primarily interested in sex; he's telling you that the sex will be really bad *for you*. (Note: Far too frequently, "open-minded" also translates to "I'll need you to understand that I'm still married.")

> I'm looking for a woman who is compassionate and who completely accepts me as I am.

The translation on this one is often "I want to be impossible, infuriating, unemployed, and generally ineffectual."

• • •

The feedback in the comments on this article made it clear to me how much these mini-analyses were resonating with women. I had an inkling there might be a much larger project and mission on which I should embark.

Being able to decode language like this is not only a dating app superpower; it's an every-aspect-of-life time-saver. I suspect some people read the above translations and thought, *Duh, I was on to all that years ago*, and others thought, *Wow, I didn't get any of that out of "I'm looking for an open-minded woman who is giving and generous."* Regardless of where you fall along that spectrum, I hope you'll enjoy learning how to employ these analytical lenses quickly and intuitively, and if you're already doing that, I hope you might still enjoy diving into the academic foundations of why these lenses are so accurate. I can almost promise that even if you're already rhetorically savvy, you'll still pick up some tricks along the way.

One trick—and it's foundational, so I want to include it early in the book—is to have a solid understanding of how **text**, **subtext**, and **context** work.

Text refers to the actual words you see. "An orange cat is up in the tree" means that there is a pumpkin-colored feline mammal sitting above you on a tree branch; the meaning is gleaned from dictionary definitions of the words used.

Subtext refers to what lies beneath the text. Subtext can be intentional or unintentional. Sometimes people intentionally embed shaded or suggestive meanings into the words they say, and other times they reveal things about themselves that they don't intend to. If you live in America and someone says to you, "It's a child, not a choice," you automatically understand the subtext of that statement to be something like "Abortion is morally wrong," even though the original sentence includes nothing about pregnancy or reproductive rights or human values. We could also say that there's a subtext here in which people who utter this statement (or who drive around with it on a bumper sticker) believe that "to abort or not" is a simple either/or scenario in which women decide whether they care about themselves or their unborn children.

Context refers to the conditions surrounding the text (the prefix "con" means "with," so literally "with the text"). Context includes things like place, time, relevant events, and so on. In the context of current-day America, we know that any juxtaposition of "child" and "choice" is about abortion. If you lived in another culture where abortion was considered a noncontroversial medical procedure common in basic health care, you might never even connect discussions of child/choice conundrums to abortion.

So that's how text, subtext, and context work together to create and reveal meaning. Every single word uttered or written contains these three dimensions and can be analyzed for them. The more you do it, the easier it gets.

Now let's apply what we just learned to a post from the Burned Haystack Facebook group.

> Dear Jennie,
>
> The word "loyalty" on dating apps bugs me. Gives me the ick. Men say they are looking for loyalty, and my immediate thoughts are *He was cheated on, he's bitter, he wants a woman who will go along with anything and stay loyal no matter what he puts her through or how awful he is.* I associated it with being unquestioning, as with our incoming president, someone who demands loyalty from his associates no matter what outrageous thing he says or does. Loyalty above all else.
>
> Currently reading Logan Ury's book,* and she says loyalty is one of the things to look for in a partner. She uses it in the sense that

> you want someone willing to hold your purse while you're getting chemo (paraphrasing). A good test is to see how many friends they have from the past or their childhood, because that means they are loyal to them. You want someone who will stick with you through hard times.
>
> Wondering what you would say on this word. I totally get Ury's point, but I fear it will take a big shift for me to be able to read past that word on a man's profile and not cringe.
>
> ---
>
> (*She's referring to *How to Not Die Alone*. It's in the Haystack Bookstack list on page 294.)

I completely understand this woman's confusion; the word "loyalty" is complicated in the entire context of dating. I, too, agree with Logan Ury that, in its purest form, loyalty is an objectively and inherently "good" quality that is vital to building a healthy relationship.

This is where that goodness gets muddied: Words such as "loyal," "generous," "open-minded," "fun-loving," and "relaxed" do not always mean their dictionary definitions (their "denotations") in men's dating profiles.

In the dating apps, those words in a certain subset of men's profiles have become "coded" to mean something else. This simply means that the implications or connotations of the words in that specific context mean something different from their purer denotations.

Here's a quick decoder key for that set of words in men's dating apps:

"LOYAL": Will always stay with me and never leave me no matter what, even if I'm abusive, neglectful, or unfaithful.

"GENEROUS": Will serve and pleasure me to your own detriment.

"OPEN-MINDED": Willing to put yourself in uncomfortable/painful scenarios if it's what I want.

"FUN-LOVING": Will never make me deal with or even think about anything serious, because that wouldn't be fun for me.

"CHILL/DOESN'T TAKE HERSELF SERIOUSLY": Will tolerate anything from me without complaint.

Obviously, not every man who writes one of these words into his profile means it (or realizes he means it) in these nefarious contexts. However, if you've been on the apps long enough, you already know full well, probably through painful experience, that many of them do.

This is why subtext and context matter as much if not more than words taken at face value. Let's do a little experiment with the word "loyal." Here's how the typical coded version looks—

> Just looking for a great girl to make my life complete. Someone who doesn't take herself too seriously and who understands that loyalty and generosity are the keys to making a relationship work.

A guy who writes things like this is to be avoided, as opposed to a man who might write something like this:

> I believe that qualities such as friendship, understanding, and common values are as important as mutual attraction. I'm a loyal person by nature who's ready to be someone's partner during the hard times as well as the easy, and I'm hoping to find the same.

See what I mean? Both these passages invoke and focus on the concept of loyalty, but the implications of what that means to each man are quite different.

When I was first on the dating apps, I spent a lot of time thinking about stuff like this—studying, comparing and contrasting, analyzing, categorizing, and making rules and guidelines for myself to follow. Once I felt I had a better grasp on a lot of the common traps, I spent some time crafting my own profile in a way that I hoped would repel the men likely to exhibit behavior I didn't like. I published an article about that experience that, in many ways, became the true kickoff of Burned Haystack, though I wasn't calling it that yet, and I had no other concrete plans to share it nor any idea of how it would evolve. The title of the article was "Want to Meet Decent Men Online? Write a Bitchy Profile," which honestly probably got a bunch of clicks simply because of the phrase "bitchy profile," but I meant it in the proactive, positive, feminist sense of the word "bitch." I published my dating app profile in that article:

> I'm a writer (humor writer, self-supporting, not a starving poet), and I'm going to write this from a different angle. Here's my Top 10 List of what I *don't* want:
>
> 1. Hookups.
> 2. "Hey" messages.
> 3. "What's up" messages.
> 4. "You up?" messages.
> 5. Anyone who's "living life to the fullest."
> 6. A 55-year-old man who "wants kids someday."
> 7. Anyone whose profile is written in "second-person directive" voice that directs me how *I* should be. Here's an example: "You should be fun-loving, honest, easygoing, and fit."
> 8. Anyone who's easily offended by dark humor (or this list).
> 9. Texting maniacs. I use texting for logistics, not actual communication.
> 10. Party boys, in all iterations. I'm a family-oriented grown-up with my life together, looking for same.
>
> Last thing you should know: I'm not a "cool girl" (if you don't know the reference, google it).

If you can get past all that, and if you're still reading, this could work.

Less prickly section of profile: I'm a runner and cyclist (more recreational than competitive these days), and I love hiking. I'm a fan of books, coffee shops, small towns, lakes, and mountains. I haven't traveled much internationally but want to. I'm funny. I know everyone on here claims this, but I'm pretty well published (internet satire) and sometimes even financially compensated to be funny, so I feel like I can claim it accurately? I guess?

I can't be attracted to anyone who doesn't know their homonyms. I'm sorry.

Posting this profile changed everything, and it changed everything immediately. I got far fewer responses, that's true, but the responses I did get were worth reading.

Dan, for instance, wrote: "I get what you're doing, thinning the herd, right?"

Yes, that's exactly what I was doing.

Wayne wrote: "'I can't be attracted to anyone who doesn't know their homonyms.' That might be the funniest thing I've ever read on hear."

Nice, Wayne! An intentional homonym error to join in on the joke! This is what I'd been hoping would happen.

Todd wrote: "Hi Jennie, I am going to assume that you likely scared off 90% of the Wisconsin men who enjoy their beer and brats. Hoping I am the last man standing. Great read, and I can tell you are way different than most out in this strange internet dating world."

I'm sure I *did* scare off 90 percent of Wisconsin men who enjoy beer and brats, but *I* don't enjoy beer and brats, so I didn't really care.

Stan wrote: "Hey (sorry, couldn't resist). This is hands-down the best profile I have ever read."

The messages continued to come in like this. For many of the matches, there were other factors that rendered the connection moot for me (they were separated but not divorced, or there was something off-putting in their physical appearance, or they'd selected "ENM" [ethical non-monogamy] or "fun casual dates" instead of "long-term relationship"). I did end up meeting someone within five days of posting that profile, and we were together for about two years. (As mentioned earlier, we remain good friends.)

Through that experience I realized that even though I hadn't found my forever person—my "needle"—I'd already done a good chunk of foundational research and initial testing and development of a set of practices that could be honed into a teachable method. So like a lot of things in life, it was one sad ending that led to a proportionately exciting beginning. And Burned Haystack as a method and community was born.

SUCCESS STORY!

A little over two years ago, I had just ended a Covid situationship, and the thought of diving back into the dating apps made me physically ill. At that point, I had been divorced for over ten years and had only dated sporadically while solo raising my kids.

March 2023, cue Jennie and Burned Haystack. As an early adopter, I have had the pleasure of watching this incredible movement truly change the lives of so many. After repeatedly making horrible relationship decisions, this method has empowered me with the tools and courage to be picky, set boundaries, and immediately recognize toxicity when I read it.

Last August, after taking most of the previous year off from dating (as I was launching my youngest into the world and caring for aging parents), I decided to dip my toe back into the dating pool. Within a few weeks, I had found my needle.

As many have said before, this experience was different from the start. My needle's initial communication was thoughtful, respectful, and curious. Our first coffee date lasted over three hours, and I felt an incredible sense of calm with him. There were no obvious fireworks, but I was attracted to him and felt a strong connection that has grown into amazing chemistry over the last nine months. I have never felt more seen, loved, or appreciated in a relationship. He shows up, in both big and small ways, and I never have to wonder how he feels about me.

We are both unbelievably grateful for Jennie and her wisdom, and I will continue to cheer on this group as we change the world with this feminist movement!

—Kim

3

COURSE SYLLABUS

Feminism and Rhetorical Theory in Contemporary Dating Culture (AKA Critical Discourse Analysis Is Sexy)

INSTRUCTOR: PROFESSOR YOUNG

COURSE OVERVIEW

This course adapts theory and methods from the discipline of applied rhetoric and contextualizes them within the practice of encountering ridiculous men on dating apps. An advanced understanding of linguistic and semiotic analytical techniques should not be required to navigate Bumble, yet here we are.

COURSE LEARNING OUTCOMES

By the end of this chapter, you should be able to:

- Define "rhetoric," "critical discourse analysis," and associated terms and concepts.
- Annoy your family and friends with your weirdly intricate knowledge of academic theory previously known only by postgraduate scholars and linguistics experts.

- Recognize red flags in men's words and behavior so quickly that you've already moved on before they're done telling you they "don't have time for drama."

REQUIRED MATERIALS

None. Come exactly as you are. I'm grateful you're here.

HOW TO BE SUCCESSFUL IN THIS COURSE

1. **ALLOW YOURSELF TO DEPART FROM THE FEELINGS SURROUNDING LOVE AND ROMANCE FOR A WHILE.** I want you to let your intellect take over for now. (Not forever!) We're going to hand things over to our brains for a little while so that our hearts can realize their dreams later—dreams that will be even more magical, and a whole lot safer, because they've been framed by knowledge and information. I realize that applying analytical techniques like these in the search for love might seem cold and calculating. But the internet is a cold and calculating place—literally. Dating platforms run on code sequences, algorithms, and money. To pretend that they're governed by angels and rainbows is not only delusional but dangerous. If you begin dating your closest friend's brother or your brother's closest friend or someone you've worked with for years, you may not need any of this knowledge or any of these tricks (though they could still be illuminating). If you're dating in any other circumstances, I feel confident in assuring you that the information in this chapter will be helpful.

2. **GIVE YOURSELF PERMISSION TO BE HIGHLY CRITICAL.** Critical doesn't need to signify "mean." Sometimes it signifies "deeply thoughtful in an informed way," and that's what we're going for here. A question I frequently get is this: "You spend *so* much time and energy analyzing men's words and pictures and behavior, but I just don't think they put that much thought into any of it, so isn't

this a waste of time?" This concern is generally valid, and its validity makes these practices even *more* powerful. Because we have all been socialized in a patriarchal culture, many linguistic patterns that reveal male toxicity and danger just sound . . . normal. Totally normal. Critical discourse analysis (CDA) has many applications, but its most powerful dating-related application is that you can use it to cull the underlying meaning from text and images in a way that reveals important information about the source—especially information that source is not intending to reveal. CDA exposes the cultural conditions that reside beneath "normal" language and enable nonsense and manipulation to fly under the radar of daily interactions.

3. **STAY WITH THIS CONTENT, EVEN WHEN YOU FIND IT CHALLENGING.** What I'm about to present in this chapter might initially feel like "a lot." You might think, *I just want to go out on some dates. I don't even know what "applied rhetoric" is, and I'm not sure I care.* Or you might read through this chapter and think, *I'm not going to be able to remember the difference between a figured world and a primary metaphor.* Later on, in chapter 5, you might wonder, *How am I supposed to remember thirty-three different rhetorical patterns? Do I even know what a rhetorical pattern is?* I am promising you this right now: You will understand and internalize these ideas quickly because you live in a patriarchy and have been encountering them your entire life. I'm just giving you language and vocabulary to put a name to the ridiculous, manipulative, and condescending conversations we've been having with men since childhood. I regularly teach this content to undergrads—to eighteen-year-olds—and they become wizards at it. I post about it on social media and people with zero formal training in this stuff will immediately comment, "Oh yeah, classic 'test and apologize' pattern," or "That's a sexual non sequitur" or (this is a real quote from an Instagram follower) "God I love critical discourse analysis." I'm saying all this now because I want you to feel empowered by this new vocabulary rather than feel intimidated (or annoyed, or bored) by it. And it's fun—I promise!

And finally, and maybe most important: On some deep reptilian level, whether through lived experience or evolutionary knowledge or women's intuition, you already know a lot of what's in this book, or you at least sense it. We all do. We've just been gaslighted into forgetting it or questioning it or thinking we're "too picky" or "too demanding" or simply "too much." That's all a pack of lies, and we're going to use rhetoric to bust it up.

Okay, ready? Let's have some rhetoric lessons . . .

. . .

I've mentioned critical discourse analysis a few times already, and we're going to get into that in detail very soon, but first I want to discuss the overall discipline of rhetoric as an academic field, at least as it concerns Burned Haystack. We can think of rhetoric as the umbrella for a set of subcategories and practices such as applied rhetoric and discourse analysis.

There are a *lot* of definitions of the word "rhetoric." For the purposes of this book, let's go with this one: **Rhetoric is the study and practice of language use.** You may have heard that "rhetoric is the art of persuasion," and that's frequently true, but it's not the whole deal and it's not even always accurate. Making the decision to craft language to persuade someone of something is one rhetorical choice, but there are other rhetorical choices. Depending upon what I'm writing, my most important rhetorical goal might be clarity, or perhaps it is to make people laugh, or maybe it is simply to create a beautiful sentence; there are many possible rhetorical goals. The other component of rhetoric—the first part of my definition above—is the study of figuring out how the language operates, what lies beneath it, what it's accomplishing or failing to accomplish, what kind of effects it's creating, and so on. We'll be doing a lot of that in this book.

There are also many subcategories of rhetoric. For example, **visual**

rhetoric refers specifically to messaging (intentional or unintentional) achieved through images. When you see an anti-smoking campaign billboard and there's almost no text but a graphic image of a lung clouded by masses, or an anti-meth campaign with an image of a young woman with teeth crumbling out of her head, these are intentional applications of visual rhetoric. You don't need someone to break down the message for you; you know that it's "Don't do [this] or you will end up like [that]." Alternatively, if you see an advertisement for a hair salon and it features a gorgeous woman, the visual rhetoric there translates to "If you come here, you can look like this." If you've ever used a dating app, you've probably relied heavily upon visual rhetoric. The pictures someone chooses to include in their profile tell us a lot about that person; sometimes this is intentional on their part and sometimes not, but that doesn't matter much to the analyzer—the information is available regardless of intent.

Related to visual rhetoric is the branch of academic rhetoric called **semiotics**, which refers specifically to the study of signs, symbols, and signification. Whereas linguistic rhetoric analyzes words, semiotics analyzes symbols and other sign systems and is concerned with the communicative and persuasive effects of those things. One easy example of a contemporary sign system is the set of emojis we now commonly use to communicate, sometimes even without any words. Semiotics can be as concrete as the set of common traffic signs and symbols we see every day or as complex as the collective elements that go into "branding" a good or service to appeal to a particular audience. Semiotics involves everything from definable elements such as color psychology to less-definable elements such as achieving a certain "vibe" in an advertising campaign's visuals.

Two other important subcategories of rhetoric as it relates to dating are **material rhetoric** and **embodied rhetoric**. If you're flipping through a man's profile and there's a Confederate flag on the wall of his apartment behind him, that's material rhetoric; he's revealing something via one of his material possessions. If there's a motorcycle in most of his pics (or if the motorcycle all by itself *is* the main profile pic, shockingly common in men's profiles), that's material rhetoric, in which the obvious conclusion is that this motorcycle has an outsize importance in his life and probably his entire self-concept. If he's sending you a bathroom mirror selfie (gag), and the toilet seat is up next to him and the whole rest of the bathroom is absolutely filthy, this is a valuable artifact of material rhetoric. Conversely, if his house is appealing and spotless and he has a friendly and healthy-looking dog lying contentedly next to him on a clean and cushy dog bed, that's material rhetoric too.

Embodied rhetoric literally means "rhetoric of the body." The guy glaring aggressively down at you in all his pics is revealing something through embodied rhetoric. The crotch shots and the pillow pics and the guys who post profile pics of themselves surrounded by stereotypical "hot girls"—all are embodied rhetoric. In real life, the guy who invades your personal space by imposing his own body too much into it is giving you important information through embodied rhetoric. The fact that Keanu Reeves famously refuses to put his hands upon women in photographs communicates something about him through an intentional act of embodied rhetoric. The man who navigates a crowd by pointlessly grazing the small of women's backs with his hands is revealing something through embodied rhetoric, as is the guy who drops to his knees and speaks softly so as not to intimidate a nervous dog.

All these are different examples of rhetoric, and all are relevant to critical discourse analysis, which is a form of **applied rhetoric.** This sounds like a fancy academic term, but all it really means is that the study or practice of rhetoric goes beyond theory, beyond ideas, and beyond the walls of the academy; it's being *applied* to the real world and employed to understand, critique, and change real life.

Early in my academic career, I wrote a textbook in which I applied CDA to a collection of high school handbooks. I used the analysis to identify and classify rhetorical patterns and to figure out what kinds of metaphors were governing contemporary high schools. My conclusion was that the massive and intricate systems of rules are making high schools so prisonlike that they're actively thwarting many important goals of education. I then used those findings to make real-world suggestions for changes to high school administration, such as implementing collaborative governance between teachers and students or restorative rather than punitive justice when things go awry. All this work is based in theoretical rhetoric, but it culminates in working toward change in the actual world, and thus becomes applied rhetoric.

I wanted to write that book because I began my teaching career as a high school teacher and was so demoralized and horrified by the system that I wanted to be a voice in dismantling it. I then got so obsessed with rhetoric that I wanted to make an entire career of it and apply CDA to a bunch of other complex, intractable problems, and then I ended up single and on a dating app, and now here we are. Necessity is the mother of invention (that's a metaphor; we'll talk more about metaphors shortly).

THE FOUNDATIONS OF CDA

Before we begin looking in detail at CDA, I want to define three other terms you may already know, but they're so foundational to rhetoric that they warrant a brief mention: **ethos, pathos,** and **logos**. These terms *do* primarily concern rhetoric as "the art of persuasion," and they refer to that art in these ways:

Ethos refers to the ethical component, to what we call "ethical appeals." An ethical appeal encourages people to do/think/be something because it is "the right thing to do," because it is aligned with the notion of "goodness." The Ten Commandments are a set of ethical appeals: "Live this way because it will make you good, because it's the right way to live."

Pathos refers to the emotional component, to what we call "emotional appeals." If you are compelled to purchase a certain brand of toilet paper because of the adorable golden retriever puppies used to advertise it, you are responding to an emotional appeal. Golden retrievers actually have nothing to do with toilet paper (other than being soft and fluffy, perhaps, but lots of things are soft and fluffy: that pink attic insulation is soft and fluffy, but no one is using it to sell toilet paper); the reason the puppies are used to sell toilet paper is that they're cute and lovable and resonate with people in a positive way. When you're at Target staring at an entire aisle of toilet paper options, you might be compelled to choose the one with which you've already formed an emotional bond. You don't need to be aware of this; it operates beneath the surface. Pathos is also being used when a speaker begins her speech by sharing a heartbreaking story from her life. This recruits her audience's emotions through sympathy, empathy, and resonance; when people are emotionally engaged, they pay more attention and are more likely to align with the speaker.

Logos refers to the logical component, to what we call "logical appeals." If I'm helping you decide which car to buy and I can definitively prove that Car A is safer, less expensive, and gets better mileage than Car B, the logical conclusion is that you should purchase Car A, at least if you're making this decision based upon logic.

The most persuasive campaigns—whether they are political, capitalistic, or personal—address all three of the appeals. For example, let's imagine a campaign to encourage people to recycle. We could build the campaign around **ethos**—recycling is the right and good thing to do; we could build it around **pathos**—this beautiful world you remember from childhood is dying and dying fast; we could build it around **logos**—research shows that fewer emissions and a reduced carbon footprint could mitigate global warming. Any of these might work, but different people are swayed more or less by different appeals, so incorporating *all* the appeals gives us the best shot at persuading the highest number of people.

From an analytical perspective, a great benefit of understanding the appeals is that it enables you to see through nefarious attempts to persuade. Women, especially widows over a certain age, are frequently the victims of dating app scammers because these scammers are highly skilled in appealing to emotions. If would-be victims are unable to see through the rhetoric, they are susceptible to being scammed for money or worse. Once you begin to think about and understand the rhetorical appeals, you will see them everywhere.

∙ ∙ ∙

Now let's get into the nitty-gritty details and break CDA into its constituent parts, beginning with the term "discourse." For the purposes of this book, **discourse** can be considered nearly synonymous with the word "conversation"; a "discourse" is the way people talk about something within a given context. We could talk about political discourses or discourses on education or discourse specific to financial institutions or legal discourse, but with Burned Haystack, we are primarily concerned with discourses relevant to dating, feminism, and women. Another word we use in CDA quite a bit is "discursive," which simply means "of the discourse" and is used to describe language that derives from a particular discourse. Within the realm of dating discourse, my example above of a Confederate flag in a photo in a man's dating profile, in addition to being analyzable in a material rhetoric sense, could be considered a "discursive artifact," one that is associated with hard-right conservativism and racism.

Discourse analysis is a term on its own without the word "critical." Straight-up discourse analysis (DA) refers to a more neutral method of studying linguistic patterns—how language is used and how meaning is constructed—and then recording and analyzing it in order to more deeply understand it. (DA is sometimes referred to as a "descriptive methodology" because its primary aim is to *define* what is happening linguistically as opposed to having the end goal of *doing* something with it.)

Adding the "critical" component—the *C* in CDA—makes the practice more pointed, more investigative, and, in the case of using it for dating—far more useful. Critical discourse analysis implies two key attributes that transcend the more neutral discourse analysis:

- CDA is used to identify and articulate what people are revealing *un*intentionally, which is why it's so useful in dating applications. Its purpose is to cull the underlying or cloaked rhetorical message from passages of text or other discursive artifacts (such as a profile with more pictures of a guy's motorcycle than of him).
- CDA implies a mandate to use what you've learned to improve the world in some way, and that's what I'm trying to do. The best comparison here is an ethnographic one, I think. Ethnographers sit quietly and record discourse patterns (ways of speaking) as they occur in real time, and they do not intervene or impose any judgments upon the discourse. The primary goal of ethnographic research is accuracy and insight, not necessarily change; with critical discourse analysis there's an imperative toward positive change, to use the knowledge gained through observation not just for understanding but for critical action.

The foundational scholars in the discipline of CDA, and there are really only a few, all share some common beliefs. Norman Fairclough, professor emeritus of linguistics at Lancaster University and the primary founder of CDA, identifies three properties of the practice: "It is relational, it is dialectical, and it is transdisciplinary." What this means is that no texts or discourses or images or bodies exist in a vacuum; rather, we're all subject to all these linked norms and forces all the time, and this is all occurring beneath the surface in a way we don't even notice—which makes it all the more powerful. This is why something as simple as a man telling a woman to smile isn't a positive or even neutral statement. Without interrogation, it might sound like it, right? *Smiling is good, who doesn't want to smile?* But the social custom of men encouraging women to smile reveals a lot of nefarious forces:

- Men are taking an authoritative position over women in which they get to direct the muscular positioning of a woman's face, thus dictating their embodied rhetoric.
- Men are assuming that a performative display (the smile) is more important than a woman's internal state.
- Even if you take the gender dynamics out of it, a smile request reveals vapid and overly simplistic cultural mandates that fail to account for human complexity. ("Turn that frown upside-down!" But what if the frown was the more appropriate response?)

Barbara Johnstone, professor emeritus of Linguistics at Carnegie Mellon and a specialist in DA, articulates the "controlling theoretical idea" behind CDA as the idea that "texts, embedded in recurring 'discursive practices' for their production, circulation, and reception which are themselves embedded in 'social practice,' are among the principal ways in which ideology is circulated and reproduced." Let me translate that into dating language: That guy who uses his profile to tell you that his mother is his hero because she sacrificed her entire life to make his father and her children happy? He's clueless about women's lived experiences, yes, but he's not *just* clueless. He's also revealing that he has been raised in an interlinked matrix of discursive practices founded upon these beliefs: The most honorable and rewarding thing a woman can be is a wife and mother. This necessarily implies sacrificing herself for others, particularly male others, and the idea that her entire worth is defined by her service to others. This man on the apps is not trying to be a selfish jerk with a limited view of women, he's simply revealing his worldview. Granted, we do wish that by the twenty-first century he'd have gleaned some evolution of insight, but if he hasn't, you definitely want to know that before you date him.

According to both Fairclough and Johnstone, our words and actions not only reflect rhetorical norms but reproduce them. For example, the guy telling women to smile is not only mimicking a practice that has existed for centuries, but if he has a son who's watching him, he's also ushering in the next generation to perpetuate these norms. This is the theory of social reproduction: Social structures and systems, if left unexamined, will naturally be handed down through the generations. When this happens without interrogation, discourses become "naturalized."

A discourse can be considered naturalized when it is taken as common sense by the community of participants who use or are subjected to it. The goal of CDA is to denaturalize discourses and ideologies—to help us pause, break things down, and understand the cultural forces and assumptions that lie beneath various discourses. This is exactly what I seek to do with Burned Haystack; I want to denaturalize the aggressions and manipulations that women are constantly subjected to in the dating pool so that we can all call them out and resist internalizing them and blaming ourselves, as so frequently happens. It might have happened to you.

Note: Discourses can also be naturalized toward health and functionality, and that too is a goal of using this method. Recall the success story you read on pages 14–15, about the young woman who broke up with her boyfriend and said, "My mom left her partner for treating her badly—I'm not afraid of being alone." In that family, the mother had naturalized the practice of walking away from disrespectful and dishonest partners so effectively that her daughter did it intuitively and confidently, rather than wasting years of her life trying to get this young man to treat her decently.

My personal favorite CDA scholar is a now-retired linguist named James Paul Gee. I like his method of CDA the best because it's meticulous and concrete, and "formalized rhetorical methodology" is my love language in the same way that "physical touch" is the love language of all middle-aged divorced men on dating apps.

In his work, Gee uses the term "figured worlds" and defines it as "a picture of a simplified world that captures what is taken to be typical or normal." For example, there is a very traditional figured world for a wedding ceremony: There is a female bride dressed in a white gown who is walked down the aisle by her father and "handed over" to her male groom. This figured world obviously carries a multitude of connotations and implications, featured among them the bride as object of beauty and purity and the groom as agent of provision and protection.

However, our figured worlds are in a constant state of flux and evolution. Over time, certain elements of typical figured worlds are violated or new elements are added. Same-sex marriage is now legally recognized, and this complicates the figured world of "wedding ceremony"; it is a change that some see as productive evolution and others see as destructive violation. Figured worlds are an analytical concept that we can use to understand the stasis or evolution of various identities and social dynamics.

The first time I taught my Rhetoric of Dating and Intimacy course, I asked my students to identify and interrogate some of the figured worlds of Tinder. They described figured worlds such as "shopping on Amazon Prime," where you can "favorite" people and "add them to cart" for later, then ignore them or delete them at will, and they pointed out how commodifying the whole process can be. A group of young women complained that too many of their male heterosexual peers try to use Tinder more like Pornhub; they want to demand certain content and have it "delivered" to them, and when relationships brokered like that translate to real-life interactions they too frequently feature violations of consent. On a day that really broke my heart, one young woman said, "We're just . . . we're just so tired of being choked." She said it matter-of-factly, and at least half a dozen other students just nodded sadly in both solidarity and resignation. More lightly, they described a dating app figured world of "going to the zoo just to see what kind of exotic or freakish animals might be in the cages." DoorDash or Uber Eats offered an example of another figured world—just order up what you want and it will appear at your doorstep within half an hour or so. Many people set up Tinder hookups in exactly this way.

This is all intellectually fascinating, for sure, but it's also rhetorically fruitful. If you're talking to some guy and you realize you feel like a sex worker or an order of nachos, that might be a sign that this particular figured world is one in which you don't want to dwell—and that's your sign to break that connection.

A concept related to figured worlds is something we call primary metaphors, which is an extended manifestation of figurative language. While figured worlds refer to one discrete scenario, such as a wedding or observing animals in a zoo, primary metaphors apply across larger planes of existence such as human relationships or people's states of mind. I will explain that in a moment, but first I want to clearly differentiate between regular metaphors (the kind you learned about in middle school) and primary metaphors.

We know that figurative language is so pervasive that it is nearly impossible for speakers and writers to avoid. If we sufficiently slow down our reading or listening, we will generally find that most people are capable of isolating and identifying many of the semantic metaphors that we use. For example, to say that "John is a pig" is a regular (or semantic) metaphor. Any native English speaker understands that by saying this we are implying that John is sloppy, or boorish, or rude. We easily recognize "pig" as metaphorical.

Primary metaphors are deeper, more comprehensive, and more powerful than semantic metaphors. They order our behavior in ways we don't even register, which is part of the reason they're so powerful.

For example, Gee uses this short sentence, in which a woman discusses her reluctance to leave a bad marriage, to demonstrate how such metaphors operate: "Why in the world would I want to stop and not get the use out of all the years we've already spent together?" This question exemplifies the "time = money" primary metaphor. The woman's use of the word "spent" and the phrase "get the use out of," as well as her tacit allusions to wanting some sort of "return on investment," reveal the ways in which she (perhaps unknowingly) subscribes to a financial model as the basis for marriage.

George Lakoff and Mark Johnson, authors of *Metaphors We Live By*, claim that these metaphors are not only central to the way we understand the concepts in our worlds, but they also "govern our everyday functioning, down to the most mundane details . . . what we perceive, how we get around in the world, and how we relate to other people. [They play] a central role in defining our everyday realities." According to Lakoff and Johnson, these metaphors are so pervasive in our everyday reality that, for the most part, we remain unaware of them. They operate below the level of text, without our conscious knowledge, and literally become embodied and embedded within us in a way that we neither take note of nor confront.

For example, most people subscribe to what is called the "up is good" primary metaphor. We tend to *feel* (not necessarily *believe* or *think*, since primary metaphors operate subconsciously) that "up is good" and "down is bad." We would rather rise than fall, and we assume that "higher" is always better than lower, that "things are looking up" means something good while "looking down on someone" implies contempt. "There's nowhere to go but up" means that things will only get better, whereas "That whole deal went south" means that things went poorly.

Primary metaphors generally relate to our embodied knowledge, what we might call "gut reactions." We use and understand them without the need to recruit intellectual explanations for them. We feel that rising up is good and falling down is bad, perhaps because we've embodied positive responses to rising—the fun of jumping or being lifted up—and negative responses to falling—pain or lack of control or humiliation. Hence, "up is good and down is bad" becomes part of our embodied knowledge that we do not question.

This combination—the coexistence of something that orders our reality while simultaneously remaining hidden from us—warrants our attention when we study the discourses of institutions, politics, and interpersonal communication. The sheer number of primary metaphors we use every day without thinking about them suggests how crucial they are to how we function as human beings. Lakoff and Johnson suggest several, of which I include just a few for the purpose of demonstration:

THEORIES AND ARGUMENTS ARE BUILDINGS: "Is that the *foundation* of your theory? The theory needs more *support*. The argument is *shaky*."

They list four different primary metaphors for ideas:

IDEAS ARE FOOD: "What he said left a *bad taste in my mouth*. All this paper has in it are *raw facts, half-baked ideas, and warmed-over theories*."

As opposed to:

IDEAS ARE PLANTS: "That idea *died on the vine*. That's a *budding* theory. It will take years for that idea *to come to full flower*."

As opposed to:

IDEAS ARE COMMODITIES: "It's important how you *package* your ideas. He won't *buy* that. That idea just won't *sell*. There is always a *market* for good ideas. That's a *worthless* idea."

As opposed to:

IDEAS ARE CUTTING INSTRUMENTS: "That's an *incisive* idea. That *cuts right to the heart* of the matter. That was a *cutting* remark. He's *sharp*. He has a *razor* wit."

These four primary metaphors for talking about ideas demonstrate the very different ways such metaphors can reflect or construct reality.

To conceive of an idea as a plant (which should be protected, nurtured, and cultivated) is vastly different from considering it as a cutting instrument (a weapon or tool capable of inflicting pain and/or death). There are many other potential conceptual structures for "ideas" beyond these four. Lakoff and Johnson articulate seven different highly complex primary metaphor options to describe the experience of love. For example, we often refer to conceptions of medicine when talking about love: "This is a *sick* relationship. They have a *strong, healthy* marriage. The marriage is *dead*—it can't be *revived*. Their marriage is *on the mend*. We're getting *back on our feet*." Another option is to see it as magic: "She *cast her spell* over me . . . I was *entranced* by him. I'm *charmed* by her. She is *bewitching*." I borrow these examples from Lakoff and Johnson because their metaphorical deconstruction of love is, number one, now foundational to how cognitive linguists conceive of the intersection of language and love, and, number two, highly relevant to the subject matter of this book. However, there are arguably an infinite number of primary metaphors we could find to describe love. Just last week, a group of undergraduate students in my "Rhetoric of Dating and Intimacy" class pointed out that we frequently discuss romantic relationships in terms of air and space: "I need some space here"; "It's like you can't even let me breathe"; "You took my breath away"; "You seem so distant right now"; "Your ego is sucking all the oxygen out of this room."

Let's return to the primary metaphor of "Love is magic" for a moment and consider what a different orientation this is from the financial model the woman in Gee's earlier example seems to suggest. Depending upon which theory we subscribe to (again, probably subconsciously), we are likely to act and react accordingly. If we perceive love to be a financial state of affairs, we will tend to make decisions based upon logic and rationality, and we will tend to believe that we, for the most part, control those decisions. If we see love as magic, we tend to watch and wait passively, to allow ourselves to be swept up in its orbit or abandoned according to its whims. This model is significantly less controllable (albeit significantly more romantic).

This is the reason that the implications of primary metaphors are so consequential for human relationships and environments. Identifying the primary metaphors operating in a dating interaction (or any interaction) gives us important clues about its relative toxicity or health.

To get to the primary metaphor level of Burned Haystack, we first need to isolate and define the semantic metaphors:

HAYSTACK = the group of men available to date

HAY = men we don't want to date

NEEDLES = men we do want to date

The primary metaphor of this method, then, might sound something like this:

Finding a partner is burning a haystack to reveal the needles

I use both figured worlds and primary metaphors when analyzing dating app language for these patterns (we'll dive into the fascinating world of rhetorical patterns in chapter 5).

. . .

Let's end this chapter by demonstrating a "hot take" CDA analysis from a very short profile to demonstrate how powerful and illuminating these analytical tools can be. Here's the profile:

> I am searching for a mate that dislikes arguing. Is as quick to accept a compliment as she is to give one. Someone who gives freely without expectation of rewards or perhaps understands the concept that giving is the reward.

Let's analyze:

"I am searching for a mate": He doesn't intend to reveal this, but you already know how he sees women from the first sentence—he views women as objects/animals/complements to men. No enlightened man in contemporary life uses the phrase "searching for a mate." His subconscious figured world is one in which women are animals to be impregnated.

"dislikes arguing": Almost everyone dislikes arguing. What he means here is that he can't handle a women questioning him in any way.

"quick to accept a compliment": Everyone likes compliments unless they're not really compliments. He's revealing here that women haven't "accepted" his compliments in the past, which means they weren't really compliments to begin with. I imagine (though I can't know for sure) that we are probably dealing with some sort of "boundary violation" figured world. If this guy is "giving women compliments" that they don't want to "accept," it seems likely that he is doing something more akin to "flinging unwanted objects into their personal spaces." Which is, of course, another metaphor. We truly can't conceive of or communicate within our world without metaphors. (Also, "within our world" is metaphorical because I'm speaking figuratively right now rather than referring to something that happens specifically within the troposphere of planet Earth; see how this never ends???)

"as she is to give one": What he's really saying here is *praise* me, *love* me, *accept* me!!!!!!!!

"gives freely": The concept of "giving freely" to a full-grown man is problematic because it invokes the notion of unconditional love, which is only ever appropriate between parent and child, not between two adults in a romantic relationship. In a romantic relationship that is a situation ripe for abuse and exploitation. We're working with a figured world of "mother-to-child" here, which does not bode well.

"without expectation of reward": In this sentence the word "reward" means basic human give-and-take; it means being two adults, but he only wants *you* to be the adult. If we were to write this in primary metaphor form, it might sound like "Feminine love is a never-ending one-directional fountain of giving." It sounds hyperbolic phrased this way, but it's a pattern I see over and over again in men's profiles. Sometimes it sounds like the profile we're analyzing right now; other times it sounds like this: "My ideal woman cares more about others than herself and always puts her partner's needs before her own." I think the men who write these things actually mean them in a "good" way, but they're revealing their concept of how women should perform in a relationship, and it's a destructive one that doesn't work for most women in current times.

"understands the concept that giving is the reward": He's taking it up a notch here. Not only are you to expect zero from him, but you're supposed to *like* it because you'll have gotten *so* much joy simply from the process of giving *to* him.

Bottom line: If you view your love life as a 100 percent charitable endeavor that will simultaneously make you feel shitty every day, this dude is your guy! If not, you need to block and burn him immediately. (Another metaphor!!)

SUCCESS STORY!

I've learned so much here and applied Burned Haystack on Bumble for almost two months now. I wanted to share my experience. (Spoiler: It works!)

I chose to use the paid version so I didn't have to swipe through the masses. Rather, I only looked through those profiles who had already liked me. I did nothing for a week. I wanted a pool before I looked at them. When I looked . . . oh my! Hundreds of likes. Way too many. So I set filters to see people who had liked me within thirty miles (my ideal dating radius), within eight years on either side of my age, and with a couple of shared values selected. Bam! Less than a hundred profiles to look at. Most profiles I B2Bd quickly due to clichés (such as "partner in crime"), the sex positivity icon, toxic or negative language, "I'm not sure yet" for what they are looking for, and so on . . .

I selected the ten best profiles to swipe right and message. Half did not respond to my initial message at all. Of the five who responded:

One couldn't naturally make conversation at all. So awkward . . . B2B.

One made comments immediately like "Wow you're sexy, let's exchange numbers." B2B.

One moved within three days from seeming to put effort into getting to know me to messaging me "wyd?" one evening.

Whether he's clueless that it's dating slang for a booty call, or whether he was just being lazy in not coming up with things to share or ask on his own and was punting the ball to me, I realized I didn't care. Both were unacceptable. B2B.

Another exchanged ten very nice messages with me telling me stories about his life and travels until I realized he hadn't asked me a single question about myself or anything in my profile. I had asked him several questions, which he responded to and asked nothing back. I waited two days not writing back to his last message to see if he leaned in and asked me anything. Nope. I B2Bd him too, with no explanation.

And then there was one . . . one who kept jumping over every hurdle I set, not moving too fast or love bombing me, never commenting on my appearance or saying anything sexual, asking me thoughtful questions, and sharing at a nice reciprocal level. One who when I asked why he had not chosen to "verify" his profile, said he could understand why that felt important and verified it immediately. One who asked if we could play a game of Words with Friends before he even asked for my phone number. We played a whole game over a few days, deciding along the way that the loser would buy the winner coffee. (When I won, he immediately challenged me again with no snark about losing. And we talked for three hours over that coffee.) One who brought a treat for my dog on our second date at the park and inquired whether she might be on a special diet and if it was okay to give her the treat. One who I have been on five well-planned dates with now and messaged with every day for six weeks.

Things are progressing rather slowly, which my therapist tells me is actually very healthy. I'm so used to in past relationships going out with someone two or three times, feeling a great connection, being intimate, and bam, you're in an instant relationship. (C'mon, I know I'm not the only one here.) We're really taking time to be friends and get to know each other (with some wonderful kissing and hand-holding included). I'm pretty sure he's a needle. Time will tell whether he's *my* needle, but I would call this a Burned Haystack success. I was able to fairly rapidly—and with very little swiping and demoralizing drama—find someone who met my criteria, with mutual attraction on several levels, who was worth spending time with. That feels like a win! I'm excited to see where this goes, and I'm enjoying the journey.

Since I am still in my paid membership period, I have at least once a week gone to check new likes on Bumble. I wasn't looking to put all my eggs in one basket so early. I am still willing to meet someone else and consider options. This isn't locked down. I matched with one other guy and chatted briefly, but really it just reinforced what I appreciate about the one I'm already seeing.

Thanks for reading about my experience. I'm not sure I have a question here—more a reinforcement that following the steps and being a bit unapologetically ruthless in B2Bing does work.

—*Lisa*

I wrote the community post below on the Facebook group page, and it's relevant to the success stories in this book as well.

> Sometimes when we celebrate a success story in the online communities, people ask, "How do we know this is really a success? They've only known each other three months" (or six months, or two months, or whatever).
>
> I remove those comments for three reasons:
>
> 1. I want to just let people be happy. Anything can go wrong for anyone at any time for any reason. People walk away from thirty-year marriages *all* the time. Pure duration is never an accurate metric of "success." (Similarly, people stay married and miserable for their entire lives, and I don't personally consider that a "success.")

2. I've been very clear that this method is strictly about using applied rhetoric techniques to make the apps more efficient and effective at finding decent matches ("needles") that have the potential to turn into long-term successful partnerships. People meet needles all the time that might not turn out to be *their* needle, but that doesn't negate the match's needle status.

3. I'm a rhetorician; I'm not a therapist or a couples counselor or a social scientist or a psychologist. I have no more qualifications to judge a "good" or "successful" relationship than anyone. My game is making my very specific expertise (applied rhetoric) work for women who are using the dating apps. After that, I'm out. Not because I don't care (I do care!) but because I'm not qualified.

I hope this is helpful—I know this is the internet and people have no problem verging out of their lanes all the time (a good deal of the most successful "dating coaches" on the web have zero professional qualifications), but it's something I still care about, and I work really hard to focus on what I can do, not make claims I haven't earned, and stay in my own lane (while recognizing I don't get this 100 percent perfect, lol).

Okay, carry on, Haystackers!

HUMOR BREAK

As a Middle-Aged Man on a Dating App, I Would Like to Show How Modern I Am by Quoting a Book Published in 1992

Hi Ladies. I get it: you're sick of meeting men who are "afraid of commitment" or "really busy with work" or any of the other fairy tales my gender loves to tell. Most of all, you're done with guys who are emotionally unavailable and unevolved.

I realize that most of the men on this app have the EQ of a cane toad and haven't kept up with modern relationship science. Not me, though: I'm cutting edge. Not only am I an expert on psychology, but I can set myself apart by quoting this hot new book that was published in 1992. Impressive, right? Kinda caught you off guard that I'd be aware of an international bestseller that's sold twenty million copies and been translated into forty-nine languages. Clearly, I'm not like other men; I am capable of reading an entire book cover to cover, especially if it has lots of bullet points and bold text.

Anyway, enough mystery! *What is this magical book*, you might wonder, *and how is it relevant to me, a single woman looking for a long-term relationship?* Well, it's called *The 5 Love Languages*, by Gary Chapman. It's wholly uninformed by research, laughably gendered, and reduces all complexities of human connection into five pithy-but-stupid sayings. Needless to say, I was hooked immediately. I'm really busy at work, so I don't have a lot of time to waste on details and nuance. And I definitely don't have time for drama!

Anyway, I'm being coy, aren't I? I'm sorry, I'll get to the big reveal here. Even if you've never heard of this megahit from thirty years ago, at this point you're certainly wondering, "But which love language is *this* guy's love language?" Well, you're probably going to be surprised, but here it is:

My love language is.......... ...

Physical touch.

I realize you probably don't see that one a lot on this app, but for me, it's true.

And rather than dragging you through the whole boring saga of my tense, sexless marriage and my absolute failure to interrogate my complicity in the dry spell of its last seventeen years, I can just tell you that "My love language is physical touch," and you'll know everything you need to know about me. I'm basically giving you the code-cracker for unlocking my tricky chemistry and finding your way to my heart! Through my pants!! Ha ha, just being a flirt!

So if you're a sexy, affectionate lady who's fit and open-minded and equally comfortable in jeans and a cocktail dress, and you want to meet a guy who's not like all the rest, LET'S CHAT (in my love language, which, again, is physical touch).

4

THE BURNED HAYSTACK METHOD RULES

When I first got on the apps and encountered the terribleness that all women encounter, I figured I must be doing something wrong, that surely there were tricks to navigating these apps and making them work better, and I just hadn't cracked the code. I looked to Google for help and found two pieces of advice again and again:

1. I should make myself as widely appealing as possible to as many men as possible.
2. I should give almost everyone a chance because it's a numbers game, and the more men I meet the more likely I would be to find a partner.

This is *terrible* advice. It *is* a numbers game, but the strategy needs to be flipped. There is no shortage of men on dating apps (they outnumber women three-to-one on some apps), but there is a severe shortage of *datable* men. This is why my method advises women to do the exact opposite of the two most common pieces of advice: According to Burned Haystack, you should present yourself exactly as you are, and you should give almost no one a chance.

So I decided to write my own rules. Here they are:

RULE 1: THE APP IS A TOOL; IT'S NOT A PLACE TO LIVE, AND IT'S NOT A GAME OR SOMEWHERE TO HANG OUT OR KILL TIME.

Think of it like your toothbrush, which you use probably twice a day, maybe three times, for a couple of minutes at a time. And then you put it away. You probably do not carry your toothbrush around with you all day constantly "checking" on it to see what it's doing, and you shouldn't do that with a dating app either.

It may be true that *some* amount of activity on the dating app affects the algorithms in a way that can benefit you, but I still recommend spending no more than five to ten minutes max per day interacting with the app itself. If you're messaging with someone or a few someones and the messaging is going well (see next rule), that's a different story.

Dating apps are "gamified" (more on that later) to keep you on them all day, but Burned Haystack requires you to resist that temptation. The goal of this method is to give you a set of guidelines for maximizing your chances of success on the apps while minimizing their effect on the rest of your life. You want to move dating app activity to the back burner so that it's not *controlling* your life. This is the only healthy, sustainable way to purposefully use a dating app to find a long-term partnership. I understand that some people really do want to use the dating apps more as a distraction or form of entertainment, and no judgment if that's you, but that's not the focus of this method.

RULE 2: FOCUS ON MESSAGING OVER SCROLLING OR SWIPING. MESSAGING IS WHERE YOU'LL FIND THE INFO YOU REALLY NEED.

Engage only with personalized messages that are worth responding to, and respond only in kind. For example, if someone says "Hi," your response should be "Hi" (or don't respond at all; I wouldn't). Do not accept crumbs of communication and serve up a buffet in response. I see this all the time. The man says something like "What do you hope to find on this app?" and the woman responds with a thoughtful and detailed answer (because women are socialized to be generous communicators who naturally pick up the lion's share of facilitating a conversation), and then she never hears from him again.

> ### "HI"—TIME TO MOVE ALONG
>
> You probably shouldn't respond to lazy messages early on no matter what; in particular, the question about your experience on the apps is a copy-paste, and if you respond to it honestly, you're essentially handing over a "playbook" to manipulate you. I realize that this might sound paranoid or defensive, but it's simply not a good idea to reveal too much intimate information to perfect strangers; you have no idea what they might do with it. It makes much more sense to keep the conversation light until you meet someone in person and can get a better feel for who he actually is. If you just cringed at the suggestion to "keep the conversation light" (I would; I hate small talk), then understand that by "light" I don't mean "fluffy and inconsequential"; what I actually mean is "not deeply personal about *you* (or, for god's sake, your children)." Go right ahead and have meaningful discussions about social or political events or celebrities or art or music or sports or books or any number of other fascinating topics; you can actually glean a *lot* of crucial knowledge about someone by talking about such things. Just don't get into inappropriately personal conversations too early.

Use this graphic to help you navigate a dating app conversation and to decide when it's time to exit it or invest more energy:

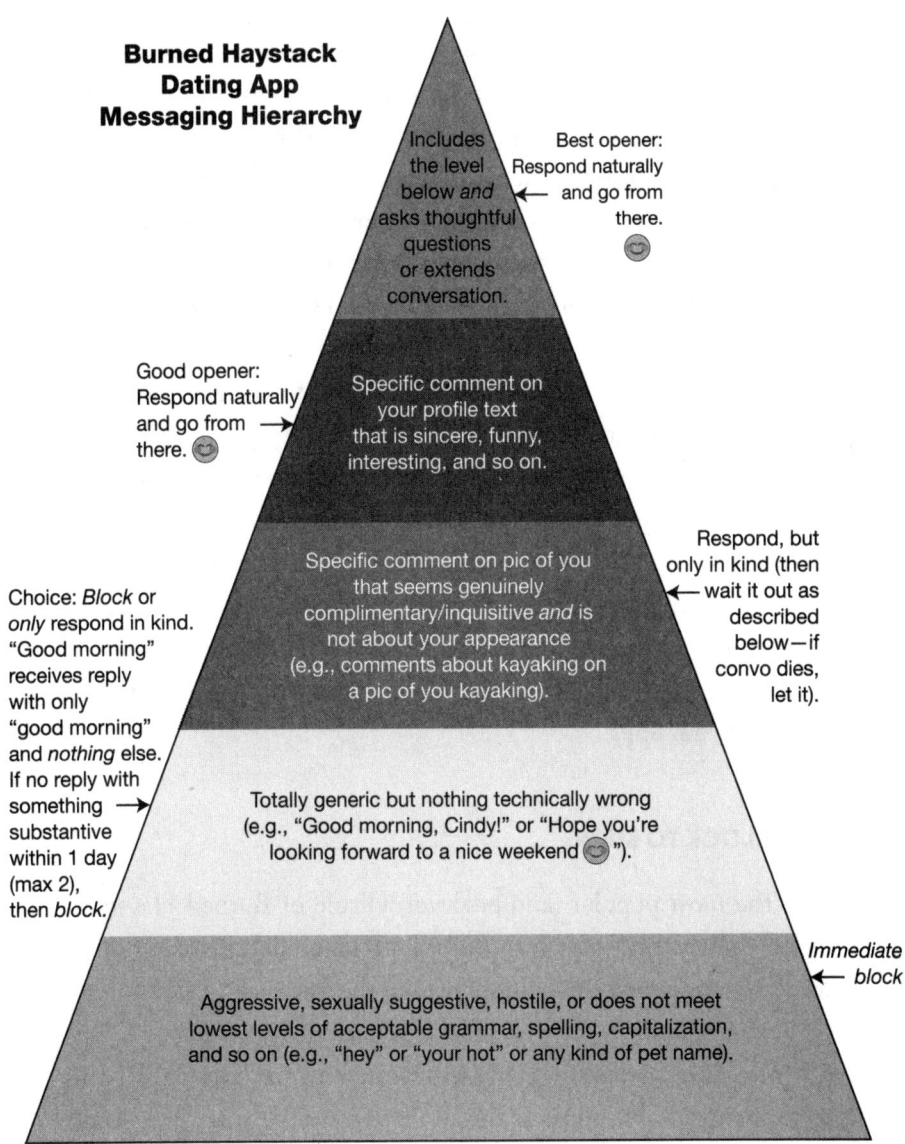

RULE 3: NO NOTIFICATIONS.

Disable them entirely. Why?

- It's not good for your nervous system to be constantly vigilant for pings and vibrations. I'm sure you get enough of that from work and your family and friends. Don't let the dating apps become an additional burden. The dating apps are working for *you*, not vice versa; it is not your responsibility to be at their beck and call. It is also not your responsibility to be at the beck and call of men. I know we've been socialized to think so. Fight that.
- You don't *need* to respond to every ounce of male attention immediately. And moreover, you *shouldn't*. Responding to every like or wave within five minutes conveys desperation, and that is not a vibe you want to exhibit on dating apps.
- If you're concerned that without notifications you'll forget to check your dating app, then so be it; that's fine and just means it's not your priority right now. I promise that if dating and finding a partner is a priority for you, you will not forget to check your apps.

RULE 4: BLOCK TO BURN.

This is the most popular (and buzzwordy) rule of Burned Haystack. A lot of women abbreviate it to B2B on social media. Blocking is the superpower and secret weapon of burning the haystack.

The dating apps "recycle" people. If you simply swipe left or X men out, you're almost certainly going to see them again. Not only is this a waste of time, but it prevents the app from sending you other people who might be better matches.

This rule requires a thought shift. With Burned Haystack, blocking is not punitive (and every app has a way to do it without negatively impacting the person you're blocking); it's used to beat the algorithms. Use it *liberally*.

Let's think in terms of burning an actual haystack for a moment. If you were to set a match to a haystack with the intention of burning it to find the needle, you'd want the entire haystack to burn down to the ground, making it really easy to spot the needle. You wouldn't want to just burn it halfway, because then you'd have to dig through scattered burned hay and piles of ashes. If you keep men you're not interested in circulating through your accounts—even if they've done nothing wrong—that's what you're doing. You're not really burning the haystack so much as moving little pieces of it to the side. The hay will keep blowing around and back in your way, making it hard to see the needles.

Here is what women who have used this method to find their needles report (over and over and over again):

- I was absolutely ruthless about blocking to burn. (A shocking number of Burned Haystack success stories feature the word "ruthless"—I've studied this.)
- The second a guy led with anything to do with my appearance, I blocked him.
- I tolerated zero words of sexual content and blocked to burn without further engagement.

Many women who've found their needles report blocking hundreds to thousands of men and, depending upon geography, sitting with no haystack at all for periods of time. If that's happening to you (it happens in rural areas a lot, especially to women over forty), it might be time to consider one of these adjustments:

- While I don't like to suggest expanding your filters in terms of the kind of partner you want, the geographical filter is the most benign one to try expanding. Especially postpandemic, many people are more mobile than ever. We have quite a few long-distance success stories at this point. This is obviously a personal decision and not feasible for everyone, but if it's even a possibility for you, you might want to consider it.

- Consider changing apps. You will get the most exposure and activity on any dating app when you initially join it; things will dwindle after that. For this reason, for women who live in rural or sparsely populated areas, I recommend using only one app at a time for one month at a time. I realize this is more work because you're more frequently setting up accounts and profiles, but it's an intervention that has proved successful for people.

RULE 5: NO FIGHTING WITH MEN.

First, I get it. I've done it. They say mean or irritating or just stupid things and you feel compelled to defend yourself, call out their bullshit, or correct them. It's human nature. Don't do it. *Block them immediately.* Engaging with this is a waste of your time. Discipline yourself not to. Do not spend one second of your one wild and precious life (shout-out to Mary Oliver) fighting with random men on the internet.

And if you can't do it with sheer discipline, think about it this way: While you're lecturing Toxic Todd about why his sexual aggression actually isn't a turn-on, you might miss an actual needle (and meanwhile you're training Todd how to manipulate other women). It's just not worth the time *or* the risk.

RULE 6: DON'T BE A PEN PAL.

This is a real problem on dating apps. You enter a conversation with a man and the conversation seems promising, but then it never goes anywhere. You just keep trading message after message, and there's nothing really wrong with the exchange (or it might even be a really great exchange), but it's not moving toward meeting in real life.

I think you need to set a limit on this. My limit was one week. If I'd been messaging back and forth with a man for a week and he didn't move it toward meeting, I blocked him.

There are caveats to this: If he's out of town, if he's taking care of a sick kid, if he's volunteering overseas for Doctors Without Borders or working on an offshore oil rig (just kidding, they are *never actually with Doctors Without Borders or working on an offshore oil rig*; this is the stuff of scammers), then okay. But if there's some legit reason he hasn't moved the exchange toward meeting, he will tell you that, and he'll tell you clearly, because he won't want to risk letting you get away. Don't give men the benefit of the doubt on this; don't delude yourself into thinking they're shy, or they're trying not to rush you, or they're busy, and so on. If a man is genuinely interested in you, he will figure out how to orchestrate meeting you in real life. And if he can't (for whatever reason: he's underconfident, he's super passive, whatever), then you don't want him anyway.

Final word: Every man I've ever met on an app who was worth dating moved the conversation off the app and into real life in less than one week. (I know right now you're thinking, *This sounds very heteronormative, old-school gender-rules-ish. Why am I waiting for the man to move the conversation off the app?* Please stay tuned.)

RULE 7: SET YOUR GEOGRAPHY, BUT DON'T SHARE YOUR LOCATION (IF YOU CAN HELP IT; SOME APPS REQUIRE IT).

I feel strongly about this. Do you know who chooses male-female pairings based upon immediate location? Animals. Wild animals. Wild animals decide whom to mate with by looking around their immediate area and seeing who's there. This is the premise of Tinder and other hookup apps; it's not the way to find someone who wants to learn about you and grow with you into a mature, committed relationship.

Go ahead and set your geographic boundaries (as mentioned in

Rule 4, those of you in small towns or rural areas might have to be willing to expand those boundaries considerably in order to get decent matches), but disable the location-sharing option on your apps if possible. Not sharing location is a great way to burn the haystack because it'll weed out a lot of men who just want to hook up.

On the apps in which location sharing is unavoidable, I recommend *only* matching with men who actually live in your datable area, for these reasons:

- Practically, there's just way more chance you'll be able to facilitate a relationship with someone reasonably close to you.
- Men who live in, say, Los Angeles and want to "date" you while they're on a business trip to Des Moines probably do not have the same goals as you (if your goal is a long-term, committed partnership).

I know, I know, I know: We've all heard those stories about fate and chance and passing ships who actually stop and remain together forever. That's possible; it is. If you're a gambler, or you're super mobile, or you just want to see what happens, then have at it, I guess. But the Burned Haystack method is aimed at stacking the deck in your favor to increase the likelihood of success based upon actions and decisions rather than the whims of the universe. That said, I'm certainly not one to rain on anybody's cosmic parade, so venture forth if you feel so moved. If you're a pragmatist like me, though, you might want to focus on the boys next door.

RULE 8: NO "LUDIC LOOPING" AND NO "ATTRACTIONS OF DEPRIVATION."

Natasha Schüll, a cultural anthropologist and professor at New York University, uses the phrase "ludic loop" to describe the phenomenon of falling victim to the addictive nature of video games or phone games such as Candy Crush. In an interview on *All Things Considered*, she described the effect like this: "It's you and the machine. . . . There's no real character development or narrative arc. Kill the monster; kill the monster again; kill the monster again. You never know when you're going to get the reward [or] how much the reward will be." This sounds a *lot* like online dating: Like the guy, swipe right on the next guy, like the guy after him. You never know when one of them is going to message or what the message might be. It'll probably be "your gorgeous" [*sic*] or "What do you hope to find on this app?" or the dreaded "How is a beautiful girl like you still single?"

The experience of endless swiping on a dating app—getting caught in the ludic loop—creates a simple stimulus-response pattern that releases dopamine (the feel-good hormone) even in a total absence of reward. This is the exact same phenomenon that keeps people playing slot machines for hours on end—even the *anticipation* of a reward becomes a reward itself on a neurological level. This pattern is *intentionally* built into dating apps and designed to keep you hooked, even without any reward.

Dr. Michael Merzenich, a neuroscientist and professor at University of California San Francisco, explains how the simple act of swiping through a dating app triggers dopamine release and creates what he calls a "chemical positive." Tinder, for example, knows this and perpetuates it; the goal is *not* to find you a good match as quickly as possible. Tinder defines "success" as "more members having more conversations," but that's success *for Tinder*, not for people who are truly hoping to find a partner. (I'm bashing Tinder because it's the worst and there's the most info on these topics available in relation to Tinder, but all dating apps have this effect.)

Avoiding ludic looping is about refusing to become a victim of the app, but people can draw us into a similar destructive pattern, and it's equally important to guard against it in app-based dating. The concept is called "attractions of deprivation," and understanding it is crucial to protecting yourself in romantic relationships. Ken Page, psychotherapist and author of *Deeper Dating: How to Drop the Games of Seduction and Discover the Power of Intimacy*, writes, "If I could only share one insight with my single readers, it would be this: Learn to distinguish between your 'attractions of deprivation' and your 'attractions of inspiration.' Then, *only* follow your attractions of inspiration. I believe that's the wisest path to love." In a *Psychology Today* article, Page describes attractions of deprivation as ones that "draw us in like an undertow and almost always get us hurt." He describes a scenario that many of us have spent far too much time in: waiting to hear from a man, trying to win him over, feeling high when we're in his immediate sphere of attention yet constantly insecure and distracted and worried when we're not.

Dating apps, of course, are also the perfect example of intermittent reward, and I am betting that the definition above will resonate with nearly everyone who's ever set up an online dating profile.

Attractions of *inspiration*, on the other hand, are stable and comfortable and predictable and secure. They unfold and deepen over time and are built upon mutual trust and support. Rather than keeping you guessing or creating a dynamic in which you're constantly "chasing" and hoping to "win" (attention or commitment or love or whatever), they make you feel calm and secure and confident and content. This obviously requires time and repeated interactions, as opposed to immediate chemistry and excitement, which is why we see so many more attractions of deprivation than inspiration being brokered on the dating apps, at least initially.

Getting sucked into ludic loops and AODs (attractions of deprivation) is *not* your fault. You are a human being with a human brain, and human brains are susceptible to such things. However, human brains are *also* capable of understanding how these things work, and this is knowledge that can help protect us from falling victim.

We must use that knowledge. It's all tied into the concept of intermittent reward systems and their potential to both create obsession and sustain abuse; this has been well documented in research on rats.

The effect of intentionally doling out intermittent rewards is cruel and heartbreaking, but *we are not rats*. Do not allow a digital app or a man to turn you into a desperate rat. (Also, no judgment if it happens; we've all been there at one point or another, but let's just try *really* hard not to stay there or, ideally, not to get there in the first place now that we understand the mechanisms.)

RULE 9: NO MEN WHO CAN'T PLAN THE DATE.

I get yelled at a lot about this one, especially from other feminists, and the argument sounds like this:

> Are you serious? It's 2026, and you're telling me I'm supposed to sit passively back and wait for a man to ask me out and tell me what we're doing?

Yes, that is exactly what I'm telling you, but not for the reasons you think.

Gendered labor inequities are still a pervasive problem, if not the norm, especially when we're talking about domestic labor and emotional labor, and dating fits squarely into those genres. I bet the reason many of you are on the dating apps and reading this book right now is that you finally got sick of doing all the work, all the time.

As I've said before, Burned Haystack is not moralistic; it's strategic. The method is concerned with *efficacy*. It's designed to teach you to use rhetorical and linguistic clues to get important information very early on so that you don't waste your time, and to help you make good decisions about whom to date. The argument for sitting back and waiting to see if a man can plan a date is that if he can't or won't, then you're going to be doing all the work for Date #1, which doesn't bode well for the interactions you have beyond that date. People usually bring their A game at the beginning of things, so if he can't plan a date during his best-self phase, he's definitely not going to do it down the road. If he can plan a good date and communicate about it well and work with you cooperatively to refine it into something that works for both of you, it suggests he can and will probably do a lot of other good things too—good information to have. He can probably navigate the grocery store, and plan a vacation, and put a meal together all on his own, and remember the birthdays of his family members, all without you directing it—and that's what you're looking for. You don't want the guys who can't plan the date.

I'm not saying that the man needs to handle 100 percent of date planning and/or that you should not weigh in. I'm saying you should guard against dynamics like this:

> **Man:** Would you want to get together on Friday?
> **You:** Sure, that sounds great!
> **Man:** Awesome, let me know what you want to do!

Or worse:

> **Man:** Cool!

Or worse yet:

> **Man:** *crickets*

Here's what's happened: He's getting you to do all the labor (emotional and practical) before you've even met. Things don't improve from this point. If you get any of the responses above, I would simply wait it out. He's asked, you've said yes, the ball is in his court. You may never hear from him again, and if so, you've just saved yourself what was almost certainly going to be wasted time. If he's truly interested in you, and he asked you out and you kindly and enthusiastically accepted, then he will figure out how to orchestrate the next moves. At this point you've said yes, so we can't give him the excuse of being insecure or uncertain or confused or whatever. Remember that men run companies and become brain surgeons and fly into space and build bridges—they are perfectly capable of planning a first date.

Here's the kind of interaction you *do* want to see:

First Date Scenario 1

> **Man:** Would you want to get together on Friday?
> **You:** Sure, that sounds great!
> **Man:** Awesome! Do you prefer a coffee or dinner date for the first meeting?

[After this a collaborative dialogue develops and you jointly plan the date—this is *all good!*]

First Date Scenario 2

He offers up an entirely planned date and asks if it sounds good to you. If it does, then great! You're good to go, and he handled all the work of this date (obviously we are not expecting him to handle 100 percent of all date planning forever—just this first one). Or it mostly sounds good to you but you want to modify something—maybe he suggested a barbecue place and you're vegetarian. In that case, you tell him the date sounds great but how about this other restaurant instead? He's cool with that, yay!! Also *all good!*

Either of these two scenarios suggest good things about this guy. It doesn't ensure chemistry or a love connection, but it does suggest you're dealing with a capable adult with good manners, and that already sets him apart in the world of online dating.

Here's one other scenario that I think is rare, but let's talk through it:

First Date Scenario 3

He offers an entirely planned date and you hate every element of it. I have a friend who met a man who suggested that for their first date they go to a video-game arcade and then out for burgers. She's a vegan who hates video games. She responded and said, "Not a video game fan, but I'm willing to try it. Could we try a different restaurant, though? I'm vegan." I think we also must recognize here that if you hate every element of what he's planned, the chances of him being a viable partner for you are not great. (My friend actually did go on the date, and it was horrible but in a cringe-inducing, laughably bad kind of way that we've cracked jokes about for years, so maybe it was worth it???)

If he plans the date and you ask for a modification and he has *any kind of bad reaction at all*—he gets angry or you suddenly don't hear from him for days or he mocks you or his whole demeanor changes—cancel the date and block him. This is going to be a waste of your time at best and a truly horrible experience at worst. If he's angry with you *prior* to Date #1, it's not going to get better from there. Cut your losses and move on.

The only acceptable response to your asking for a reasonable modification to the first-date plan is to graciously and immediately respond positively and make the modification.

Everything related to Rule 9 is a great example of using language—people's words and sentences—to analyze the likelihood or potential of their future behavior. Our whole purpose here is to use language to burn the haystack, so we have to be willing to do that with honesty and courage that is grounded in demonstrable reality: We cannot read his actual words and then assume he didn't really mean to come across that way. It doesn't matter how he meant to come across; the words reveal his reality. Since the endeavor of dating is aimed at merging *your* reality with someone else's, there's no room to misjudge it. Read the words and burn the haystack.

RULE 10: TREAT THE PROCESS OF ONLINE DATING AS A JOB SEARCH, NOT A TAKE-OUT ORDER.

The apps are definitely designed to feel more like ordering from DoorDash or Uber—they're offering nearly immediate gratification. But tacos and rides to the airport are inherently short-term things: You'll be done within minutes, so there's not much at stake. If you're trying to meet a *human being*, with whom you'd ideally like to forge a lifelong commitment, you have to be willing to play a longer game, which is not what the apps are built for or profit from.

The average job search for a professional position takes five months—which means it often takes longer. If you were on the job market, you'd spend a significant amount of time writing a résumé and cover letter and start working your network, and then once you'd applied for multiple positions, you'd sit back and wait until you heard from someone offering you something that sounded like a good fit. You wouldn't sit there staring at your email inbox and then immediately agree to take the first shitty job that wants to hire you. You'd probably be insulted that at this stage of your life someone even thought you would be interested.

What you'd do instead is send out those applications and then walk away from the computer and do other things—whatever else you want to do in your life. You'd tell yourself that job searching is a long and protracted process that involves myriad factors you can't control, but you've done all the work and made all the connections necessary to kick it off, and the right job for you will eventually come through. It happens exactly this way in real life all the time; I'm suggesting you apply the same mentality to your dating life.

• • •

One thing I'm frequently asked is this: "If I actually follow all these rules, there will hardly be any men left to date." That might be true, and it's definitely true that using Burned Haystack you will meet far fewer men and go out on far fewer dates; however, the men you *do* meet and spend time with will be much better candidates for long-term, monogamous partnerships, which is the goal of the method.

When I started burning the haystack myself, instead of juggling twenty-five different men engaging at various levels from "viewing" to "winking" to "favoriting" to messaging, I was instead managing perhaps two or three conversations that were actually worth having.

For me, this was a good thing. I don't want to contend with a large number of dating app men; I don't have the time or the interest, and most women in the Burned Haystack community feel similar. The goal of these collected rules is to minimize the expenditure of time and energy to the degree that you're wasting zero time engaging with men who aren't clearly demonstrating long-term partnership potential. I'm a minimalist in all elements of my life, and I developed Burned Haystack method in accordance with minimalist principles. You have to Marie Kondo these guys; if they don't spark joy, get rid of them.

SUCCESS STORY!

Hi Jennie,

Thanks for the opportunity to share my success story.

I've always been told that I'm too picky, and was almost completely single for a decade.

After a six-month "situationship" with lots of chemistry but lots of flakiness, I embraced Burned Haystack wholeheartedly. It took me four months and I found my needle.

When I got home from our first coffee date I knew Doug was different. He didn't sexualize me, he was super respectful, and his questions were relationship and compatibility oriented.

This wasn't "chemistry," but something different. I felt safe, heard, and respected. We took our time getting to know each other, and it took a month (seven dates) before we got intimate (this is a record for me!).

A major green flag is that he'd taken three years out from dating to work on himself. He's kind, compassionate, mature, and emotionally intelligent and shows up for me every single time.

We've just celebrated nine months together and I get on really well with his kids (and as someone who's always been happily child-free this is huge for me!).

I'm a sex coach and I regularly tell my clients about Burned Haystack because I see so many women getting gaslighted and I see the devastating impact it has on their self-esteem.

Occasionally I see some colleagues who claim that Burned Haystack is "not sex positive" or that it's anti men. In my opinion this is a red flag, as these colleagues promote some dogmatic gender/polarity ideology that can be incredibly harmful.

Thank you for the amazing work you're doing, and the incredible community you have built. I'll keep recommending Burned Haystack to everyone!

—Mangala Holland

FREQUENTLY ASKED QUESTIONS

Q: Is Burned Haystack dating method too strict?
A: It's a fair question. Many people believe that Burned Haystack is too picky, that it empowers women to be too selective.

On Instagram not long ago, someone asked, "Should we just resign ourselves to spinsterhood?" This was my response: "I don't know. What I know for sure is that spinsterhood is a way better option than dating terrible men. For a lot of women, spinsterhood is a fantastic option. There is an increasing population of intentionally single women who have built rich lives that involve amazing friends and vibrant activities and adventurous travels."

Another version of a similar concern:

"If I *truly* hold men to standards this high—if I employ all the method rules and apply all these filters and block to burn at the first sign of even slightly unacceptable behavior—then there won't be anyone left to date, and I'll end up all alone."

To be fair, if you use this method faithfully, you will meet far fewer people and go out on far fewer dates. That's true. But the dates you *do* go on will be better, and you won't end up wasting your time and energy with men who do not have the potential to meet your needs.

When you use this method (and, as mentioned, especially if you live in a rural area), there's a very good chance that you will literally burn that haystack down to nothing and have zero matches on your dating app. At this point, the app will encourage you to "expand your filters." You can certainly do that, and in some cases you should. (I frequently encourage women to expand geographical filters and to be open to men without college degrees if they aren't already; what I *never* encourage women to do is accept bad behavior from men.) If you decide you're absolutely not willing to expand your filters and would prefer to just wait it out, I think that's a perfectly valid response. This is one community member's response to this conundrum and her advice to other women: "Hang on in there. . . . I live in a big city and followed Jennie's advice to the letter and ended up with the dreaded 'expand your filter.' Do not expand your filter . . . expand your patience; it will pay off. My stack was burned so low I was digging a hole, when one day up popped a really good profile, and his first question to me was 10/10. Very early days but he was worth waiting for and I might have missed him in among a big crowd."

Here's an analogy I like to use to respond to the "Is this method too strict/Are we being too picky?" questions: If I were wandering through the forest and I was super hungry, and I came upon some clearly poisonous mushrooms, I would not eat the mushrooms just because they were there. I would acknowledge my hunger and keep on movin'—and that's not a terrible way to conduct yourself on the dating apps.

Q: This method is hard to employ! Is it too hard? Also, it seems very judgy!
A: Blocking to burn, and Burned Haystack in general, *is* hard. It's really hard! I do know that, and I just want to acknowledge and affirm it.

It's also definitely judgy, but I don't see that as a negative. I love to judge things. I consider myself an excellent judge. It *is* judgy, and it *should* be. You are choosing a *human being*, potentially for the *rest of your life*. There is no scenario that calls for more discernment. Being judgy keeps us safe, protects our boundaries and our time, and results in far better selections. Judge away, I say!

Meeting people online is different from meeting people in person over time. Meeting people in real life is better. That doesn't mean we should give up on the apps; it means we must force them to operate more like real life, which means slowing down the whole process, maintaining boundaries, and taking a wait-and-see approach.

It also means we need to trust women's (and our own) gut reactions on the apps as much as we do in real life. If a friend of mine met a guy at a party and told me that she felt really creeped out by him in a way she couldn't name and that she didn't want to encounter him again, it would not occur to me to question her judgment. I'd affirm it immediately. I believe we can trust women's intuition on the apps as well. What *does* take longer on the apps, though, is determining needle status, which is why we need to control the pace a bit at the beginning. The guys who are worth it will reveal themselves over time by displaying patience, integrity, and depth.

I'm a teacher, so I understand the inclination to give everyone the benefit of the doubt and to seek common ground, to operate more on "potential" than "current reality." You simply have to cut this off on the dating apps (I know it's not easy, but it *is* actually simple). Initially, while you're using the app, you must become ruthless. You must get out of your emotions and firmly into your brain. There's time for feelings later. Right now, you need to be a judge.

Q: Is it okay to contact a man first or ask him out first?
A: I think this is a 100 percent personal call. I almost never do, but that's probably because I was brought up in the 1980s and there are some cultural norms I just haven't succeeded in overcoming. That said, I also think there's a very logical and pragmatic reason to sit back and see if men will make the first move. Most of that is contained in Rule 9 in the previous chapter, but consider this as well: It's pretty hard to tell from scrolling and swiping how serious any individual man might be about dating. There are a shocking number of people who download and then hang around indefinitely on the apps without any real intention of finding a partnership, so you could waste a *lot* of time sending thoughtful messages or crafting amazing date plans for men who never wanted that in the first place. Letting him reach out or ask you out first

offers some degree of mitigation for that reality. I also like to think of this as one way I can help to correct the labor imbalance that is still the norm in too many heterosexual relationships.

Q: You spend all your time talking about when to block to burn men. It seems like there's no man's profile that would be good enough for you. Why don't you show us examples of good male profiles?

A: A "good male profile" is a profile that doesn't violate the rhetorical patterns (see chapter 5) or turn you off in some way. That's really it. We use the Burned Haystack method to rule men *out*, not *in*. That's literally the premise of the haystack metaphor: if you burn all the hay away, you don't have to go looking for some sort of unknowable-perfect-needle-thing, because the needles simply emerge on their own. A man's profile doesn't need to "wow" you; it just needs not to violate the patterns. Consider this statement from one of our recent success stories:

"I found a needle! But wouldn't have necessarily guessed based on his profile. His bio was only this brief couple of phrases. And he said 'short term open to long,' which I normally swipe left on. But his pictures drew me in because he looked happy, kind, and fun in a good way. He has a bachelor's degree and owns a business, which seemed to reflect the stable part as well, so I gave it a try. It turns out his sister created the profile because they were traveling overseas and she wanted him to meet someone. He's a widower and had an amazing marriage, so he knows what it takes to have a healthy, stable relationship. I've never been happier or felt I was in a better relationship. (I'm divorced after a twenty-year marriage and have been dating for a year.) I randomly tried Tinder after a friend convinced me the pool of men was larger. He was only on Tinder because of his sister. I'm the first person he has dated from an app. Just wanted to share my success story. I don't think there were any red flags on his profile, but also it wasn't what I'd call a 'great' profile either."

I've heard more versions of this story than I can count, and I've experienced it myself. There are all kinds of reasons a man might have a lackluster or sparse profile—but if he has a toxic profile, it's because he's toxic.

I do, however, appreciate that a list of "ideals" in terms of men's profiles and male behavior is helpful, so after many, many requests, I did publish a list of characteristics that I consider clear "needle behavior" from men:

1. He sends you a message that directly references your profile, and the message is respectful, well written, and engaging.
2. He does not reference your appearance or anything sexual in this first message.
3. After you respond, he responds again within a reasonable amount of time (let's say at least within a day), and he not only speaks directly to whatever you said but extends the conversation in some way—he asks you relevant questions about yourself, he comments on things you've said, he introduces new topics in a way that feels natural and organic.
4. The messaging goes on for a few days at the most before he suggests meeting in person.
5. He gives you his full name if you ask for it, and it's clear this transparency is totally fine with him; he doesn't make a big deal out of it. Bonus points if he in some way recognizes that dating apps are potentially scary for women.
6. He suggests an actual date, with a place and a time.
7. He works with you on any adjustments to this date, and this process happens like any adjustment would happen between two healthy adults—without drama or hurt feelings.
8. He shows up for the date on time and looking presentable, and the conversation flows naturally and easily.
9. By the end of the date, in person or shortly thereafter in text or by

phone, he lets you know that he had a great time and would love to see you again.

10. And then this dynamic continues and builds, and here's the very key part: You're never left to wonder if he's into you; you're never frustrated by ridiculously long wait times in responses to texts; you feel calm and secure and at peace with the whole thing; and you feel like you're spending time with someone who could be a legit partner—who adds to your life and supports you and lifts you up.

Here's a post shared anonymously in the Burned Haystack Facebook group; it reflects a lot of what I'm seeing in my inbox:

> Hi Jennie, I have a needle story I'd like to share anonymously please. I'm going to highlight his green flags along the way:
>
> I connected with a wonderful man on Hinge after he replied with an actual thoughtful comment (not a passive like) to one of my written prompts (not a photo). ✔
>
> We messaged at a steady pace, short thoughtful messages, not too many, appropriate convo, nothing sexual, no requests to send him pics, and he asked me on a date nearly a week in advance. ✔✔✔
>
> He lives about an hour outside of my city (I had broadened my radius on the app); he arranged to drive to meet me and initiated the date and details. ✔✔
>
> That date night, he initiated the second date, and again he planned, seemingly researched options, and drove to my city. ✔✔✔
>
> We had a great second date based on something I said in my profile that I enjoy, that he sought out and planned while living out of town. ✔
>
> It's tbd whether or not he's my needle but he certainly seems like someone's needle so far.

About his dating profile:

✘ Shirtless pics

✘ Bathroom selfies

✘ Fish

✘ Weird power/intimidating angles

✘ Sexual references

✘ Directives or weird language about women ("don't be drama, be loyal, etc.")

✘ Negative language ("I hate the apps") etc.

✘ His prompts speak to his interests in cooking, his dog, nature walks, music—HIS interests, not who the other person "should" be

✘ His profile could be perceived as BORING—which at this rate, bring it

✘ Pics are of him, fully dressed (!), outside with his dog, doing nothing particularly interesting (no extreme sports or 600th country visited or a midlife-crisis car or whatever else)

✘ He selected Liberal, not "Not political" or Moderate

All this to say, his profile looks perfectly neutral if not "boring" compared to much of what's out there—and this man seems to be a needle so far who is very interesting and full of life.

In contrast, an allegedly 50+ year old man also from the apps messaged me while I was on a date with this needle man.

The message in full: "Hey."

Enough said. Thank you for Burned Haystack!

Q: If I'm only interested in finding a long-term monogamous relationship, shouldn't I block anyone who selects any option other than "long-term relationship/marriage"?
A: I would not, and here's why: What I know from interviewing men (some of whom are men I know personally and who are definite needles) is that many people on the apps (this is a genderless problem) are simply too quick and too high pressure in terms of moving to commitment. For that reason, many people (again, of all genders) pick options such as "short term open to long" or "friendship first" to guard against that and to slow down the process. I don't personally see this as always being a red flag (sometimes it is, but they'll show you that on their own anyway).

Q: I know exactly what I want, so I filter for all those things: geography, degree status, height, income, and so on. Why do you encourage women to lower their standards on these things?
A: I encourage women to change their filters on certain metrics because I don't believe those metrics give you the information you think they're giving you. The best example of that might be degree status. I have a PhD and have worked with hundreds of men who also have PhDs. I'm telling you they are not necessarily "smarter." For me personally, I care about intelligence and literacy and humor; I don't care about degree status. I've dated men with zero degrees who could not only hang with me and challenge me intellectually but who make a lot more money than I do; I'm just not convinced degree status tells you that much. In the United States, I think it tells you far more about someone's level of privilege and/or family socioeconomic status than it does about individual worth or capabilities. That said, if this is a deal-breaker for you, then it's a deal-breaker; I'm just saying it's worth considering.

The other piece of my response to this question is that I've now heard endless "I thought I knew what I wanted but I was surprised" stories. Women who thought height was a nonnegotiable for them found that with the right mix of other qualities, they couldn't care less about a guy's height. Other couples who were not initially open to long-distance relationships or dating people with young children somehow fell into those things and found themselves happier than they had ever imagined.

Consider the accompanying note of a recent success story featured in the Facebook group:

"I think I found my needle, and it's all because I took a chance on somebody I would've swiped left on in the past, before I learned from all the wise women on this group. I'm a well-educated, well-traveled woman who works for a local school district. My needle is a biker/union electrician from a small town in Montana. He has the most incredible emotional skills I have ever experienced with a man, genuine communication skills, and is incredibly kind and generous. He listens to me, cares about my feelings, is never jealous of my time, and understands my need for quality time with my female friends. Thank you, Wise Women."

Bottom line on this: I think there's a difference between "lowering your standards" and "thoughtfully changing your criteria," and I think it's worth some time to parse that difference.

Q: This method seems prudish and not sex positive. Why are you so judgy about men saying anything sexual at all?

A: Burned Haystack is not anti sex; it is anti objectification. The most common way for men to objectify you is sexually, and there's no world in which a man who objectifies you is going to be a healthy partner. Therefore, we use "going to sex too early" as a key indicator of which men should be blocked to burn immediately, before they can wreak havoc on your life. If men bring any sexual content into very early discussions or if they talk about your body at all in very early discussions, you should see this as serious red-flag behavior, for two reasons: First, they're objectifying you—literally conceiving of you as an object—from the very beginning. Second, they don't have the sense to know that this kind of behavior is considered offensive, aggressive, and nonconsensual in the contemporary dating arena. If they don't know this, what else don't they know? In what other ways have they not evolved? I believe it's totally fair, in a rhetorical sense, to thin-slice this sort of behavior to these eight conclusions:

1. This guy has poor social skills.
2. This guy doesn't understand boundaries.
3. This guy objectifies women in general.
4. This guy is 100 percent out of touch with modern dating discourses (so what else is he out of touch with?).
5. This guy has zero empathy for or concept of what it's like to be a woman on a dating app.
6. This guy isn't smart enough to increase his own odds on the dating apps simply by avoiding what nearly every dating coach and article published in the past five years has told him to avoid.
7. This guy is too lazy to look up tips about how to succeed as a man on the dating apps, or he already knows that he's working against himself and doesn't care.
8. This guy is going to be really bad in bed (because poor social intuition, lack of boundary recognition, disrespect for women, unwillingness to listen, and laziness all = bad in bed).

So, this is why we block to burn. It's not because we're prudes. It's because we're uninterested in socially inept, lazy men who are going to be bad in bed.

Here's another way to think about it: As I've said before, Burned Haystack is pragmatic; it's not moralistic. So when I advise blocking men who lead with anything sexual, it's not coming from a place of judgment or prudishness or political conservativism or religious mores; it's coming from reading powerful rhetorical indicators that a man is not egalitarian, long-term-relationship material. We're looking for the exceptions with this method—for the needles. It's not hard to find a man on the internet who wants to sext with or have sex with you. You don't need a method to find those kinds of men. If what you're looking for, though, is a long-term monogamous partnership, then you want to focus your attention only on men who lead with integrity, respect, and self-control.

Q: What can I do to nudge men toward more respectful behavior on the apps? Do you have responses or scripts I can use to indicate that I want to take things more slowly or don't want to talk about sex right away?

A: I can't answer this clearly enough: No. *No no no no no no no no,* one million times *no.* We're talking about adult men here; the second you find yourself trying to "strategize" how to get them to be more communicative or less toxic or gentler or [fill in the blank], the game is already over. Block to burn. The only useful information is raw; it's how men present to you without coaching, bargaining, negotiation, or "tips." The other really important point here is that any tips you do give these guys will most likely simply be used to exploit or manipulate the woman they encounter after you. Don't do it. Let these guys reveal themselves transparently. Have the courage and wisdom to recognize it for what it is and move on.

In the early days of Burned Haystack, I would constantly get comments that sound like this: "I already knew I was going to block to burn this guy because he was super clueless and toxic, but before I did, I gave him a couple of tips because I like to help people and I thought it could help him to do better in the future." *Don't do that.* You're not helping him do better in the future. You're helping him *appear* better, in a totally superficial way, and all that's going to do is allow him to misrepresent himself and be more effective in manipulating the next woman he encounters on the apps. Remember that dating apps are a technological tool; they are not a charity event. If you have the time and energy to do charity work, I think that's wonderful, but don't choose the dating apps as the site of your humanitarian efforts; that's actually going to make things worse.

Q: What if a dating app conversation is dying? Are there things I can do to keep it going?
A: Maybe, but there's no point in it. It's the same reasoning as above: If you have to do this, it's already over. A Burned Haystack community member once shared that a convo was dying and that she "performed no CPR." This is a good rule: "No CPR. Let the dying convos die."

Q: The whole point of being on a dating app is to find love, but a lot of your method seems sort of cold and calculating; it doesn't seem very romantic or fun at all to employ this method.
A: This is an excellent observation. Employing Burned Haystack requires a "switch-flipping" kind of act in which you approach the process of dating in "professional" or "strategic" mode; once you've successfully navigated the apps and the algorithms to lead you to safe, healthy, and viable human relationships, then you need to toggle off those modes so you can allow your humanity and values to preside. That's when it's time for love.

I've said this before, and I will keep saying it because I think it's crucially important: I'm a realist and a pragmatist, and I operate within that orientation. It's definitely at the heart of this method, which I know is not for everyone. However, the success stories keep stacking up. When women bring their dating app profiles and behaviors in accordance with Burned Haystack principles, they are suddenly finding better matches.

To help with getting into the proper mindset to employ this method, I offer these three pointers:

1. Trust and work the method.
2. Get out of your heart and into your brain (or out of your feelings and into your intellect).

3. Don't expect the vetting process to be fun. It's going to be a drag because most men on the dating apps are a drag. However, if you get the vetting process right, the dates themselves should be fun, because you'll be meeting kind and respectful and interesting men, whether or not one of them turns out to be your needle.

Q: Why do you have a different set of standards for men than women (e.g., men have to plan the first date according to Rule 9, and I've said online that women have a right to men's full names in advance of meeting but not vice versa, and that women can require a video chat in advance of meeting but men cannot)?

A: That's true. I do have different expectations for women and men, and here's why: When we're talking about the dating arena (or almost any arena), the playing field has never been even. To pretend that it *is* even is not only delusional but dangerous. Men simply aren't in danger from women the way women are in danger from men. I'm interested in introducing *equity* to the dating process, not *equality*. If our world evolves to a point where gendered labor imbalances no longer exist and where women are no longer in any kind of danger from men, then it would make sense to revisit a lot of Burned Haystack guidelines. Right now, we are nowhere close to that world.

5

RED-FLAG RHETORICAL PATTERNS

Run!

Burned Haystack uses something called "rhetorical patterning" to vet men's profiles. The benefit of learning the rhetorical patterns is that they function as "cheat codes" to navigating the apps so that you can block to burn problematic men immediately, without wasted time or energy or bad experiences.

Although I've used rhetorical patterning extensively in my academic writing, I stumbled upon it somewhat by accident when I first started using the dating apps. It happened when one of my first dating app conversations went like this:

> **Man:** Good morning, how are you today?
> **Me:** I'm good, you? I love your dog 😊
> **Man:** I like festivals and cuddling and am looking for an open-minded, generous, fit and active lady to spoil with dinners out, good wine, long talks, and breakfast in bed. You never know if you don't try. I believe in work hard/play hard and living

life to the fullest. How has your experience on this app been so far?

Wait, what? Did I miss something here? I tried again.

Me: How old is your dog?

I had a lot of conversations like this. Three days into my first adventure with the dating apps, I was walking around in a fog, demoralized by trying to figure out what was going on and what was wrong with me. I'd had so many pointless, confusing, and go-nowhere conversations that it felt like I'd entered some sort of bizarro universe where everyone but me understood communication patterns. I assumed it must be me—I must be the problem. I was also beginning to question my sanity. But then I thought, *I don't have communication problems anywhere else. I talk to people all the time, all day long, and I never struggle to understand anyone, and no one seems to struggle to understand me.*

Let me share another example from my early days on the apps:

Man: Hi there, hoping you might be open to chatting!
Me: Hi, and thanks for connecting! I love *The Office* too, by the way! What's your favorite episode?
Man: Hmmmmm . . .

[Several hours go by, during which I don't respond, because how does one respond to "Hmmmmm"?]

[The next day]
Man: There are so many . . .
Me: I know, right? The dinner party episode is right up at the top for me.

[Three days later]
Man: Love dinner parties!

I blamed this one on myself too. I assumed I must have confused profiles and seen a bunch of mentions of *The Office* on some other guy's profile, so I took a second look. Nope, there it was, plain as day.

What I didn't understand yet is that this communication pattern is so common it has a name, and the name is **breadcrumbing**. People talk about it on social media all the time. It's a manipulation tactic employed to provide just enough "crumbs" of communication to keep someone's attention, but not enough to "feed" or sustain a relationship. It's a pervasive pattern on the dating apps; people use it as a way of increasing their odds by engaging as many matches in conversation as possible—it buys them time before engaging in meaningful communication, and it creates a set of fallback matches while they're continuing to look for someone who actually captures their attention.

Once I realized there was a name for this pattern, I was able to quickly see through the frustration to what was going on and just cut off the crumb-droppers immediately. It made me feel better, and it gave me a tool for becoming much more efficient.

Because I think about everything in rhetorical terms, I realized that breadcrumbing was simply a predictable pattern that could be "mapped" into its constituent ordered parts. In this case, the pattern is:

1. Make contact with woman on dating app that you're just interested in enough to keep as an option.
2. If she writes back, respond to her just enough to acknowledge her, but briefly and barely.
3. Keep doing that for as long as possible, so that if you decide you want to meet her, she's already there and ready.

Breadcrumbing is of course a metaphor, and we could use other metaphors to describe the same effect: "keeping someone on the back burner," "keeping lots of irons in the fire," "not putting all your eggs in one basket," and so on.

I realized that I could do the same kind of analysis with a whole bunch of other problem patterns on the dating apps, and now **rhetorical patterning** has become one of the most powerful tools in Burned Haystack. I began to track and analyze rhetorical patterns that are ubiquitous on the dating apps and then name and describe them so that people can recognize them immediately and block to burn the matches who exhibit them. Identifying Burned Haystack rhetorical patterns is a shortcut to quickly and safely navigate the dating apps and move through people's profiles wisely and decisively.

Let's go through the most common problematic rhetorical patterns, what they reveal about a man who uses them, and why you should learn to identify them. Here I share thirty-three different rhetorical patterns. This is not an exhaustive list, and new patterns will emerge over time, but right now these are the problematic patterns we see most frequently. All the examples shared in this chapter are taken from actual profiles and interactions.

RHETORICAL PATTERN 1: TEST AND APOLOGIZE

12:17 a.m.
Jim: Hello. How are you. Is getting a boner looking at someone's photo a compliment?

12:18 a.m.
Jim: I'm sorry that was inappropriate well you look like you have a sense of humor

Notice that the woman Jim addresses does not respond between these two messages; he sent the first and then immediately the second. Here's what's important to know about this pattern: The test is real; the apology is not. The test is exactly what it sounds like—he wants to see what he can get away with. The apology comes in to soften the test and provide plausible deniability so that if the woman he's addressing has a bad reaction, he can say, "Oh, whoa! I was kidding, you're just overreacting!" This is, of course, trivializing and gaslighting and generally manipulative, but women get this on the dating apps all the time.

Here's another example of "test and apologize" in a dating app message:

> You look quite . . . chesty.
> Okay it wasn't a question
> It was a compliment/creepy observation

[Directly after sending this message, he sent a gif of a man slinking down in his chair and hiding his face in embarrassment.]

Despite the image he includes, this guy is *not* embarrassed. He's the one who wrote this. People who do "test and apologize" are boundary violators. Boundary violation is a hallmark sign of abuse, and at the dating app stage it's low-key, for sure, but that's how all abuse starts. It starts at the soft end—so soft you might not notice it, or you might "just be overreacting," but it's a sign of things to come.

RHETORICAL PATTERN 2: ARE YOU MY MOTHER?

> About me
> I'm a good person, and have been unlucky in love but still hope to find my soul mate. I'm looking for someone who isn't too high maintenance, isn't too proud but can still be feminine, and can motivate me to become the best version of myself.

There is a lot of "mother language" here. He wants someone who will demand and expect nothing of him but also motivate him to be better—just like a mother. It's good that he wants to do better, but he's an adult and it's *his* job to motivate himself, not the job of a romantic partner. The fact that he's asking for someone who's "not high maintenance, not proud, and still feminine" is also very revealing; he's telling us what his conception of a woman is, and it seems she's primarily to be a backdrop and support structure for men, and preferably someone who doesn't think too much of herself.

> Green flags I look for: I'm into women who aren't so into themselves. In other words they're more interested in others and being kind and genuine. I mean you definitely have to love yourself and be confident. But get over yourself lol . . .

When a man says, "I'm into women who aren't so into themselves. They're more interested in others and in being kind and genuine," he is telling you he wants you to care more about *him* than about *yourself*. This dynamic would be totally appropriate in a mother-child relationship. Mothers do love their children sacrificially, and they should. You're not supposed to love random-man-from-the-internet sacrificially—that's inappropriate and unhealthy.

RHETORICAL PATTERN 3: I'M A VERY BUSY MAN!

> About me
> Busy, single and with a job that often has long hours.
> I'd love to spend some of my free time with a fun
> person who likes to seize the moment and explore
> what this city has to offer.

> All I ask is that you
> Have a full set of photos on here. This is a visual medium.
> Limited time prevents me from contacting you if you don't 🙁

The "I'm a very busy man" rhetorical pattern is ubiquitous on the dating apps. It usually sounds something like "I have a busy life and a demanding job, but I can make time for the right woman." It comes in several varieties, though, as in the two examples above. It's also frequently totally made up, coming from men whose ex-wives are still doing all the parenting and childcare. It's a fairy tale written by men who think too highly of themselves and/or have poor time-management skills, and those two things frequently intersect.

Additionally, this pattern is manipulative. Leading with "I'm a very busy man" language establishes a hierarchy with him at the top. It's also presumptuous. In advance of meeting a woman, he is assuming that his time is more valuable, more limited, and more important than hers. Additionally, it frames him as a treat or reward that can be attained if the woman is worthy enough: the "right woman."

Frequently, this pattern doesn't even make sense. Note the example above that seems to suggest that his amount of disposable time is directly related to the number of photos women include on their dating apps. That's not what he means, of course; what he means is this: "I won't bother to interact with women whose entire bodies are not displayed to me" (that's what "full set of photos" refers to here), but he's not going to say it that way, so he frames it in terms of being the dreaded "very busy man."

RHETORICAL PATTERN 4: DISCIPLINARY/DIRECTIVE

READ!!!!!!!!!!!!!! SAY SOMETHING BEFORE YOU GET BUSY!!! IF YOU CAN ONLY TALK WHEN A MAN TEXTS 1ST THEN DON'T MATCH WITH ME!!!!!

I'm honest and looking for a very particular woman

READ CAREFULLY

You too old to be playing childish games! FYI I DELETE women that match and don't say hello

I WILL DELETE YOU!!!

When 2 people are meeting in the middle there is no chasing!

Be a grown woman and don't play little girl games!

I will terminate communications with people who show a consistent pattern of bad behavior, I like people who are considerate of my human feelings, I'm not interested in things that I have identified as bad habits, rude or thoughtless endeavors, I don't like to waste my time on things that work against a productive and positive future, I don't judge you by what others have done

---

Are Women On here.REALLY SINGLE? Or Just Post Pics, Social Media . . . or Lying bout Ages

I'm age 50.and

I Don't Care How GROWN "You Say" You are.

Have YOUR OWN MONEY and RESIDENCE!!!

I Need a Woman Who Can

"REAP with Me—Not Just SLEEP With ME"

^^

(Ladies Did y'all Read That?)

Why does Distance & color Matter?

(Where's The single Women whos NOT GAY?)

I LOVE JESUS & SEX

If you ask me to telegram, or Instagram, you are wasting my time.i use Facebook and my cell, and only local to me

If you don't look like your filtered pics in person, you're blowing me until you do. Sarcasm people . . . come on

Seeking a pleasant to be around, feminine lady.men don't want masculine boss women it's the most unattractive trait in a female for a man with his crap together, don't want 2 men in the same house ya dig?

Im tall, fit, intelligent, laid back yet I work hard, raised 2 kids on my own, not a simp.

If you only have face shots don't hit me up. If we decide to go out on a dinner date you can choose the place but I will pay for my meal and you will pay for yours. If you smoke I'm not interested. If you don't have a car I'm not interested. I don't date women that hop around I ain't trying to catch anything. I just want a loving God fearing women that know how to treat her man. I don't want a woman that's always in the streets sit your asses down your getting to old for all that!!

About me

PhD Engineering

Incredibly motivated

Multifaceted

Well traveled

Dating with purpose

If kids aren't in your future, don't bother.

100% don't give a shit about your Instagram!

Be financially literate!

Convinced most are using this to network and for attention, that is NOT what I'm here for.

> First up you tell me your overview of a realistic weeks schedule with me in 10 years time
>
> fyi: straight up if you're non-responsive, over controlling and/or mallipulative; have a can of take it somewhere else.
>
> Moving forward, myself: never married, no kids, no unhealthy addictions

This pattern is so ubiquitous on dating apps that it's alternately hilarious and terrifying. We need to be clear about the implications, though: This kind of language is not a show of strength or clarity. This is not admirable. It's social ineptitude at best but more likely a bright red flag of toxicity. The other consideration here is that all these examples were taken from the "About me" section of men's dating app profiles. These guys are revealing that the most important thing *about them* is that they're angry *at you* and that they feel comfortable yelling at you before they've even met you. Imagine that in real life.

The examples above are at the strong-toxic end of this pattern, but I want to share a sneakier version of it as well. A Burned Haystack community member recently posted this question along with two screenshots: one of his profile and one of a messaging conversation with her: "Please tell me what I overlooked here because I sure misjudged this one. We exchanged a few texts and one telephone conversation over four days. Then he asked to change my name! I felt this was his first step to change and control me. I never answered. Just B2B."

Here's the guy's profile:

> About me
> Are you tired? I am. I just want to meet one woman who I can relax with and have fun with. If it leads to

> something more, great. If instead we simply remain friends, that's cool as well. 😊 Take a chance, otherwise, you may be passing up a great time and perhaps the right person.

From their message conversation:

> I have a question for you. As you may recall, I mentioned to you I like the name Katherine. It is such a beautiful name.
>
> Now I don't mean to offend you, however, if our friendship should blossom, may I call you, Katherine?
>
> If our friendship blossoms, I have a name you can call me as well.

The woman who posted this is asking the right question—"What did I miss?"—and the answer is contained in three short words: "Take a chance."

"Take a chance" is a directive. This man, whom she does not know, is *giving her a direction*. Although it comes across as lighthearted and benign, it still falls into the "disciplinary/directive" rhetorical pattern, which is at the high-toxic end of the spectrum. (Some of the patterns in this chapter lean toward annoying or frustrating or boring, some toward toxicity and danger; the pattern we're talking about right now is the latter.)

The way he phrased it in this case—"Take a chance"—is low-key, which is why she missed it, but that actually doesn't matter because the rhetorical reveal is the same: This is a man who assumes authority and directorial control over women.

And look how quickly he confirmed that: He literally asked her to *change her name* after one phone call. The audacity of this is almost shocking in its extremity and impropriety, but it's a *great* example of how deconstructing text—reading for words and patterns rather than glossing the surface—gives us tons of crucial information.

Here's another sneaky, more low-key variant of the disciplinary/directive profile; I call it the "Please be" variant. Here's an example:

> Hello ladies! So I have to say that I love confident, beautiful, and sexy women that are completely comfortable being feminine! Somehow we are missing that in today's society. Are you healthy, fun, and fit? Please be secure, positive, flexible, giving, intelligent, outgoing, and fun.

Adding the word "please" does not change this rhetorical pattern; it just makes it sound nicer because it softens it and dresses it up as a question or a request. Rhetorically, though, it's still just a man telling women (whom he doesn't even know) how to be (or how to present, or how to "perform").

RHETORICAL PATTERN 5: *MANIC PIXIE DREAMER*

> In search of a remarkable woman who exudes strength and allure. I'm drawn to a chemistry that feels like an intriguing dance—effortless yet charged with energy. If you're authentic, witty, and ready to escape the confines of dating apps, let's craft our own story. Life is a thrilling adventure, and I believe the right connection can turn every moment into an exhilarating escapade whether snuggling on the couch for a movie or traveling the world. Let's see where this journey might lead us.

The problem with the MANic Pixie Dreamer guys is that they don't seem to be living in the real world. It's unrealistic as an adult to believe that *every moment* can be an "exhilarating escapade." That's not only unrealistic but it also sounds exhausting and dramatic. I assume a lot of these guys are single because living in the real world just wasn't fun or entertaining enough for them. I imagine many of them have ex-wives, probably still caring for their children and taking out the trash, who would roll their eyes into the back of their heads if they saw these guys' profiles; it's probably why they're divorced. The MANic Pixie Dreamers simply seem incapable of or unwilling to contend with the basic responsibilities of adulthood, many of which are not fun or exhilarating.

RHETORICAL PATTERN 6: MAN'S PLANNING

This one is related to the MANic Pixie Dreamers, but it applies to planning actual dates. The label "Man's Planning" is a play on "man-splaining," since these profiles take the form of a man being weirdly directive and detailed about how a hypothetical day with a hypothetical woman might go. We *do* want men to plan dates, but the "man's planners" plan them hypothetically in advance of making an actual connection, which renders this pattern presumptuous and awkward. Here's an example from Mike:

> Typical Sunday—would be our time to be as lazy as you want. Leave your hair tousled with no makeup as we float into the kitchen to make crazy awesome lemon ricotta pancakes, with a hot cup of coffee and leave the dishes till way later!

If Mike here were talking to a woman whom he already knew intimately, this might be romantic because we could assume that his words are grounded in knowledge and experience. We would assume that he already knows that she wants to skip hair and makeup in order to go "floating into the kitchen" and that she actually likes "crazy awesome lemon ricotta pancakes and coffee." But since all of that is made up in Mike's head, we have to question his thought processes: Does Mike want to meet an actual adult human woman, or is he crafting some sort of avatar or fantasy girl? It's a strange and disembodied (since there's no woman yet present) form of preplanning that I don't believe bodes well for his ability to navigate the *actual* world.

RHETORICAL PATTERN 7: MY KIDS COME FIRST

This is another pattern on the dating apps that's so common it's easy to miss its significance. The phrase "My kids come first" is stated verbatim in countless profiles and early messaging conversations. It's also an excellent one to analyze for text, subtext, and context, so let's review those terms quickly.

Text is the actual words you see.

Subtext is what lies *beneath* the text—the hidden/implied meanings and the intentional or unintentional reveals. (What critical discourse analysis does especially well is train you to quickly detect what people are telling you without intending to.)

Context is the conditions surrounding the text (the prefix "con" means "with," so literally "with the text").

Now, let's apply these terms to "My kids come first."

Text: Taken literally, this is a neutral-to-positive statement. This person's children are their priority.

Subtext: The word "first" implies the words "second, third, fourth, last," and so on. Suddenly the statement is more complex, right? The subtext now becomes more shaded, more hypothetical, and more negative. Before he even meets you, this person is saying you will not be first.

It's a defensive statement, and we should ask why. It's also an *unnecessary* statement. "Kids come first" is literally the definition of the parental and societal contract. It's assumed. It's like saying "I really love my kids. They're important to me." Of course they are!

But that's not how it's phrased in the dating apps. Phrasing it as "My kids come first" is *also saying*:

- "Don't expect too much from me."
- "Don't expect me to prioritize you."
- "Things in this relationship are going to be on my terms."
- "I'm assuming the 'director' role in this relationship *before we've even met*."

The person who writes this is making assumptions about the person who reads it, and those assumptions range from fear (*This person is going to put too much pressure on me and demand too much from me and make me feel smothered!*) to unchecked egotism (*I'm the more desirable person in this relationship, and this person is clearly going to want to spend more time with me than I will with them*).

Note that these meanings are unintentional even to the person who wrote them. They're also understandable. I've certainly felt smothered and even threatened in relationships and defensively put up walls from people who weren't at the scene of the original crime. But that's not a great way to forge healthy connections. If this is in *your* profile, spend some time thinking about why. Consider whether there's a more accurate way to say it.

Writing something like "Family is really important to me" or "I'm a family-oriented person" communicates the same message while also making room for someone else to enter that family circle (at some *much later* and more appropriate point!), which is ostensibly why you're on a dating app in the first place—to find a partner who will be an integral part of your life. At the point you meet someone you want to build a life with, it's actually psychologically *inappropriate* to lay out a hierarchy of who's most important to you; family systems thrive in interdependence and in the *absence* of those hierarchies.

Context: What's "with the text" here is a situation in which you're talking to unknowable strangers. There's a time to discuss things like your children, your scheduling preferences, and so on, but that point is not your profile text in a dating app. It's inappropriate to start discussing your daily schedule (which is what "My kids come first" implies) with total strangers on the internet as though you're just presuming that, number one, your schedule will be relevant to them, and number two, you've already decided to deprioritize them in said schedule.

This rhetorical gambit is very similar to the "time to talk about sex" debate. Too many people, especially male people, lead with sex. Their reasoning is that sex is important to them and they want to know right off the bat if there's going to be a lot of it. But the women they're attempting to force into those conversations are complete strangers and don't have nearly enough information to know whether they're going to be interested in *any* sex with this person, let alone a lot of it. If the two people in question feel a connection and decide to proceed into relationship development, then yes, of course they should have all those discussions, but it's inappropriate in a dating app profile or early messaging conversation in the same way it would be inappropriate for a coworker to stop by your cubicle on your first day to introduce himself and also to just let you know that he wants to sleep with you.

RHETORICAL PATTERN 8: OPPOSITE-IMPOSSIBLE WOMAN

> I go crazy for
> A strong yet feminine woman. Someone who puts on her game face and gets things done, yet will make time to snuggle and cuddle with me and talk about life. Someone who will do her nails and then go camping

The men who write this rhetorical pattern seem to want impossible women; they want a "traditional girl" with advanced degrees. But women with advanced degrees don't identify this way because those things simply don't go together. These men want the proverbial "Bring home the bacon and fry it up in a pan" woman.

A humorous aside: One of my social media followers shared the following comment on Instagram: "I saw a profile today where he said he's looking for a mermaid. Also, he wants her to stand on her own feet. Dude! Mermaids don't have feet. He was clueless about the contradiction."

RHETORICAL PATTERN 9: BOMBASTIC SYNTAX (OR, SIMPLY, BS)

> Meet a charismatic middle-aged gentleman with striking good looks. This individual is not only captivating in appearance but also possesses an insatiable passion for engaging conversations, staying abreast of current events, and exploring the complexities of human connection, including the intriguing realm of intimacy.
>
> No drama. Casual. Safe. Respectful. Won't do any moves until agreed upon. No strings attached.

> Good morning radiant soul!
>
> Just wanted to sprinkle a bit of sunshine into your day. May your morning be as bright as your smile, and your day unfold with unexpected joys. I couldn't resist reaching out after noticing your striking beauty. If you're open to a conversation, I'd love to get to know the person behind that captivating smile.

Bombastic syntax (BS) is the pattern of scammers (frequently due to poor translation) and men using AI to handle their dating app communications, and it should always be a B2B.

Here's a quick crash course in language analysis: There are primarily three components to the presentation and aesthetics of language, specifically sentences in this case: **semantics, lexicon,** and **syntax.**

Semantics refers to meaning. The meaning of the bombastic syntax rhetorical pattern is frequently vague and abstract. It's difficult to visualize what people are actually saying when they use this pattern.

Lexicon refers to personal vocabulary. The lexicon of BS is ornate, unnecessarily elevated, and just sounds goofy, like a student letting a thesaurus loose on their essay.

Syntax refers to writing style or word arrangement. This could include sentence structure, number of adjectives, use of punctuation, and so on. It's what makes language sound a certain way if read aloud. "Bombastic" means elevated and flowery and artificial and over the top, and that's exactly how the BS rhetorical pattern sounds. It also sounds like the other BS!

RHETORICAL PATTERN 10: "WERE YOU AT THE CAPITOL ON JANUARY 6?"

> A true alpha knows that he's responsibility for all those that loves him . . . that Responsibility is to protect, provide, and to serve . . . And to serve means to take care of all emotional, Physical need and some need requires understanding, a gentle touch, unforgiving . . . And when it's time to defend his loved ones from outside forces . . . he can do that as well!! That's what makes him an alpha male. Any idiot, maniac, fool can destroy, boss, control and terrorize People around him . . . he's not an alpha male, he's a weak man that's afraid! The same definition applies to a woman . . . That's why two alphas can coexist because they give what it takes to make it work.

About me
Pureblood stuck in a sea of liberal tears and mRNA spike proteins, please don't shed on me. I'm trying hard to win the popularity contest in my area, can you tell? It's very important to me to have everyone's acceptance and understanding. Please be patient! The response to my profile is often overwhelming and it takes a while to sort through all of the beautiful ladies and check their vaccination records. I hardly have time for anything else! Guys like me are hard to find in this city. Lets riot

My bio
I'm a strong-willed, strong-minded man who's ready to protect, fight for, and even die for the woman by my side.

Men who write things like the examples above think that regular everyday life is way more exciting than it actually is. These are the guys who accuse women of being dramatic while they go on about "defending their loved ones from outside forces." That skill set was relevant in a certain time and place; it is not relevant to middle-aged white men who live on the cul-de-sacs of suburban America, and that is where 99 percent of this nonsense is coming from. When you encounter men talking about anti-vaxxing and conspiracy theories and defending loved ones from outside forces, that is a serious set of red flags.

This kind of talk is associated with aggression and violence and misogyny, but we could take all that out of the equation and there are *still* major problems here that render these guys undatable. They have extraordinarily poor critical thinking and decision-making skills, which would obviously impact all aspects of their lives. They are dangerously susceptible to misinformation, manipulation, and con artists in a way that renders them (and you, if you're partnered with them) vulnerable to toxic and destructive people. They are unable to root themselves within basic reality, and that is an unstable and unsafe scenario for everyone involved.

RHETORICAL PATTERN 11: FLUENT IN SARCASM

Similar to "My kids come first," labeling oneself "fluent in sarcasm" is one of the most common and most problematic patterns on the dating apps. Sarcasm is the lowest form of humor. It resides at the intersection of "lazy" and "angry." It takes something obvious or something someone else has already said and repeats it in an angry tone of voice. At its *most* sophisticated, it might incorporate irony by stating the opposite of what is meant and adding an "eye roll" tone of voice (for example, "Oh, yeah, I *love* getting root canals").

To be clear: Everyone is sarcastic from time to time, and sarcasm applied appropriately can be funny. That's not what we're talking about here. We're talking about men who claim sarcasm as their *identity*.

The other problem here is that uttering this phrase reveals a serious lack of imagination, like saying "partner in crime" or "no drama." If you're considering dating someone who is still using phrases that have been the punchline of dating jokes for more than a decade, it's probably a good idea to question what else about contemporary life they might be missing. It suggests a level of social cluelessness and lack of attention to other human beings that should be highly concerning to anyone who might be considering entering a relationship with these guys.

RHETORICAL PATTERN 12: SIX FLAGS OR RED FLAGS?

> Dating me is like
> An amusement park.

Dating me is like
Non-stop adventure

Dating me is like
A friend told me I was like a roller coaster ride through a teddy bear factory lol

About me
Dating me is like riding a roller-coaster with amazing snacks and a killer soundtrack

About me
I'm like a Rubik's cube, fun to play with but frustrating to figure out; but it won't be boring.

About me
There are two types of people in your dating life the ones that make rules for you and the ones that break rules for you. The latter person says "hell yes let's do it" because it's about you not about the venue the activity it's about you. I am in search of my HELL YES WOMAN. Be safe God Bless

Dating me is like
Being inside a comedy club at six flags but with better rides.

Dating me is like
Riding a bolt of lightning.

Exhilarating

> Dating me is like
> Driving down a mountain without brakes. You have control only as long as you don't try to push the brake pedal. You have to juke and jive around obstacles and be ready for anything, including ninjas.

> I'm a real nerd about . . .
> I'm a dash of mystery and a splash of adventure. Autocross adrenaline, Netflix and chill nights, and being present exploring nature.

As you can see from the samples above, these aren't just guys who like amusement parks; these are guys who think they *are* the amusement park. Rhetorically, this indicates immaturity, a lack of tolerance for the requirements of living an everyday adult life, or perhaps a misconception of how adult life typically plays out. There also seems to be some compensation going on here. If you need to go to such extreme lengths and make such histrionic comparisons to prove how interesting you are, you might just not be that interesting.

And hey, amusement park rides are fun, but only for a few seconds to a few hours—you wouldn't want to *live* in an amusement park. That would be stomach turning (in a literal sense) and destabilizing (in a literal *and* figurative sense), and really just kind of insane and creepy—think clowns in funhouse mirrors and things moving at high speed while upside down. Now think about the associated metaphors of those two things: You can't get your feet beneath you; you don't know what's real and what's distorted; you can't take a deep breath or find any peace; and all your senses are constantly being bombarded. Amusement parks are specifically designed to mess with our nervous systems; that's literally one of their primary purposes, because it's fun to be scared every now and then. But most people don't want that as a way of life.

RHETORICAL PATTERN 13: LET'S BE CUDDLE BEARS

Ask any woman on a dating app how many invitations she's gotten to "cuddle" (or snuggle, or curl up on the couch, and so on), and she'll roll her eyes straight up into the back of her head. There is a weird amount of hypothetical cuddling and snuggling going on in men's dating app profiles and in early messaging conversations.

I've gotten a lot of messages from women that say, "Can you explain why, in a rhetorical sense, the cuddle talk is so icky and revolting?" I think this is why: The words "cuddle" and "snuggle" are words that we associate with little children. With familiarity and warmth and coziness and being at home. These are the associations and connotations of those words, and these "submeanings" are frequently more powerful than the dictionary definition of words. This is the difference between "connotation" (associated meaning) and "denotation" (dictionary definition).

In contemporary dating discourses, these words "cuddle" and "snuggle" are now coded for sex (similar to how the term "Netflix and chill" quickly became coded for sex). I suspect that enough men have been advised not to go straight to sex on the apps, but they still kind of want to, and so they're doing this substitution thing instead.

So why is it so off-putting, so creepy?? When we're forced to put two ideas together that we know shouldn't go together, it sparks a cognitive clash, a deep level of discomfort. This happens beneath the level of consciousness. So when we're forced to pair something like "nurturing little children" with "men we don't know on the internet demanding sex," of course it creates an intense visceral "eew."

RHETORICAL PATTERN 14: DESIGNING MY AI GIRLFRIEND

> About me
> I am a professional investor and have become quite well off now—enough so that I will never have to worry about money for the rest of life. I bring a lot to the table in so many ways and want a somebody who is my complimentary equal.
>
> Looking for a traditional girl to settle down and have a family with. She must be pretty, easy-going, low maintenance, naturally happy, and educated with a professional career. Personality fit is the biggest factor for me, but looks is the gatekeeper.
>
> Asian girls welcome.

There are apps where people can literally design an AI girlfriend (or boyfriend, or whatever). They can pick out body type, hair color, eye color, weight, age, ethnicity, personality traits, and so on. The ethics and social ramifications of such technologies are well beyond the scope of this book, and because the technologies are so new, we don't know what the long-term benefits or consequences might be. But here's what we do know: Treating living human women like sex dolls or fantasy-driven AI creations is unhealthy and unhinged. The guy in the example above wants a "traditional girl" who also has a professional career, and oh, "Asian girls welcome."

Men who seem to be "designing" their prospective dates lack a mature and even basic understanding of what it means to be fully human. What we're talking about with the "designing my AI girlfriend" pattern is different from having preferences; everyone has preferences. But laying them out the way this guy is in the example above is objectifying and fetishizing. A dating app is used to meet another living, breathing human being; it's not the same process as shoe shopping on Amazon and filtering for features.

RHETORICAL PATTERN 15: LOOKING FOR A TRADWIFE

> Entrepreneur—Proud Dad of 4—Faith-Led Life
>
> I own my own business and love being a stable, supportive presence for my kids. I'm on the lookout for a Proverbs 31 woman who shares my commitment to faith. If you are fit and have a nice booty, that's huge plus also ☺.

> The way to win me over is
> Be sweet, not overweight, submissive, let me lead, no kids with other men, and want to start a family.

> The world would be a better place with more
> Masculine men who aren't afraid to lead

> Do you agree or disagree that
> That relationships should go back to the way they were. I'm looking for a wife that wants to have lots of kids and be a stay at home mom. Even home school the kids all the way through high school. Should believe in god also.

The tradwife phenomenon is quite literally a figured world made real again—a social movement in which young women are willingly embodying the caricature of the old-fashioned housewife. In the dating sphere, it's associated with conservative Christianity and being propagated by social media influencers, some of whom actually dress to emulate housewives from the 1950s or even earlier, wearing long, calico dresses reminiscent of the American pioneer days. While much of this is being employed in the name of content creation and algorithm chasing, there is a very real (and very disturbing) contingent of men who are actively seeking women who want to "submit" and to "serve"—women who will accept being "led by their husbands" while they "rest in femininity." This seems a fairly obvious backlash to women's increasing success and autonomy, but it's a concerning trend whose signal flags you should be aware of.

The examples above are fairly explicit in terms of this rhetorical pattern, and many "looking for a tradwife" profiles include obvious terms such as "Proverbs 31" or "godly marriage" or "biblical womanhood," but watch for these signal words as well: humble/humility, grace, soft/soften, wholesome, simple, vintage/retro, obedient, Christ-centered, equally yoked, home-centered, old-fashioned, nurturing.

The juxtaposition of requiring both a "Proverbs 31 woman" and a "nice booty" in the first example is particularly revealing. Everything about the tradwife movement is objectifying and misogynistic and exploitative, but those effects are usually more cloaked and embedded; this guy just calls himself right out.

RHETORICAL PATTERN 16: RESCUE PUPS AND EEYORES

> It looks like we may have a few things in common. As you can see from my profile I'm in a tough situation. Not impossible, but pretty tough. Hey, it's helping to build character, lol.

> In their own words
> I live in isolation
> It's much like I imagine prison is
> I did not commit a crime

> I am just not able to fit in
> I see all the profiles of so many great people
> It reminds me that I just can't fit in anywhere, ever

> My bio
> I'm really just a regular guy. Nothing special. I work, I pay bills, I don't get arrested, and I travel occasionally. I'm getting old, fat, and probably out of touch, but that's life.
>
> I'm just me. If that's not good enough, then I'll just stay single.

There are a lot of Eeyores and rescue puppies on the dating apps—men who've been left, who've been cheated on, who've fallen on hard times, who've been widowed and can't figure out how to make a sandwich because their wife did all the work, and so on. It may not even be their fault, but it's not yours either and it's not your responsibility to fix or save them.

If someone enters a situation in which they have nothing to bring to the table, then they're only there to eat your food. And by food I mean your other resources—time, energy, money, and emotional well-being. There are a lot of women who end up being drained to the point of illness and injury because they're overly supporting men. And let's not entertain any nonsense about how he's providing fun or emotional support or friendship. You can get all those things from your actual friends, and you should.

Bottom line: If you want a rescue puppy, get one with floppy ears and a tail.

RHETORICAL PATTERN 17: CULT LEADER LINGO

> About me
> My philosophy is intimate relationships take work.
> Communication is the #1 success factor, hands down.

RED-FLAG RHETORICAL PATTERNS 117

Followed by an equal balance of mutual give and take, aka Compromise. Trust should be 💯 to your new prospect until your natural instincts tell you otherwise. Now let's have some fun doing it

---

We'll get along if . . .
You prioritize sex into your daily routine, consider and respect your partners boundaries and point of view, trust your partner has your best interests at heart

---

Greetings ladies and skanks.

I understand all mysteries.

Come, sit at my feet and learn.

NASA lies with CGI.

Evolution is nonsense.

Dinosaurs never existed.

The earth is a stationary plane.

Outer space is fake.

Leviticus 19:28 Ye shall not make any cuttings in your flesh for the dead, nor print any marks upon you: I am the LORD.

Again, I say, come sit at my feet and learn.

About me
I give up. It's better to be alone, than to settle. I cannot live a lie just for companionship. Why would I want a woman in my life? I have not had any good

experiences yet. Men love. Women just want the bigger and better deal. Will God save this evil world? Another reset is coming!

Cult leader language in men's dating app profiles tends to come in two varieties:

1. Demanding a weird and inappropriate level of trust and control. In the examples above, we see these sentences:

    "Trust should be given 100% to your new prospect."

    "Trust your partner has your best interests at heart."

    Putting 100 percent of your trust in an absolute stranger is not only unnatural, it's incredibly dangerous. This is exactly the kind of thing cult leaders demand, and these guys are demanding it in their dating app profiles. Deconstructing the systems of rhetorical manipulation used by cult leaders is far too complex an endeavor to address in this book, but I do want to share one particularly relevant line from Amanda Montell's book *Cultish: The Language of Fanaticism*, in which she refers to "a type of conditioning most of us have experienced: the conditioning to automatically trust the voices of middle-aged white men." This is the demographic who appear most likely to invoke this tenor with women on dating apps, and it makes sense; we have all been raised in a patriarchy that's privileged the voices of middle-aged white men, the group of people assigned to categories such as "father," "pastor," and "doctor." The discourse of "middle-aged white man as leader" has become naturalized to a degree that it's sometimes easy not to question it, but we *need* to question it—we need to denaturalize it—and one way to do that is to call out the more nefarious rhetorical patterns it engenders. And as with all toxic rhetorical patterns, when we see them in a man's dating app profile, it's a good reason to block to burn.

2. Things that just sound completely insane. In the examples above, we see these phrases:

   "Come, sit at my feet and learn."

   "Dinosaurs never existed."

   "Outer space is fake."

   I suspect that men who write such sentences are suffering from a mental illness, and we should have empathy for that, but we should absolutely not date it.

Whatever the genre of cult leader language these guys engage in, your next step is the same: block to burn. They have power and control issues and/or have departed from reality; you cannot build a relationship on a foundation constructed of aggression and untreated mental illness.

RHETORICAL PATTERN 18: CRAZY-MAKING COMMUNICATION

> **Woman:** There are many gendered tropes about the "old ball and chain" so anything resembling that is not a dynamic I'm interested in. That's how I read what you said.
> **Man:** I hope you have a nice weekend. I'm staying in tonight. I'm marinating some chicken thighs that I'm going to grill this evening. It's Mediterranean style . . . yum! 😊

The one thing you should know about me is
The one thing you should ask me about

> **Man:** What's your week looking like? Do you think you might be available Friday? Maybe meet up and grab a bite or a drink or both?

> **Woman:** Yeah I am free Friday! There is a cool place in [blank], would you be up to meet up there? 😊
>
> **Man:** Anyway, as a single man, I keep thinking about someone new exciting and beautiful

> My bio
> I'll probably make you laugh until your cucumber is pickled.

I love a good word puzzle, and I am totally susceptible to spending *way* too much time trying to render nonsensical things into clarity—it's like a game to me. But it took me awhile to realize what a stupid game this is to play on the dating apps, and I now dedicate my word-puzzle time to *The New York Times*'s Games app.

Crazy-making communication happens for a variety of reasons. Maybe you're talking to a bot, maybe it's a scam, maybe the man has a cognitive impairment, maybe he's just talking to so many women he's confusing you with someone else, maybe he's mentally ill, maybe he's intentionally messing with you. But the reason doesn't matter, because every single one of these reasons is a block to burn.

Protect your sanity and your precious time and don't waste either trying to figure out why a man is threatening to "make you laugh until your cucumber is pickled" or because he's responding to your questions as though he is an actual space alien. If you have to work that hard just to decode what he's saying, there is no hope for a productive relationship anyway. Block to burn and move on.

RHETORICAL PATTERN 19: RECEPTACLES FOR RANDOMNESS

I want to introduce this pattern by using a question from a Burned Haystack community member. She writes:

"I have a few single guy friends whose communication style leans toward narrating their days. They'll message me with little context and just start sharing pics of their breakfast or their lighting fixture installation project. There's no reference to previous conversations we've had or questions about how I'm doing. They just send these things and assume I'll be interested."

I also encountered this kind of thing on the dating apps, and from the comments online it was clear most other women had as well. One group member labeled the phenomenon "receptacles for randomness," and it clearly resonated.

Let's talk for a minute about **discourse communities** and **discourse norms**, because this is an important concept in rhetoric in general and on the dating apps in particular. A discourse community is simply a group of people who share common experiences, understandings, and ways of speaking. We could talk about the discourse communities of feminist academics, of legal scholars, of serious gamers, of men's locker rooms. Within such communities, there is a built-in framework for what forms of communication are acceptable, and this applies to content, to vocabulary, to tone, and to value systems. Each discourse community, therefore, has its own "discourse norms."

Let's apply that concept to a real-life example: I might very well text my inner circle of girlfriends a pic of my closet that I'd just cleaned. That's within the discourse norms in our own discourse community; we've known each other forever and are genuinely interested in the minutia of one another's lives. This kind of sharing of everyday mundanity is also normal and healthy in long-term partnerships or marriages.

But let's change the discourse community and ask if it still falls within the norms. Imagine that I have my neighbor's phone number. I don't know this neighbor at all, but we met one time and exchanged numbers just in case someone needed to borrow a cup of sugar. Now imagine that I send that neighbor a random picture of the inside of my closet. That's weird. They would probably have some questions about me, and rightfully so.

It's even weirder on the dating apps; at least I'd met my neighbor in the example above. On the dating apps, we're talking about total strangers.

I don't know why so many men use women on dating apps as receptacles for randomness. My best and most generous guess is that some of these men have been in long-term relationships, and this is simply the only way they know how to communicate with women. Maybe it's just an awkward attempt to connect.

Women in the Burned Haystack community shared their own interpretations, and I want to share a few that strike me as valid.

One woman states, "It's just another form of using a woman. She nods, she smiles. It's a porn-like release, with their pent-up words into our ears, and then they move on."

Another contextualized "receptacles for randomness" within gendered labor imbalances writ large, noting that women tend to bring our A game to the apps—we agonize over building our profiles, we try to be engaging, we edit and proofread and polish, whereas too many men seem to pick the first three photos on their phone and assume that "Just ask" is a complete bio.

Another group member likened it to a specific form of grooming, in which pics of men's days lead to selfies, lead to pillow pics, lead to nudes, and so on.

A few other group members suggested that many of these guys tend to suffer from main character syndrome, and I tend to agree with that. You'd have to consider yourself pretty fascinating to assume a stranger would want to take time out of their day to hear about what you bought at Target.

As far as rhetorical patterns go, receptacles for randomness might be more closely aligned with boredom than anything toxic or aggressive (unless you experience inflicted boredom as a form of aggression; I've certainly been on dates that fit the category). But enough about receptacles for randomness; it's a problem, and we don't know why they do it.

RHETORICAL PATTERN 20: THE GREEK TRAGEDY OF FUNNY GUYS ON THE APPS

Here's what happens in a Greek tragedy: The tragic hero tries *so hard* to outrun his fate yet somehow ends up running right into it. This is how I feel about all the men loudly insisting on their profiles that they're funny. Many of them engage in such bizarre displays of nonsense that they end up proving how unfunny they are *while* trying to prove they're funny, hence the Greek tragedy reference.

We're going to look at some examples so that we can watch these micro Greek tragedies play out in the dating apps, but first, I think we should establish a very basic principle regarding humor:

Truly funny people don't have to tell you they're funny; a legit sense of humor makes itself apparent naturally. I *never* believe the guys who say, "I promise you'll laugh," or who otherwise explain to me that they're funny. My personal rule for men claiming comedic talent is that in order for me to take it seriously they have to have some kind of credential. If he writes for *The Daily Show* or *The Onion* or something, then okay. Otherwise, if you're funny, just be funny.

Let's look at some Greek tragedies . . .

About me
I funny . . . I floss, I travel, I hike, I read, I bike, I restaurant! I empty nest, I tech biz own. I spiritual! Meditate, pray, and work on earthly skills daily. I loyal. I truthful. Did I mention I funny?

The guy above thinks he's demonstrating how funny he is, but he's really just demonstrating that he can't use helping verbs.

Here's a somewhat random sampling of other humor-related Greek tragedies on the apps:

In their own words
Unemployed, live in my mom's basement, collecting disability, therapy 5 days a week, a professional protester, blame everyone for my problems, take no personal responsibility for anything, aaaaaand (last but not least). . . . president of the Star Trek fan club . . . . . . (lol!)

Jackpot, right!!!!!

My bio
I'm just here looking for my parents. They disappeared one night a few years ago and I thought I might be able to find them here . . . . . . Having trouble though. . . . because seriously? Gross! Who tries to date there parents!

My bio
Seeking beautiful young super model. Prefer wealthy to rich. Must be highly educated, prefer a PHD but a Masters will do with the right lady. Super good looking. Must be obedient and willing to be spanked. Brunettes only! NO Redheads, leave me alone! Artists welcome. Must have a great sense of humor

The other really interesting thing about Greek tragedies in a literary sense—and also in a dating app sense—is that hubris always plays a significant role in the downfall of the tragic hero. Hubris refers to excessive pride or arrogance, to an overestimation of one's abilities. We're seeing that here too.

In conclusion, I have advice for both profile writers and profile readers on the apps:

For writers: If you're authentically funny, that's a highly desirable trait, and you should capitalize on it in your dating app profile. But maybe run it by a few other people—people who will be honest with you, people who will intervene and protect you from meeting your own tragic end even as you try to outrun it.

And if you're a *reader* of a Greek tragedy on the dating apps, I would block to burn, because those endings are either tragically boring or just tragic.

RHETORICAL PATTERN 21: PET NAMERS

Most women on the apps encounter this constantly, which is baffling to me. Here's a post from the Facebook group:

> Community member: How does everyone feel about men calling you sweetie or sunshine or silly or sweetheart when you have barely even been texting let alone talking on the phone or in an actual dating relationship? Is it now the norm that men throw those pet names out there? I'm not even sure why but it gives me the ick something fierce. Is it to be expected with online dating?
>
> My response: Literally 100% of women I know hate this. Nobody knows why they do it. Super ick.

We're going to turn this one into a grammar lesson, and we're going to go over the definitions of the word "pet" in its noun, adjective, and verb forms. Ready?

PET AS NOUN: a tamed animal that is kept for companionship.

Women who are online dating do not want to think of themselves as tamed animals that are being kept for any reason. Super terrifying.

PET AS ADJECTIVE: an object of affection

This one is contextual, because after people have developed a fondness for one another, the adjective definition makes sense within the context of an intimate relationship. Most people use pet names all the time for their children or their spouse, as a show of love and affection and connection.

PET AS A VERB (this is where it gets super icky): to stroke something

It seems obvious that people shouldn't use pet names with strangers, but men do all the time. Rather than spending too much time trying to figure out why, let's focus on what calling women pet names reveals about the men who are doing so:

- That they are presumptuous enough to assume women will be okay with this and/or like the pet names they choose.
- That they view women as objects and animals rather than complex human beings whom they do not know.
- That they've somehow missed sweeping changes to discourse norms for the past several decades. It's true that there was a time when men could get away with calling women they didn't know "honey" or "sweetie pie," but that time is *long* past.
- That they are socially clueless and insensitive.

Any one of these revelations suggests a man is undatable. Block to burn the pet namers.

RHETORICAL PATTERN 22: ONTOLOGY OF FITNESS BROS

Ontology is a nerdy academic word that refers to a system of characterizing and classifying things, and it's a helpful tool for our consideration of the many, *many* varieties of fitness bros on the dating apps. Visual rhetoric, the branch of analysis that involves reading images to glean important info, is also going to be used here. Enjoy this handy guide of words and image descriptions of actual men's profiles to help you parse the nuances of fitness bros and decide whether they're a yay or a nay for you depending upon your own preferences.

THE GUY WHOSE MAIN PROFILE PIC IS TAKEN AT PLANET FITNESS: He's telling you this is a big part of who he is. He spends a lot of time at the gym, and it's really important to him. He's holding a protein drink, and he has a physique that suggests he works out a *lot*. If that's important to you too, then this might be a good fit. If this would drive you insane, then probably not.

THE SUPER-BUFF GUY POSING IN HIS UNDERWEAR: This guy is also telling you that working out is important to him, but there's an additional consideration here because he's telling you that he's okay with his profile pic (which is essentially a public artifact) being taken in his bikini underwear. You have to ask yourself, "Is this guy making decisions that I would feel good about if I were his partner?"

THE WEIRDLY FIT MOUNTAIN MAN: This one is a little more complex. This guy is outside, he seems outdoorsy, and he likes nature; many women find this appealing. He also has an almost otherworldly physique, and that's maybe the important part here. If, say, a fifty-five year-old man has the body of an uber-shredded thirty-year-old, there are implications to consider. This kind of physique on a middle-aged man does not just happen. It takes a lot of time, and a lot of energy, and a lot of focus, and a lot of resources. If this is your lifestyle as well, then this guy might be a great match because you have the same interests and abilities. The flip side is that he may live an incredibly strict and demanding life. Does he not eat carbs? Can he never sit and watch TV? Would all vacation accommodations be based upon quality of the hotel gym? This is beyond health and fitness; there's a level of vanity here that should at least be considered.

Note: I realize I'm sounding pretty judgy about Bikini Underwear and Mountain Man, which is revealing my personal preferences; I couldn't deal with either of these guys, because number one, put your clothes on, and number two, I want to eat carbs and lie around on vacation!!! But that's me. As I've noted, Burned Haystack is not intended to be morally judgmental; it's intended to be pragmatic—to reveal information. You have to be clear-eyed and honest about what you're seeing, and then extrapolate that data to make predictions about other aspects of people's personalities. If you do that accurately, then you get better matches (for you specifically).

EXTREME SPORTS GUY: There are a lot of men on the dating apps who are skydiving and climbing Mount Everest and jumping over things on their motorcycles. If you do those things too, or have a respect for daredevils, these guys would be a good match. We should also ask ourselves, *What else does this imply? Is this guy an adrenaline junkie? Does he have a constant need for intensity and excitement and danger? What might that mean?* Just things to consider.

INDOOR ADVENTURE SPORTS GUY: The guy whose profile features him in a CrossFit gym or on an indoor rock-climbing wall might spend a lot of time in such facilities or with the relevant crowd. That could be good or bad, depending upon what you want.

MARATHON MAN: Marathons are sort of extreme, and they require time and energy and focus and commitment. These are objectively good things in many ways—men who are disciplined and able to tolerate hard work over a period of time frequently make good partners. These guys tend to present differently than the guy in his underwear—less performative in terms of body presentation and more about communicating his value system and how he spends his time. This could be a good match or it could be really annoying, because those weekend long runs really do take a lot of time. It's all information to consider.

OUTDOOR FUN GUY: Depicting oneself in activities such as social mountain biking and group hiking usually signifies "I like to be active and outdoors." As long as this is okay with you—either because you also enjoy these activities or because you don't mind your partner engaging in them without you—then these guys might be wonderful partners for you.

• • •

This ontology of fitness bros is intended to be lighthearted and somewhat fun, but engaging in these kinds of practices and using these rhetorical tools is a serious superpower and a shortcut. And the more you use them, the sharper you get.

RHETORICAL PATTERN 23: CONDITIONAL DECENCY

> Look, I don't have time to fuck around, I want a good woman who understands life is complicated. I want good sex with a woman who likes home cooked meals and a good message and movie. Not playing games, time is limited. Act accordingly. I don't have a 6 pack. I work my as off. So I'm chubby with no butt 🤷 I will treat you like a queen if you treat me like your king. 😎 👳 old enough to know nothing lasts forever. Prove me wrong. . . .

> What's something I wouldn't know from your profile?
> **Man:** That I'm a big ole teddy bear once ya get to know me.
> **Woman:** Ahhh, but can I count on you to score me those elusive

> top shelf items? I wasn't exactly kidding about being asked not to climb shelves 😂
> **Man:** Well yes but, I can be kind of a shit. I mean I might grab it, but then still hold it just high enough you can't reach it. But I mean for a simple kiss or a slap on the ass I might give it up. 😊

Men who signal conditional decency conceive of intimate relationships as transactional arrangements. We're not talking about a healthy give-and-take, which is normal. These guys are telling you that you must earn the "privilege" of him treating you like a human being, that he will not dole out basic human kindness "for free." You shouldn't even be friends with a person like this, let alone date them.

RHETORICAL PATTERN 24: BORED TODDLER

> How are the big Bs looking this next season?   11:01 a.m.
>
> And how's Bumble treating you?   11:24 a.m.
>
> Somebody has had a really busy day 😢   2:56 p.m.

Note: "The big Bs" refers to a sports team in this conversation, and the third message is him crying because she hadn't responded to him quickly (it was still the same day; she was at work).

This rhetorical pattern is short and sweet, just like a real toddler (not a grown-man toddler).

She hasn't even met this guy, and he feels entitled to demand her time and attention. This is the equivalent of a grown man following you around and tugging on your sleeve all the time. Can you imagine what that would be like in real life? You need to Ferberize these guys and let them go cry themselves to sleep. Block to burn.

RHETORICAL PATTERN 25: WEAPONIZED SPIRITUALITY

I want to first differentiate between valid statements of spirituality on the dating apps and weaponized spirituality. Let's use the concept of weaponized incompetence for comparison: Imagine that your boyfriend does the dishes one night, and he breaks all the dishes. In this case, he is clearly incompetent at washing dishes. But now imagine him saying, "Can you always do the dishes? I'm just not good at it like you are." That's *weaponized* incompetence. Those are two different things.

It's possible to have or to be a thing without weaponizing that thing, and that's the difference I'm interested in with spirituality. It's totally fine to say that you're a spiritual person or that you belong to a particular church or faith community. This rhetorical pattern becomes problematic when a man suggests you need to "soften" in order to spark his attraction, that you must guard against being "led by ego," that "desirable women keep sweet" or "reside in grace" or "understand that unquestioning trust in her man" is the key to receiving love. You should consider any championing of "purity" a red flag; men who do this reduce a woman's entire value to how many men she has been with and how those men have treated her. This is total erasure of women as autonomous human beings, a conception of women as mere vessels for men. You should absolutely avoid men who nod toward hierarchical family structures that place the man as the "head of the household" or "spiritual leader" for his wife, even if (perhaps especially if) he seems to suggest that this hierarchy is a prerequisite to love.

I want to address one other form of weaponized spirituality that fits into this pattern. It's what I call a "middle-aged white Buddhist" effect. (I label this a "MAWB alert!" online.) That's not as specific as it sounds, because they're not all claiming to be Buddhists and they're not all white. However, there's a phenomenon on the dating apps in which men, usually long-term-problematic middle-aged men whose wives have finally left them, stumble upon some sort of god or gods. They spend three months or so listening to Dude Bro podcasts about cold plunging or biohacking or stoicism and suddenly consider themselves spiritual gurus. Sometimes they claim to be on "spiritual journeys" or to have "done the work" or to be "peace-centered," or a whole bunch of other nonsense-coded phrases they've recently encountered. I ran into this a *lot* on the apps, and it quickly became a weeding-out nonstarter for me. I'm not necessarily saying these guys should be automatic block to burns, but I am saying they might be annoying to date if what they're talking about (generally nonstop) is not your particular jam.

RHETORICAL PATTERN 26: I'M THE PRIZE

A Burned Haystack community member shared this screenshot of a message she received from a man and asked, "How do I respond to this?"

> Hi Tasha, i read your profile and i am thinking wow she is asking/expecting a lot . . . But What is she offering ? At least as much as What she is asking ?

You don't respond to anything like this. *At all*. Ever. This is an "I'm the prize" pattern and an auto block to burn.

I completely get that when we are challenged on things such as our very worth, we feel compelled to respond, to prove ourselves. That's human nature. I'd want to also. But you shouldn't. There is no world in which this guy is datable, and any single second you spend engaging with him is a waste of your time.

If it helps you to think of it this way, remind yourself that while you're trying to prove yourself to this egomaniac, someone else might be connecting with a decent human being who would have been a good match for you.

I'm now going to interrupt this chapter for a moment to make an important point. That sentence you just read—the one about the danger of missing decent human beings while contending with jerks—speaks directly to the subtitle of this book, which is "Decode Dating, Torch the Duds, and Make Room for Men Who Matter." Subtitles are important, and this one was settled upon after a great deal of consideration. I want to address it explicitly here.

If I were a toxic man who was also an expert in critical discourse analysis, how would I analyze this subtitle? I might say something like this (probably using ALL CAPS): "Do you understand what Jennie Young is IMPLYING HERE?! She's implying that if we don't pass Burned Haystack rules, then WE DON'T MATTER!"

Yes. Bingo. That is exactly what I'm saying, and it is 100 percent intentional. I'm not saying these men don't matter as a human beings; just that they should not figure in the dating sphere of any woman looking for a healthy partnership. Any man who is still aggressing women on the internet, facilitating totally one-sided conversations, weaponizing laziness and incompetence, and flying red flags all over the place as though he's his own personal opening ceremony of the Beijing Olympics simply doesn't matter in the context of dating. He's a nonfactor. He can change this if he wants, but that decision, along with engaging in the emotional labor it entails, is entirely up to him. He can do that on his own time while you're meeting men who *do* matter.

Let's return now to the "I'm the prize" guy trying to bait Tasha into proving her worth. It sounds as though he's asking questions here, but he's not; he's making statements, and these are the statements:

1. You think too much of yourself.
2. I will change that.
3. There is a hierarchy here, and I am at the top; it's your job to prove yourself worthy of me.

This guy is attempting to *begin a relationship* with abusive tactics, and it is not going to get better from here. There's nothing reportable here; his interactions do not rise to anything technically or legally registerable, but I would bet money that down the road, and probably not too far down the road, he becomes explicitly abusive.

Please do not entertain these guys, not for one second.

Here are some additional examples of "I'm the prize."

> **My bio**
> I'm a confident quite often cheeky buggar that'll make you laugh daily. Looking build a good connection, having some fun dates and see where things go.
>
> Non-subtle, but honest boast. I don't remember the last time a woman didn't openly tell me I was the best she'd ever had. Maybe you'll be the first, but I doubt it.
>
> You'll need to stimulate my mind if you want me to stimulate your body. You don't just get given good D, you need to earn it. Passion & Intensity guaranteed.

> **My bio**
> . . . making you figure this part out for yourself will be more rewarding for you and less of a pain for me to sum myself up in a paragraph.

The "I'm the prize" pattern frequently intersects with the disciplinary/directive pattern, and I consider it equally toxic and indicative of nondatability. On top of all the problems we already discussed (using their own profiles to tell *you* what to do; feeling comfortable taking a disciplinary role with women they haven't even met; revealing potential for abuse), these guys are game players who lack the maturity, sensitivity, and emotional skills to participate in a relationship at an adult level.

There's a subtler manifestation of this rhetorical pattern than those depicted above, though, and it's especially easy to miss because it tends to show up with men who are objectively desirable because of their social status, their profession, or their wealth. I experienced this myself in two specific instances that are worth sharing for the sake of exemplifying how "I'm the prize" can be detected with this subset of men (sometimes referred to as "high-value men," which is a problematic term for describing an actual human being, but I see it a lot on social media and in particular from exploitative dating coaches).

Physicians and attorneys for sure, but also finance executives, tech bros, and CEOs of [whatever], get a disproportionate amount of attention from women on dating apps. I understand why. Among the crowds of men instructing matches to "text me, I can't see messages" (because they're not paying for the app) and men clearly living in their elderly mothers' basements, the notion of a successful, financially secure if not wealthy partner is appealing.

So I'm certainly not blaming anyone for being drawn to the doctors and lawyers, nor am I suggesting you shouldn't date them. I *am* suggesting, however, that you don't give them extra chances you wouldn't give other men, and I'm also suggesting you not tolerate bad behavior and poor treatment that you wouldn't tolerate from men of less lofty professions.

I ended up blocking one doctor and one lawyer within a relatively short period of time, and I still feel good about both those decisions.

I met the attorney on Hinge shortly before starting Burned Haystack. I was getting savvier on the apps and experimenting with rhetoric, but I hadn't totally formalized the method yet. Sometimes I'm suspicious of attorneys, but this guy claimed to be a human rights attorney, which compelled me. I quickly found him on Facebook, and then on the news, being interviewed about a high-profile case he had litigated (and won). His Hinge profile said he'd climbed Mount Kilimanjaro, which is usually something that makes me roll my eyes, but the other claims he'd made were checking out, so I gave him the benefit of the doubt.

His Facebook profile pic was a shot of a silhouette of his head backlit by the sun rising over Kilimanjaro itself. This struck me as pretentious, but I decided that wasn't sufficient reason to disqualify someone; maybe he knew it was pretentious and was sort of mocking himself or something. There was a time when I entertained these kinds of possibilities.

He'd set up one of those "two truths and a lie" options in his Hinge profile, which is my favorite because I almost always get those right—if you know enough about critical discourse analysis they're super easy to crack. He was impressed I got his right and asked me how I figured it out. I told him I had a PhD in applied rhetoric and that "these kinds of games are child's play to me" (lines like this almost always work with male attorneys, I've found; they fancy themselves smarter than everyone else, and they frequently seem intrigued if a woman does anything smart at all).

His response to that was to send me his phone number. He said, and I quote, "I give most women my burner number, but you seem different, so I'm giving you my real one."

I should have blocked him then, because that's obnoxious, not to mention disrespectful of other women he was meeting, who I assume were no more threatening than me, but for some reason I didn't. We had one phone conversation, which went well, and set up a date for the following week. The more I thought about it, though, the more I didn't like something about him. He was exhibiting not only an "I'm the prize" vibe, but the other side of it, which is "I have deemed you a prize and will therefore treat you differently/better than I do other women." This part I couldn't get over, so I canceled the date.

A few of my friends thought I'd acted rashly, which was potentially valid, but then a few weeks later he messaged me on LinkedIn. The message said, "Hey Jennie, how're you doing? Just letting you know you're still on my A-Team."

This really did make me laugh. I was on an A-Team of single

women? Like in a Robert Palmer video? Can you imagine dating that? I was so glad I'd opted out.

The doctor I met in "in the wild." We had both moved to the same town during the same month, and we met in a coffee shop. I had two girlfriends with me at the time, and they were immediately captivated by the Hallmark-movie/meet-cute potential of this narrative: "You both moved to the same adorable town at the same time, and he's a single doctor and you're a single teacher and you both love cats!"

We had exchanged cell numbers at that first meeting (I did look him up and verify his identity as well; I do research on all prospective dates!). He texted me the following day and said, "Great meeting you. Just so you know, I'll be at the coffee shop around 8:30 on Sunday morning." This wasn't exactly a date invitation, but it seemed fine to me at that point—it was no pressure and a place we both liked to go anyway. I showed up.

We chatted easily for half an hour or so, and then he had to leave to pick up his daughter.

He texted me the following Sunday right at 8:30 and said, "Just so you know, I'm down at the coffee shop." This I didn't love because it felt more like a directive. I texted back and said I already had plans.

This happened three more times, and I never showed up at my assigned time. Several weeks later I just happened to be in that coffee shop at 8:30 on a Sunday morning, and he was in there sitting at a table talking to a woman. So maybe this was his shtick? He just notified women of his whereabouts and some would show up?

Rhetorically, this could be revealing. This man doesn't seem to realize that the women he's asking out might have a life and a schedule that's as relevant as his own.

To sum up, neither of these guys did anything horribly toxic, and if my number one goal was to find a man with a good job, I might have blown it, but that never was my goal anyway. I realize single women face a lot of pressure to "lock these guys down" or whatever, but that's misplaced. It comes from an era in which women were expected to make emotional compromises for partnership, to sacrifice their independence at the altar of financial security. We don't have to do that anymore.

So go ahead and block to burn those guys if you want to. Above all, I think you should trust your gut. I trusted mine in both these cases and have never regretted it a bit.

RHETORICAL PATTERN 27: PEACE SEEKERS

> Starting over is weird! I don't want much but I need peace I don't do drama or people that R NEGGO's which means negative thinking people! I made up that word btw! I love positive people so I tend to read Ur entire profile, memes, pics etc! Im looking4 a woman 2B my peace, my joy, my desire, my love! Amazing in bed in all ways! Passion that's never lazy! I want a Ride with me woman that's has my back loyal 2 me/US no matter what! I need a woman that can figure this out!

There is a current trend of men demanding "peace" or "peaceful women." What they mean by "peaceful" is "compliant," and those are two different things. I recommend taking them at their word. If what someone wants more than anything is total peace, then the best way to give them that is to simply not interact with them at all. So when you encounter these guys, I think you should tell them to "Peace out, Boy Scout" and block to burn.

And finally, here's a great profile (from a physician named Gavin who was educated at "Enough Schooling") that brilliantly encompasses both "peace seekers" and "I'm the prize" in one profile:

> 57 not 47. Pics current. Married 32 years. Divorced 2 years. Casual/fun dating & companionship stage. If more

develops, fine. Great relationships take time, as does avoiding mistakes & bumble has many mistakes. I DO NOT CHASE WOMEN. Busy men rest where there is peace. If you are peaceful say hello.

We're going to go line by line in analyzing this one:

"Gavin, 47," who is actually "57, not 47."

Gavin just kicked off your relationship by lying to you and disrespecting your boundaries. Keep that in mind. Also, he's trying to meet younger women, which should be taken into account as well.

He's an attending physician who was educated at "Enough Schooling."

Do not question Gavin! If he says it's enough, it's enough. Here's what makes this even funnier and more revealing: No one has to fill out the "Education" question on Bumble. If he didn't want to talk about it, he could've just skipped it. But Gavin-57-not-47 here actually took *more* time to fill out a question he didn't want to answer just to make the point to you that he will not be questioned. He's above it.

He's looking for "casual/fun," and "If more develops, fine."

Gavin wants casual fun, with "more" being a way-distant preference. He says that more would be "fine." I absolutely love sweet potato fries and become genuinely excited at the prospect of getting some. I think boiled sweet potatoes are "fine." There's a difference.

"Great relationships take time..."

Gavin, a single, middle-aged white man screaming at hypothetical women on a dating app, is mansplaining "relationships" to you. Listen up!

"...as does avoiding mistakes & bumble has many mistakes."

Please understand that Gavin is framing *you* as one of the "mistakes on Bumble" before he's even met you.

"I DO NOT CHASE WOMEN."

WHO ARE YOU YELLING AT, GAVIN??? Seriously, this is a strange rhetorical choice. If I didn't want to chase someone, I simply wouldn't chase them. I wouldn't scream "I'M NOT CHASING YOU" so that they would understand that I wasn't chasing them. That's actually kind of like chasing them, isn't it?

"Busy men rest where there is peace."

This is a new (but uninteresting) spin on the "I'm a very busy man!" rhetorical pattern, which is always a fairy tale. Women are way busier.

"If you are peaceful say hello."

Only space aliens come in peace. When men demand "peaceful women," what they mean is "compliant women" and "women who are willing to tolerate all kinds of my bullshit."

Conclusion

Gavin is a disaster. There is not "Enough Schooling" or enough money in the universe to overcome the egregiousness of his personality flaws, I promise.

RHETORICAL PATTERN 28: SEXUAL NON SEQUITUR

> **Woman:** [*sends cat picture*] Belle is shy but warms up quickly. Both are cuddly and very playful
> **Man:** Prettiest pussy I've seen today

> **Woman:** I have my child in the week so those evenings are never exciting 😂
> **Man:** I disagree
> **Man:** Your curves make them exciting

> **Woman:** Love the city, and the village is such a fun area. As a theatre person thought I might end up there some day, but it was never in the cards.
> **Man:** Hi! Oh I was only there for grad school, I wanted to move home and stay in metro Detroit 😊
> I lived in LA as an actor for seven years too!
> **Woman:** Really? I was there for three years. But probably before your time;) (99–2001)
> **Man:** Oh why miss Kristine, are you flirting with me?? 😉
> I'd hate for you to get yourself into any trouble now . . .;)

The sexual non sequitur pattern doesn't require much analysis. These are the guys who will turn *anything* into a sexual discussion far too early, including things such as women's pets or, in the second example, *caring for a small child*. On top of being disrespectful and too sexually forward, this just reveals a disturbing lack of social awareness. You can't date "Horny + Clueless."

RHETORICAL PATTERN 29: BLUE RIBBON FOR BARE MINIMUM

> Fact about me that surprises people
> I never hit a woman in my whole life

> A random fact I love is
> I never hit nor will ever hit a women
>
> (Wait do spankings count) 🤔

> My bio
> I am a SWM who is looking for a fun well grounded woman. I do have all my teeth and brush daily, plus bi yearly cleanings. I have three pairs of bed sheets and change them regularly. 😊

> I chew with my mouth closed, rarely smell. For those with higher expectations I know the difference between there, their and they're and I always put the seat down. I can be an insufferable optimist, funny and low key nerd

"Blue ribbon for bare minimum" is also self-explanatory, but from an analytical perspective the concern here is twofold: 1. These guys might need constant praise and encouragement for carrying out the most basic behaviors and actions of adulthood. 2. They're probably extremely lazy and low effort if they believe activities such as maintaining their own bodily hygiene is something to brag about.

RHETORICAL PATTERN 30: PERFORMATIVE SENSITIVITY GONE HORRIBLY WRONG

> My bio
> Women are like apples on trees. The best ones are at the top of the tree. The men that don't want to reach for the good ones because they are afraid of getting hurt. So the apples at the top think something is wrong with them, when in reality, THEY'RE amazing.

This next example is from a man's profile that contained only one image, which is a drawing of a nude heterosexual couple having intercourse. Written across their bodies are the following statements:

- I'm proud of you.
- I feel safe with you.
- I want only you.
- You're beautiful.
- I trust you.
- You make me happy.
- I appreciate you.

Both of these guys (neither of whom created this content themselves—the pic is taken from somewhere and the apple story is a copy-paste) think they're displaying something positive, that they're revealing a level of sensitivity that would be appealing to women. When I shared these images online, members of the community who'd been on the apps awhile collectively groaned and then responded swiftly and astutely. One woman commented, "Besides the performative part, there's an implication that women are wounded or desperate for love. It's condescending." I agree with that wholeheartedly.

This sort of curated performative sensitivity is not real, and it doesn't mean anything, at least not anything good. If you want to observe whether a man is sensitive, you must observe how he interacts in real life and in real time. Is he responsive to you? If you display vulnerability, does he hear it reflectively and respond with support and comfort, or is he dismissive? Or does he make things even worse?

Remember that people's words always reveal their underlying beliefs. A Burned Haystack community member shared that on an early date, she (regrettably, because this was way too soon) told her date about her abusive marriage. He looked her in the eye sincerely and said, "How could anyone abuse a woman as beautiful as you?" He thought he was being sensitive, but what he actually revealed is that he ties women's worth and right to safety to physical attractiveness. The implications of his words suggest that a less attractive woman would be more deserving of abuse.

Another crucial set of questions relates to how they treat people other than you. Are they kind to people in the world? Do they have sustained relationships with their family and friends in a way that suggests people trust and depend upon them? These are the actual green flags of sensitivity.

The men whose profiles we just analyzed are not good at performing sensitivity and therefore easy to see through; however, men who are particularly rhetorically crafty can perform sensitivity so well that it's almost impossible to see through very early on, so my best advice with this pattern is to take your time getting to know people, to be vigilant (and honest!) in your observations, and to take a multiperspective approach to forming your opinion of someone. This meme from social media sums this up nicely:

> never judge a man based on how he treats women
> when they are coddling or praising him. Look closely

at how a man reacts when a woman displeases him, stands up to him, or draws a boundary with him, and you will find out who he really is.

RHETORICAL PATTERN 31: AT HIS EARLIEST CONVENIENCE

I'm going to use a story from my own personal dating history to demonstrate this rhetorical pattern.

I met Jeff on Hinge. Single dad, senior financial adviser, no red flags in his profile, nondrinker like me, fit and good-looking. He complimented my profile and asked me if I would like to meet for coffee. I told him that I might like to do that, but that I didn't know anything about him.

He responded to that as well as any man could: First, he said he thought I was smart to be cautious, and that he imagined online dating could be pretty awful for women. His messages were thoughtful, articulate, and grammatically correct—yay!! He gave me his full name so that I could background check him or verify other ways. I immediately found him on LinkedIn, and then on his company's website; he was clearly who he said he was. I even read online reviews from clients who'd worked with him, and they practically glowed: "He's kind, he's honest, he had our best interests at heart, he's trustworthy," and so on.

We exchanged a few more messages, and then I said I'd be willing to meet for coffee, but before we did, I wanted to be sure he truly wanted to pursue a connection two hours away (he lives in Madison, Wisconsin; I live in a city two hours away from Madison). This was his response:

> In reality, it would have to be a pretty special connection for that to happen. I didn't look at the distance until halfway through our chat. Chances are slim that I would make it your direction, but if you happen to travel to Madison, I would love to get coffee.

Jeff has just told me everything I need to know about Jeff.

This is what dating Jeff would be like: on Jeff's terms, convenient for Jeff, and opportunistic. Jeff is saying, "If you magically materialize in front of me due to no effort on my part, I will be happy to engage with you; but I'm not going to go out of my way."

Being willing to meet halfway (literally or figuratively) is the most baseline requirement for any viable relationship. Jeff isn't willing to meet halfway for a coffee. For a coffee that was his idea.

To be clear, I don't blame him at all for not wanting to start a relationship with someone two hours away; I don't want that either. The right way to respond, however, would be to say something like this: "Oh, I'm sorry, I didn't realize we lived that far away. I'm not in a place to take on a long-distance relationship right now, but it's been nice chatting with you, and I wish you all the best!" That's what I would have done in his position. I wouldn't have just assumed it was okay to kick off a relationship in such a lopsided way. Doing so reveals a level of entitlement and ego that doesn't bode well.

I actually do go to Madison for work fairly often, and I usually have downtime between meetings while I'm there, so I could easily reason that since I'm going there anyway, I might as well meet up with him and see what happens. Who knows, maybe once he meets me, he'll be so taken with me that he *will* want to start a long-distance relationship. And anyway, What's to lose? He seems like a really good guy.

Let's break that down:

"Maybe once he meets me, he'll be so taken with me that he *will* want to start a long-distance relationship."

First of all, this is unlikely to happen. I'm a realist, and this sounds like a plotline from a rom-com. But let's let ourselves be delusional for a minute and say that it happens exactly like this: He actually does fall head over heels for me and decides that distance means nothing in the face of his fascination with me (I'm laughing as I type this, but for the sake of argument I'm going to keep going). Then what? I've landed a super-inconvenient long-term relationship with a guy I already know is selfish? Awesome.

"What's to lose?"

I don't know—an hour? Two hours? Whatever it costs in gas to drive to wherever is most convenient for him to meet? The opportunity to do something or meet someone else? My dignity? My credibility in leading a project about haystack burning? It seems like there might actually be a lot to lose.

"He seems like a really good guy."

For sure. Just ask him. He's such a good guy that women flock to him from across the state for the opportunity to drink coffee in his presence.

I wished Jeff well and then blocked him immediately without waiting for a response because he's a perfect example of the "at his earliest convenience" rhetorical pattern. I suppose it's possible that Jeff could be a decent match for someone. Maybe there's a woman out there who's willing to pick up her own life and relocate to where he already is and to accept that everything will run according to his schedule. He appeared to have lots of money, and perhaps that's an acceptable trade for someone. It wouldn't be for me, and I know that about myself, so it would have made no sense to continue.

It's *also* possible that if Jeff had been more captivated by me, he would have suggested meeting halfway and said something like, "I didn't really intend to meet someone two hours away, but two hours still seems doable at least initially if we split the drive time in a way that makes sense." But he *didn't* say that, and to wish that he said it, or to conceive of it as something he *might* say if I proved to be that compelling in person, well . . . that's kind of living in a fantasy land, isn't it?

Final note: This pattern should not be interpreted as "long distance isn't worth it"; we actually have many Burned Haystack success stories that started out much longer distance than two hours. And in *every single one* of them, the man offered to either drive to her town or to meet her halfway from the beginning. Jeff didn't, so he got blocked and burned, because I know that if I'm going to get involved with a guy I need someone who can meet me (at least) halfway (in all ways).

RHETORICAL PATTERN 32: FINAL PIECE OF THE PUZZLE

> Former teacher now regional director! Looking for someone to help me enjoy my kingdom I built

> I own a home and have a great job, and have my stuff together. I just need a great girl. My kids are grown. Exploring the world one step at a time. If I know you, I'm swiping right just to make it awkward.

> I am working on me. I've got everything I need in life. Now I'm just looking for my Princess Buttercup. As you wish! I'm also a pretty funny guy.

> My bio
> Let's lay it all out. I am successful in majority of my life, I have great family, good close friends, awesome pups, and an amazing career. Looking for someone with the same. I don't plan on messaging too often on here so I'll be quick to ask to meet for a meal. Not a big coffee date person.

These are the guys who have everything else in their life figured out. They have good jobs, great kids, amazing friends, a big house that's paid off, a fancy car, and so on. They're just looking for the final piece of the puzzle, which is always a woman.

Before we analyze what this pattern means for you, the woman he'd like to date, we're going to return to our discussion of primary metaphors from chapter 3.

The relevant point of that discussion to this rhetorical pattern is that primary metaphors structure our lives and dictate our actions. We conduct ourselves in accordance with the primary metaphors to which we subscribe (subconsciously—nobody thinks about these things explicitly, which is what makes them so powerful).

So let's come back to our rhetorical pattern and discuss what the primary metaphor of "Final Piece of the Puzzle" means.

The person who's making these claims is positioning *himself* as the puzzle. The puzzle is complex and intricate and beautiful; it requires a foundation and attention and precision. In this conception, he is all of these time- and energy-intensive things.

You are the missing single piece. The piece that means absolutely nothing out of the context of the puzzle.

If you look at a puzzle that's complete except for one piece, you can tell exactly what it is. You can admire its beauty and how well it all comes together.

A puzzle piece on its own is just kind of pointless and worthless.

So from this, a primary metaphor emerges that we could call "I am the puzzle. You are a piece."

This is similar to a primary metaphor that has existed for centuries in classic literature; it's called "Men are the sun, women are the moon." Over and over again in literary symbolism, men are associated with the sun and women with the moon. If you think about the connotations of those celestial bodies, there are some interesting implications: The sun is strong and powerful and the provider of light and heat. The moon is small and has no light of its own; it merely reflects the light of the sun. It also orbits the Earth, which orbits the sun, while the sun maintains its position. The sun is stable, while the moon is associated with things that swing wildly, such as ocean tides, such as women's cycles, such as the moon's own appearance. The word "lunatic" is derived from "luna," which is Latin for "moon."

It's important to say here that there's no writer or creator of a culture's primary metaphors; they develop and evolve over time, and we are *all* subject to them. So these guys who are out there on the apps looking for their missing piece are not necessarily being intentionally trivializing or misogynistic, it's just that they live in a patriarchy like we all do, and they are subconsciously operating according to these metaphors that govern our existence. It's worth considering this when you engage with them.

RHETORICAL PATTERN 33: PROBLEMATIC PROMPTS

This final pattern is kind of a metapattern, in that every element of it is going to reference one (or more) of the patterns you just learned. What I've discovered over time, and it's been affirmed and reiterated by women in the Burned Haystack platforms, is that a man's selection of certain dating prompts can be a red flag in itself. Or, more precisely stated: the men who select these prompts are revealing their own red flags. The following is not an exhaustive list, but I'm sharing here my Top 10 (in no particular order) red-flag dating app prompts (with reasons). I should also say that especially sophisticated or humorous or literary writers can manage to make these prompts work really well for themselves, so there could definitely be cases where these prompts are *not* red flags.

You should not go out with me if . . .

Anything overtly negative in someone's dating app should be considered a red flag, and this one frequently takes the form of a low-key threat. It falls into the "disciplinary/directive" rhetorical pattern.

The way to win me over is/The quickest way to my heart is...

This one falls into both "disciplinary/directive" and "I'm the prize" patterns.

My love language is...

We know. It's "physical touch." This is almost always a way to introduce sexual content way too early, but even if it's not that, there are just so many other problems with the love language talk. For one thing, saying "My love language is physical touch" is such a joke at this point; I have serious concerns about men who are so out of touch with contemporary discourse that they still think it's a valid thing to say.

Don't be mad if I/Don't hate me if...

This is the male dating app equivalent of a "get out of jail free" card; it's excusing bad behavior in advance so that when it happens he can say, "Hey, I told you so." It's also directive in that it's literally directing women about what kind of emotions are acceptable.

I'll know I'm dating an adult when...

This is a very judgmental prompt. It's also an unnecessary one. In a veiled way, it's the "disciplinary/directive" pattern in that it's essentially instructing women on their behavior.

I'm weirdly attracted to...

It's always going to be "feet," for one thing. And truly, if a statement from a strange man on the internet begins with "I'm weirdly attracted to," I can almost guarantee you're not going to want to hear the rest of it. I think it's typically employed as a boundary tester (potentially a "test and apologize" pattern).

First round is on me if ...

"Conditional decency" pattern. This is highly transactional and commodifies women's behavior by pegging it to drink purchases. I think most men think this is a humorous prompt, but in 100 percent of the times I've encountered it, it reads as either offensive and objectifying or just dumb.

My red/green flags are ...

This one can go either way: Sometimes it's a totally reasonable list of qualities anyone would want in a partner, but it's definitely one that should put you on alert for these patterns: "disciplinary/directive," "designing my AI girlfriend," "I'm the prize," "looking for a tradwife," and "MANic Pixie Dreamer."

I'll brag about you to my friends if ...

This feels . . . infantilizing, doesn't it? There's an implication that women need to "perform" in some way to be worthy of being bragged about by the man who selects this prompt. It's potentially "disciplinary/directive," "designing my AI girlfriend," "I'm the prize," and "conditional decency."

The best dating advice I can give you is ...

I don't know a single woman who would appreciate dating advice from a single man on a dating app. The very idea is presumptuous and sort of hilarious, right? We do not need this kind of mansplaining from stranger-men on dating apps.

. . .

Now that we've discussed these rhetorical patterns, how they operate, and how much time you can save by learning to recognize them, let's go over the emotional and psychological benefits of rhetorical patterning. Identifying a rhetorical pattern grants you two things: intellectual grounding and emotional distance. As I said at the beginning of this chapter, when I was first on the dating apps, I was constantly and intensely frustrated with the communication problems I found. I didn't understand why I was being ignored or, conversely, yelled at. I didn't know why nothing made sense, and I was sick of being objectified and the target of men's aggression. Until I engaged in rhetorical patterning, it all blended into one foggy soup of distraction and demoralization.

The second I'd identified and catalogued the patterns, however, I felt much better. It depersonalized the entire thing. And once I started identifying and explicating the patterns on social media, a whole bunch of other women on the dating apps reported back that they immediately felt better too.

This is the benefit of rhetorical patterning: it depersonalizes and objectifies the pattern itself—"objectify" in this case meaning to literally "make it into an object." We're turning this behavior into a concrete "thing" that's identifiable and recognizable so it's no longer this unknowable and unsettling dark force that chips away at your psyche in a way you can't quite name. As most of us know, it's difficult to effectively tackle problems while in the midst of an emotional maelstrom. Rhetorical patterning gets you out of the maelstrom and back into your intellect so that you can make confident decisions (and block to burn!). It gets your heart out of the way and engages your brain, and this is *super* important when you're dealing with the early stages of romance.

There's a time and place for pure feelings, but not every time and place is a time and place for feelings.

This is true on the dating apps more than anywhere else. People want the process to be feelings-based because it's about love, and I get that, but if you lead with your feelings on the dating apps (or, more accurately, let your feelings lead you), you're probably going to end up wasting time and money, or even being ensnared in deceit and exploitation, assaulted, or dead. I'm sorry to be so blunt, but this is true: Meeting strangers on the internet is an incredibly high-stakes and high-risk endeavor, and you have to conduct it with your brain. If you do a really good job with your brain and if the stars line up (I don't want to pretend there's no element of luck here), then *at that point* (and that point only), it's time to begin operating in heart mode.

Identifying rhetorical patterns and making decisions based upon that knowledge is wildly empowering. Instead of wondering "Why am I feeling so put off by this guy?" you can just say, "Ah, he's trying to design his AI girlfriend. Next!"

SUCCESS STORY!

After a divorce, a few years of aimless dating, and the end of a dead-end 1½-year relationship, I took some time to reflect and came to the conclusion that something (read: I) needed to change. And man, looking back on who I was eight months ago, I had a *lot* to learn. So I checked out a few dating coaches (some good, some meh, some blatantly terrible), then noticed that some of my Facebook friends had joined this group. I joined, and can honestly say that Burned Haystack gave me a brand-new perspective on dating, but I had some work to do on myself. I read, I followed and listened, I reflected and journaled. And after rejoining Bumble and Hinge last September, I burned! Pretty soon, Bumble told me there were no more profiles, but I was okay with that. I did match with two politically "moderate" guys who admitted either while chatting or on our first date that they were voting for Trump. One announced during the first date that he was a proud conservative. I asked, then why did he state in his dating profile that he's a Moderate? He didn't have an answer for that, and I didn't need one.

    Then, I met my needle. We've been together about six months at this point, and he has *always* been up front and open with me. I feel like I can bring up any topic with him and feel heard. One thing that would've given me pause early on is that there wasn't a "spark." Luckily, before our first date, I'd read Logan Ury, so I knew to "f*** the spark"—that the "spark" is not a reliable determiner of whether the person will make a good partner.

Here's my green-flag checklist that I think applies to any relationship:

✔ He offered his full name and phone number before we met, and encouraged me to google him. (I did.)
✔ His dating profile was pretty bland, but there was nothing B2B-worthy, and he was clear that he was politically liberal—so not a Trumper in sheep's clothing.
✔ There were no sexual innuendos whatsoever before we became intimate.
✔ He planned the first few dates, but asked for my input and gave me a few different choices.
✔ He compliments me not only on my appearance, but also on other (more important) aspects of who I am.
✔ Based on what I've seen and experienced, I can't even imagine him ever being disrespectful to anyone.
✔ He hasn't ever told me he's a gentleman, honest, funny, intelligent, well traveled, and so on, because he doesn't have to. He is definitely all those things, and he's also humble.

Some things about him/his profile that would've turned me away before this time around:

✘ Like I said, his profile was bland. Before, without a "hook," I would've swiped left.
✘ He lives about an hour away from me but works in my city. I learned that, with the right person, this really wasn't a deal-breaker after all.
✘ He's ten years older than me. (I'm in my mid-forties.) But hey, at least he's not one of those middle-aged men who's still

contemplating having children, lol. Turns out our age gap is not the problem I thought it might be.

✘ Like I said, I didn't feel the "spark" when we met in person, but I've come to understand that's because my nervous system is completely at peace with him.

Hope my story helps other folks.

—Wendy

HUMOR BREAK

What It Means When a Woman Says She Is "Sex Positive," According to Brian from Hinge

Previously published in McSweeney's Internet Tendency, *December 5, 2023.*

Sex-positive women are kinky and down for anything with anyone, all the time.

Sex-positive women take a strong positive stance on having sex with me, instead of being wishy-washy like my ex-wife.

Sex-positive women are hot. Not all hot women are sex-positive, because I have met some hot women who do not want to have sex with me, but I'm pretty sure all sex-positive women are hot. That's why Bumble uses the chili pepper emoji to indicate sex-positivity, which is appropriate, because a small red vegetable commonly associated with hotness is definitely adequate to represent the entire spectrum of sex-positivity.

Sex-positive women are open-minded, and by "open-minded," I mean accepting of me and not saying, "That's weird, Brian," like my ex-fiancée.

Sex-positive women are impulsive and adventurous. They don't say things like "Could we do a phone chat first?" or "Would you be willing to share a last name before we meet in person?" Looking me up on LinkedIn is not sex-positive.

Sex-positive women are politically liberal, which means generous with sending pics and stuff.

Sex-positive women are 100 percent pro-sex, 100 percent of the time. They don't "get headaches" or "need some space from Brian," and they don't suddenly get "the ick" like my ex-girlfriend from college.

Sex-positive women keep a positive attitude about having sex with me. They have a cheerful and hopeful outlook regardless of the quality of any particular encounter or the ongoing totality of encounters they might experience while in bed with me.

6

TOXIC DATING COACHES

How to Spot Them and When to Block Them

It's time to address the toxic and misogynistic advice that dating coaches frequently dole out, including how it works against you by wasting your time and energy. This is by no means a comprehensive list of their terrible advice, but you'll get some excellent practice in decoding rhetoric and honing your bullshit detector. Let's get to it!

A Burned Haystack community member wrote to share with me a frustrating experience she had working with a dating coach. She'd met a man on the apps, and he led their initial messaging exchange with a comment about her profile and a "compliment" about her ass. (To be clear, in Burned Haystack this would be an auto block to burn without further words exchanged.)

Her dating coach advised her to first "express gratitude for the compliment" and then to explain that she wasn't comfortable with the word "ass" and would prefer he talk about her "curves." She was then to thank him *again* for "being willing to hear her preferences." She was also encouraged to decorate her messages with smiley faces so as not to appear confrontational.

She followed the coach's suggestions, and the man responded by saying he completely understood and that he thought she had beautiful curves. He also thanked her for sharing her feelings. The dating coach considered this a "win," that the advice had "worked," because the guy appreciated the feedback.

Let's be real. The guy did *not* appreciate the feedback; it just showed him that this particular game wasn't going to work with this woman, so he pivoted to a different tactic: manipulating her rather than openly objectifying her. We know that "thank you for sharing your feelings" is performative rather than sincere, because if this man was sincerely worried about women's feelings, he would not have initiated their conversation with a line about her ass; a truly respectful man simply wouldn't do that. We should not give this guy any credit for saying exactly what she told him to say. You can teach parrots to do this.

Your goal in using Burned Haystack is to meet men who *don't disrespect you in the first place*. It's not to "fix" random weirdos on the internet.

This woman's dating coach also told her that she was giving up way too soon on her matches. I guarantee she wasn't; if anything, she was hanging in there way too long, probably because, like all of us, she'd been told to give all these guys the benefit of the doubt, and now here she was fending off this misogynistic moron.

THE "FRAUDULENT FIVE"

Blocking to burn isn't only a helpful tool in culling matches—use it for the coaches perpetuating out-of-touch advice too. When dating coaches use the following words and phrases, they've already revealed themselves as uninformed, unprofessional, unqualified, and usually misogynistic. It's important to remember that their advice to women is *far* more revealing than how they label themselves. I know a lot of men who self-identify as "feminist," yet the way they conduct their lives does not support that label. What they believe about themselves is irrelevant when compared to their actual words and actions, and the same is true for dating coaches. A male "dating coach for women" who is simply teaching women how to appeal to men (or how to be more like men) is not truly "for women"; he's for women conforming to and accommodating men, and that's a super-important distinction.

Here are my "fraudulent five" phrases you'll find being used by these toxic dating coaches:

1. **HIGH-VALUE MAN/WOMAN:** These are relatively recent designations that get tossed around a lot in internet-dating discourses. They frequently refer to superficial criteria such as physical attractiveness or income but can also refer to character traits such as kindness, loyalty, self-discipline, and so on. The problem is that the former is not a great way to sum up a human being and the latter is simply too subjective to be useful. In both cases, whether the value markers are superficial or meaningful, the whole thing is a false construct. People are complex, and they change and grow over time and across different life domains; labeling someone either "high value" or "low value" conveys a lack of understanding of the inherent complexity of life, and it's also objectifying and commodifying to attach a "value rating" to a person. Dating successfully requires a humanity and a grasp of nuance that cannot be reduced to high or low value, and I would be extremely skeptical of the qualifications and efficacy of any dating coach who defaults to such a reductive notion of what it means to be human.

2. **FEMININE ENERGY/MASCULINE ENERGY:** If you've spent any time online in the dating sphere recently, you have undoubtedly come across phrases such as "You need to stay in your feminine energy in order to allow him to step into the masculine." These mandates are primarily being issued by the most conservative and patriarchal (and least educated and evolved) dating coaches. In an era when the entire existence of biological gender has been called into question both socially and scientifically, any dating coach who still buys into this totally binary, outdated expression of gender is revealing to you that

they are either uninformed, patriarchal, misogynistic, or all of the above. Gender exists on a spectrum, not only across the population but within individual human beings: we *all* have both feminine and masculine energy, and that's a good thing; it's part of what makes up our personalities and expresses our abilities and passions, our vulnerabilities and limitations. To attempt to artificially divide half the population into feminine energy and half into masculine energy and then to use those designations as a way to order and control bodies and minds is archaic and counterproductive to forging true connections between and among people.

3. **ALPHA, BETA, OR ANY OTHER GREEK LETTER USED TO SUM UP A PERSON'S ENTIRE BEING:** Again, these labels are just too simplistic and reductive to have any kind of meaning. They're also troublingly hierarchical; I would not take any advice from a dating coach who's willing to rank human beings according to what's essentially a numerical scale.

4. **KING/QUEEN LABELS:** These designations, while not always problematic, are not appropriate terms for dating coaches to be applying across the board. In African American vernacular, for example, the terms connote prioritizing one's partner and treating them well. More often than not, though, I'm seeing dating coaches employ these terms in ways that range from "uninformed generic application" to cultural appropriation. And like the problems I've identified in the three previous terms, the "king/queen" labels also are reductive and overly binary and do not account for the complexities of real-life human pairings.

5. **LOVE LANGUAGES, ENNEAGRAMS, NLP (NEUROLINGUISTIC PROGRAMMING), AND OTHER PSEUDOSCIENTIFIC, PSYCHOBABBLE NONSENSE:** There are other items we could add to this short list, but these three come up a lot, the first two claiming relevance to romantic connection and the third as either a weapon for men or a scare tactic for women. As mentioned earlier, *The 5 Love Languages*, a 1992 bestseller authored by Gary Chapman, a Baptist

pastor with zero credentials in psychology, has now been thoroughly debunked as the completely unfounded nonscience that it always was. Any dating coach who is not up-to-date on this is not someone from whom anyone should take advice. (Sidenote: Listen to the *If Books Could Kill* podcast episodes on both *The 5 Love Languages* and *Men Are from Mars, Women Are from Venus*. Even if you would never fall for either of these goofy ideas [love languages or planetary gender comparisons], do yourself a favor and listen to both episodes. I laughed so hard I had to pull over while commuting to the university.) The Enneagram is a personality typing system in which everyone is defined as being one of nine personality types. It's not a scientifically valid system and is prone to so much error and subjectivity that even the most experienced practitioners cannot achieve an assessment that would be considered psychologically valid or practical. Any dating coach using it as part of their practice should immediately be suspect for dabbling in quackery. And neurolinguistic programming (which I address more thoroughly in chapter 7) has two specific manifestations within the sphere of dating discourses. The first is that Incel groups (men who identify as "involuntarily celibate" and who blame women for that status) attempt to weaponize NLP to teach men how to manipulate women into bed using language; the second is that some dating coaches try to convince women that NLP is being used against them all the time without their knowledge, breeding paranoia and distrust where it may not even be appropriate. In both cases, the recruiting of NLP is somewhat moot, as most linguists and psychologists now consider it a pseudoscience. If you encounter a dating coach who's framing it as anything other than that, I would steer clear.

In order to avoid wasting time and money, you should disqualify dating coaches who use these phrases and frameworks. Many coaches, however, are savvy and nuanced enough not to include such blatant discursive red flags while still being ineffective and problematic. You'll also do best to avoid these common phrases and pieces of advice:

"You need to grant men grace."

This is tricky because "giving grace" is inherently a good thing—it appeals to our desire to be "good," to be "kind" and "patient" and "tolerant." I would argue that in most other aspects of life, this is decent advice: You should probably give your children grace, you should give it to your elderly parents, to your normally even-keeled colleague who's having a bad day, to the cashier at Target who keyed in the wrong coupon code at the end of a long shift.

I do *not* think you should give strange men on the internet talking about your ass any grace, because you know what? They're not giving you any.

The "grant grace" advice is particularly exploitative and insidious because it taps into deeply held values for people who belong to communities of faith. Recruiting "grace language" in this case is a form of weaponized spirituality—another Burned Haystack rhetorical pattern to avoid; see page 131—and you should block to burn it with dating coaches the same way you would with men.

"You need to confront your scarcity mindset."

Women are often told, especially by dating coaches on social media, that we need to ditch our **scarcity mindset**, which, they tell us, is why we're alone. This is a **thought-terminating cliché** and a **red herring,** both rhetorical terms relevant to scarcity mindset conversations. A thought-terminating cliché is intended to quite literally stop thought; it casts the external problem back onto the upset or complaining person in a way that suggests the entire problem resides within them and therefore is unworthy of discussion or examination. A red herring is a distraction from the actual issue.

Imagine a woman says something like "It seems like there aren't a lot of datable men in my age group," and her dating coach, rather than admitting this is true, instead suggests that what she *really* needs to work on is her scarcity mindset. This introduces a distraction (the mostly made-up scarcity mindset) to avoid confronting the actual problem (the lack of adequate men), and it also implies that her being alone is due to her "failure" to be optimistic, or to "have a good attitude," or to "develop an abundance mindset" rather than to the fact that too many men are too horrible to date.

I like to use an analogy to address the "scarcity mindset" concept:

Imagine that I'm in the grocery store, and I go to the cereal aisle and there's almost no cereal, just two boxes of plain puffed oats that are months beyond the expiration date—that's it. If I look at that situation and say, "There's a shortage of good cereal options here," it's not because I have a scarcity mindset and it's not because I have a bad attitude. It's because I'm looking at reality with my actual eyes and accurately describing it.

Bottom line—there are simply more datable single women than datable single men. The reasons for this are social, cultural, political, and individual—and they're also beyond the scope of this book. That said, we could easily point to some obvious reasons: the predominance of women seeking therapy, engaging with higher education, and committing to self-improvement, while men are screaming in ALL CAPS on one tab and downloading Joe Rogan podcasts on the other. As a (male) psychologist I interviewed for this book told me, the scope of this problem is wider than the dating pool: "There's simply a shortage of adequate men."

We're not going to pretend that reality is different than it is, and we're also not going to participate in our own gaslighting by constantly wondering if we're the crazy ones, or if we're just "too demanding," or if our "expectations are too high," or if we're "intolerant," or any of the other things women are constantly accused of. Look around you. Think back through your life and think about what you and other women have all tolerated from men. And then try to convince yourself that women are too intolerant. We've tolerated exploitation and abuse all the way to the grave (literally, in far too many cases, but also figuratively).

"You need to work on yourself first if you want to attract a man."

This is tricky because "working on oneself" is arguably a good thing for anyone to do on an ongoing basis. The reason it's problematic in dating discourses is that it's premised as causal, explanatory, and rooted in worth. Here's what I mean:

There's an implication here that if you just work on yourself enough, you'll find a partner (not necessarily true), and by extension, that if you *can't* find a partner it can be explained by the fact that you haven't worked on yourself enough (or successfully enough). In either case, this "work on yourself" mandate assigns blame to the single woman. It's a thought-terminating cliché that operates by shifting the conversation from a lack of adequate partners to a discussion of how women can just keep getting better and better until we are deserving of good men. And this is the third problem—attaching it to personal value, as though your value as a human being (and your worthiness in the dating arena) is wholly created by "working on yourself." There's an implication here that women must attain some level of perfection in order to be deserving of a healthy partnership.

"If you want to attract men, you need to learn how to think and act like a man."

Many dating coaches, especially male dating coaches, peddle some version of this message (think Steve Harvey's *Act Like a Lady, Think Like a Man* or Matthew Hussey's *Get the Guy: Learn Secrets of the Male Mind to Find the Man You Want and the Love You Deserve!*). This is a deeply misogynistic message because it positions male ways of thinking and being as the goal, the ideal, and the secret code to discovering love. It orients men as the prize and women as the prize seekers who need to crack the code and then follow its rules if we want to find love.

This is one of the definitions of patriarchy: to hold up maleness and male thinking and being patterns as the mode by which everyone else will be judged and to which everyone else must conform. It equates maleness to success. But just as in the broader world, this is a double-edged sword, because while women are expected to accommodate men's thinking and to navigate within men's spheres, if we take it one step too far and they're—god forbid—*too masculine*, that will render them "undatable."

"Be his peace."

In the dating arena, the word "peace" equates to "compliance" and "submission." On the soft end, it means you must never complain, disagree, challenge, or disrupt. At the hard end, it means you'll be tolerating abuse. As we know from our discussion of peace seekers in chapter 5, there are a lot of men demanding "peace" or "peaceful women" on the dating apps right now. These should always be block to burns. Ditto for any dating coach who's saying it too.

"Men are simple creatures."

This is usually followed by a line that says something like "You just need to inspire him to lead" or "Men just need food, sex, and freedom!" or some other nonsense. At the core of this rhetoric is the idea that "men are simple creatures," which warrants some confrontation.

Men are philosophers and brain surgeons and rocket scientists and psychiatrists and single parents and artists and musicians and dancers and theologians. Men are not simple creatures any more than any other human being of any gender is a simple creature. Human beings are inherently complex, *all* of us, and reducing men to the "simple creature" caricature is not only insulting to men but gaslighting to women, and it's too frequently leveraged to give men a pass on bad behavior.

"Dating is a numbers game, so in order to be successful you should message and meet as many men as possible."

This piece of advice shows up in a few different forms. There's the age-old "If you want to find the prince, you need to kiss a lot of frogs." Not if you do it right. You might need to swipe away or block to burn a lot of frogs, but if you employ Burned Haystack properly, you should not have to kiss them. Another manifestation of this message occurs when women are told that "Going on lots of dates is never a waste of your time. You gain good dating experience." I have never bought this argument; I don't believe that grown women need "dating experience." To frame it that way is to suggest that interpersonal dating interactions are somehow separate from the rest of life, and I don't believe that's true. A man who's nice to work with could be good to date; a man who's a kind and helpful and protective neighbor could be good to date; an auto mechanic who explains exactly what's wrong with your car and lays out what needs to be fixed right away versus what can wait for later could be good to date. There's a specific reason this advice is coming from so many coaches, and I'll unpack it at the end of this chapter.

"You attract the energy you bring" or "You need to raise your vibrations" or "alter your frequency" or any other line that suggests women are responsible, in a cosmic or electrical way, for the endless stream of online creeps.

We're just not going to keep holding women responsible for male toxicity. If any of the above lines were rooted in reality, then we'd have to assume that 100 percent of women are dysfunctional and broken. On top of being ridiculously insulting, that doesn't hold up in an evolutionary psychology sense: If a major problem preventing human beings from mating is that a critical mass of women are not "vibrating at the right frequency," we would have died out eons ago. As one Burned Haystack community member put it, "Like it's my fault that I attract toxic men when toxic men are attracted to everybody!" Yes. Enough said.

"Never accept a coffee date."

The argument here is that a man "needs to invest in you" to prove his worth as a date, but I think this is stupid advice. I actually *prefer* coffee first dates because they're lower pressure and don't take up as much time; if the coffee date goes well, then there can be more elaborate or prolonged dates in the future. I also think it's a weird way of commodifying the dating process, to attach the potential value of strangers to their preferred first-date modality in a way that doesn't translate to actual information. The implication, I guess, is that a man who offers a coffee date either can't afford dinner and a show or is too stingy to pay for it. But I know that I can and would afford all of that and *still* prefer a coffee date for the first date, so why couldn't the same be true of men?

"You need to rewire your anxious attachment system" or "How to deal with your avoidant boyfriend."

Attachment theory is fascinating, and I do frequently recommend the book *Attached* by Amir Levine and Rachel Heller, but many of the discussions I see online are reductive and/or misinterpretations of the theory. Too frequently, it's either exploited as another way to blame women for driving away men or recruited as information that can be used to manipulate someone into a relationship they're not actively choosing. My recommendation is that if you're interested in attachment theory, take the time to read the actual scholarship rather than consuming it as a set of "dating tips." It's definitely useful for understanding some aspects of relationship dynamics, but it's too complex to be adequately covered in social media, which I've seen a lot of dating coaches attempt to do.

"It's hard for men out there too" or "Men just aren't comfortable with feelings, so you have to moderate your expectations" or "Men just say stupid things, don't read too much into it."

First, it's hard for everyone out there, and from what I see online, we're not excusing bad behavior from women, only from men. Second, in response to men not being comfortable with their feelings, neither are women necessarily, but women have been socialized and conditioned to tolerate and push through discomfort for the benefit of the group (or the couple, or whatever), and we have always done so. It's fair to expect men to do the same, and any dating coach who's giving men a pass for bad or neglectful behavior because engaging in an authentic manner "makes them feel bad" is not anyone you should be listening to. And finally, to address the "don't read too much into it" directive: that's literally the entire point of Burned Haystack. A critique I hear frequently is "But he didn't mean it that way!" I know he didn't. I also know that his words, sometimes unconsciously, reveal underlying values and belief systems in a way that's more accurate than anything he *did* mean to share. This is the superpower of CDA—its ability to reveal what the person speaking doesn't *intend* to share. My deeper concern is that "reading too much into things" is frequently recruited as a way to discount or minimize women's intuition, to trivialize what are almost always valid concerns.

"You teach people how to treat you."

There's an interpretation of this common saying that's valid, but it only applies to people we already know and are required to interact with. If you have a difficult coworker or a problematic family member, clarifying and maintaining boundaries with that person is vital to establishing your interactions with them going forward. But you certainly do not have to teach strange men on the internet how to treat you. And if it appears that you do, then that's actually your sign to block to burn, not an indication that you need to be a better teacher.

• • •

Everything we've discussed in this chapter culminates in some tough realities about dating, and why I believe that most of the dating-coaching industry ranges from predatory to pointless.

Too much of dating coaching is comprised of offering women "tips" about "how to get men to act right," often through systems of manipulation, which is what most women want more than anything to avoid! Trying to avert manipulative men by preemptively manipulating them doesn't actually work, and it generally just wastes more of everyone's time. Nudging full-grown men toward acceptable behavior is *never* a good use of your time. The *uncoached* interaction with men is the only meaningful one, even if it isn't the nicest one. If a man can't conduct himself appropriately completely on his own, then he's inherently undatable.

Please consider the implications of the paragraph you just read: what it means is that you don't need a dating coach. I said earlier in this chapter that I would unpack the reason dating coaches are doling out so much horrible advice. Here's the reason: Individualized dating coaches are compensated only if their clients are going out on enough bad dates to rack up billable hours. Most of them know full well that the vast, vast majority of men are not datable, but if they admit that, then guess what? Not enough dates, and therefore not enough money. So they've created this entire framework of "strategy" for women to employ that not only doesn't work, but revictimizes, regaslights, reexploits, and remanipulates women, which is exactly what was happening on the apps and the whole reason women sought coaching! It's a form of digital cannibalism.

If those coaches were to give Burned Haystack–adjacent advice, which consists of quickly and easily weeding out matches, saying, "We've already identified that toxic rhetorical pattern, block to burn," then they couldn't justify charging anyone for their services. That piece of advice took three seconds, and you can't effectively monetize three seconds of consultation. If, however, you can convince women that we need to "confront our scarcity mindset" or "learn when to grant men grace" or "unpack the ways in which feminism is harmful to men" or "learn to reside in our feminine energy and spark his masculine energy" or "rewire our anxious attachment system" or "learn how to think like a man" or take an Enneagram test or a Myers-Briggs test that we can analyze for dating, or any other number of things women are being told we must do . . . Well, that takes a lot of time. That's super billable.

Two of the most meaningful comments I've received online are these:

- "Honestly, out of all the dating podcasts and all the information out there around dating, this is the advice, data, and information that actually *works*."
- "You are the only one who tells the truth and doesn't blame women."

Here's the truth about Burned Haystack: For the most part, neither I nor this method is telling you anything you don't already know or feel on some level. What the method, and perhaps the community more than the method, does, is validate that deep, intuitive, "something is off but it's hard to say what" kind of knowing that women hold in our bones, whether through generational knowledge or painfully learned life experience, or something more primordial and mystical than either.

The final question I want to answer in this chapter is this: "Are you saying *all* dating coaches are con artists, that the entire industry is fraudulent?" No, I'm not saying that. I believe there are some good ones, and I understand that some people simply prefer to work one-on-one with a coach. If that's not a financial hardship and the coaching itself is effective and not predatory or exploitative, then there's no problem, and I can certainly understand how this could be a good and productive experience. But everyone should be aware that there are a lot of unqualified, unscrupulous, exploitative, predatory, and misogynistic dating coaches out there. If you feel like something is off, then trust that intuition and block to burn.

SUCCESS STORY!

Jennie, thank you for Burned Haystack! It's wonderfully powerful, and I found a needle in great part because of what I've learned from you and your followers. I think it's important for you to hear as many success stories as possible to confirm that your method works.

    I'm sixty-four this year, and my wonderful husband of thirty-two years passed away in 2022. I decided in the fall of 2024 that I was ready to try dating again but soon learned how unprepared I was for online dating. So many unsavory men flood that environment, drowning out the few great guys. The number of scammers and insincere men is shocking. I had no idea how to navigate such a toxic swamp. I was slogging through the Silver Singles dating app.

    My daughter connected me with Burned Haystack, and very soon I felt empowered, aware, and confident, taking control of the process. I was able to critically read profiles and toss out all the crap without second-guessing or a second thought. The numbers are interesting . . . I quickly waded through about two hundred matches and chatted with maybe six who seemed worth the time. Two turned out to be sophisticated scammers, two were dull as dirt, and two were worth meeting for coffee. Both were nice men, but one was too conservative for me and the other is the man I've been dating for the last six weeks or so.

He wrote his profile with clarity and good grammar, and did not mention anything physical or sexual in his profile or during our initial conversations and meeting. His profile included insightful information that told a bit about the type of man he is: well read, open-minded, politically liberal, engaged with the world around him, and self-aware. He had good photos from various locations that were taken by others (not selfies), which I felt demonstrated he enjoyed fun times with friends and family (which is true). Prior to our first meeting and without me asking, he offered his full name, where he worked, and where he lived and did not ask me to provide him the same information. Our first meeting was out of the way for him yet at a location that was known and convenient to me. He even had to wait for me for two hours because I had to wait at my home for a critical repairman who was delayed. I felt terrible, but he was understanding and gracious, and we had a great first meeting. He's fun, chatty, and interested in me, my perspective, and what I have to say.

We are two seniors with grandbabies and achy joints trying to find joy, peace, connection, and purpose in this next chapter in our lives. I'm not sure he and I thought we'd find a suitable partner at our age, so we are grateful to have found each other.

It was luck that we were both on that darn app, but I would not have zeroed in on him without Burned Haystack. I would have been pulled into dozens of fruitless, frustrating encounters. And, knowing me, I would have thrown in the towel after a few months and not pursued partnership. I had one terrific husband already, and I have wonderful kids and grandkids, lots of lovely girlfriends, an old kitty, and a cute young dog. I'd like a partner but I certainly don't need a man to feel fulfilled.

I'm so grateful for my long, loving marriage to a good man. I'm lucky to really know what a true partnership looks and feels like. And I'm glad I took those two-plus years to grieve his death. He wanted only the best for me, and I think he'd be happy that I'm seeing a kind, honest man.

I keep on the lookout but I'm happy to say I've seen no red flags. Chemistry sparked once I felt comfortable and confident I was with a truly authentic person. Now we will let time and experiences reveal if this needle is *my* needle.

You posted a video that I found really helpful. It describes the five situations that will help reveal a person's true character: when they're bored, when they're wrong and corrected, when things go badly, when something good happens to you, and how they treat others who can't directly benefit them. I love this clear approach and I'm happy at how my guy has responded in each of these situations.

Thank you, again, for your insight and clear, focused, powerful methodology. I find that I now use it IRL all the time! And thanks to your followers and their comments—they add so much! Keep up the good work!

—*Sheila*

7

MORE TACTICS AND TRICKS TO GAME THE APPS

(So They Can't Game You!)

There are many terms in rhetorical theory that are precisely applicable to dating and that can be easily taught. This chapter offers context for those terms and explains them in a way that will help you to identify danger, uncover problematic dynamics, and protect your boundaries. I'll also go over some strategies I've developed specifically for employing the Burned Haystack method. Consider this chapter an additional tool kit of skills, tactics, and tricks that you can use to level up your game and become a smarter, savvier, more discerning, and safer dater.

Some of the terms here may be unfamiliar, but I promise that if you take the time to read and understand them, you'll internalize them quickly and begin to use them intuitively to navigate dating and probably other aspects of your life.

Let's dive in.

HEURISTICS

The first term I want to discuss is "heuristic," an academic term that refers to a somewhat ad hoc form of analysis or problem-solving. Heuristics are employed in the moment of wondering about something to glean insight that leads to deeper understanding. Heuristics or heuristic processes are rarely quantifiable—it would be inaccurate to claim, "This heuristic works 78 percent of the time"—because they're used more organically and subjectively than that. However, heuristics can be highly illuminating when used strategically.

A shorter definition more precisely targeted to dating might be to call a heuristic an informal and flexible "test" that gives you quick information about someone. This will become clearer when we talk about actual examples of heuristics, so let's do that . . .

"Translate it to real life"

One of the most powerful heuristics we use in Burned Haystack is called "Translate it to real life." This heuristic helps us to judge men's behavior on the dating apps in a way that reveals whether it's okay or not. For example: On the apps, men demanding "pics" from women they've not yet met has become naturalized and considered "normal" (see page 43 for a refresher on how behavior becomes naturalized). But *is* it normal? *Should* it be normal?

Let's translate it to real life. Imagine that you have a good friend who wants to set you up with her cousin. She tells you he's a great guy with a bright future, she completely trusts and respects him, and she thinks you two have so much in common and would really connect. Also, he'd like to see a picture of your breasts before you meet.

Did you have a jarring reaction to that last sentence? You should! Because it's *not* normal to demand intimate pictures of people we don't know—it's creepy and intrusive and threatening and objectifying. You probably would immediately opt out of that meeting. Yet on the dating apps, these requests have become so common that too many women are being gaslighted into thinking, *This is just how things work now, so I guess I should go along.*

I'm telling you that you *shouldn't*. This request tells you everything you need to know to block to burn a man. I'm also telling you that almost every Burned Haystack success story includes a line about how the "needle" in question did not remark on her appearance, did not lead with discussions of sex, and did not ask for pictures of her (also, there are pictures on the app, so this request is always redundant and should always be met with suspicion, then blocked).

To help you practice this exercise, think of the best man you know. Is it your brother? Your father? Your friend's husband? Whoever it is, ask yourself if he would ever open a conversation with a woman he doesn't know by asking her for a nude. I am going to bet he would not. Anwar White, a popular dating coach on Instagram who works with Black and brown women, suggests asking yourself, "Would my husband do that?" If you envision a future husband, and if your future husband wouldn't do whatever the thing is, that alone is enough reason to block to burn.

Let's "translate" another common behavior. Many men want to immediately get sexual information in advance of meeting because they don't want to waste any time getting to know a woman as a person; they just want sex. So they lead with things like claiming to be "sex positive"—usually while revealing that they have no idea of what that term actually means (remember the Humor Break on page 158?)—or they ask about preferences related to desired frequency of sex, sexual positions, number of previous partners, and so on. Taken out of context, this all sounds pretty easy to identify, but many men are adept at cleverly working these topics into very early communications in a way that makes it harder to call out. That's why we need the "Translate it to real life" heuristic.

Imagine you go to a neighborhood block party and run into the cute guy who lives two doors down from you. You're so excited to have a chance to connect naturally, and you ask him something about his dog, but instead of responding appropriately he says, "You have a really great ass, are you okay with being choked?" (If you think this is a hyperbolic and out-of-left-field example, then you've not spent much time as a woman on a dating app; see the sexual non sequitur rhetorical pattern on page 141.) But when you translate it to a real-life scenario, it seems somewhere between off-putting and threatening, right? I suspect you'd run away from this guy at the neighborhood party. Even if you didn't feel aggressed upon and objectified by this response, you'd have to seriously question his social skills and ability to read a room, both of which seem like necessary components of healthy adult interaction.

In this next example, we'll take a man's dating app profile and "translate it to real life" by thinking of it as a résumé and a job interview. After all, if you're on a dating app, you're essentially "applying" to be someone's partner in some fashion. Let's assume this guy's résumé is mostly blank. There are no words, just a picture of him, shirtless, holding a fish. That's weird, right? And instead of listing his education and experience, in the section dedicated to that, he's written "Just ask." Let's imagine that you for some reason decide to proceed anyway, and you ask him what kind of role he's looking for with this organization, and he says, "You know, I don't really like labels. I prefer to just keep things chill and go with the flow and see what happens." And then maybe you ask him, "When would you be available to start work?" and he says, "Ummmm, I don't really know, could you just let me know if you relocate your business to my neighborhood and then if I'm around and not busy I could work?" Your last question might be "What questions do you have for me?" and he just stares at you, because of course he has no questions. Or he has one question, and it's "What made you interested in my résumé?" which is really just an invitation to talk more about him.

You would not hire this guy, because he is clearly an unserious man—immature, disorganized, lazy, and entitled. And this is the kind of partner he'd be as well, which is no partner at all. Yet men behave exactly like this on the dating apps all the time, and too often we let it go because, again, this has become naturalized.

Let's do two more translate-it-to-real-life heuristics, one that uses grocery shopping and one that uses car shopping:

Imagine you're in the produce aisle and some guy comes up behind you and says, "Hey." And nothing else. You try to ignore him and go about your shopping, and then he says, "You're gorgeous," or "You have a great smile." None of these things seem to be *about* you so much as they seem to be targeted *at* you. Without any encouragement to continue, he asks, "How has your experience in this grocery store been?" And then,

"What are you looking for in this grocery store?"

"What, are you too busy to talk about this lettuce?"

"You shouldn't go to a grocery store if you don't want any apples."

"Do you think you're too good for this grocery store?"

Every single one of these quotes sounds both irritating and insane when put into a real-life context, yet men behave like this and ask versions of these questions on the dating apps all the time. They're not okay there either. Block to burn.

Last one—and this is about not buying what you don't want. It's as much leveraged at dating apps as it is at men because, as you probably know, you can tell Bumble or Hinge that you want to meet a politically progressive nonsmoker within sixty miles of Chicago, yet the app will be happy to introduce you to Greg from Fargo with his MAGA hat and a cigarette hanging out of his mouth.

So let's translate this to car shopping. If you went to a local dealership and told the salesman you wanted a small, ecofriendly, hybrid hatchback, you wouldn't leave with a gas-guzzling monster truck. It's not what you want, and you don't have to change what you want to align with what happens to be there that day. You have a lot of options here. You could go to a different dealership; you could decide to just wait it out for a while; you could decide that there are tweaks you can make without compromising on fundamental values—maybe it could be a wagon instead of a hatchback, or perhaps fuel efficient is close enough to hybrid. I think everyone on a dating app should be open to finding someone unexpected with whom they connect or to making minor compromises in the name of love. However, you get to decide what you compromise on.

"How else could this have been said?"

Another heuristic we use frequently is "How else could this have been said?" It's an incredibly powerful analytical tactic to use on the dating apps, especially when something doesn't sound quite right to you but you can't put your finger on why. Let's go through some examples.

A group member had a first date planned with a man she'd met on Bumble, and she was really excited to meet him. The day before, he texted her with this message: "Would you be mad if we postponed our meeting?"

She queried the group:

> Why is this not landing well with me? He's not saying anything offensive. And I wouldn't have been mad because I'm a reasonable person who understands that things come up, but because of the way he phrased it I feel like I have two choices: to be either falsely happy about it or to be "angry."

I think most women would have felt exactly like this. In order to figure out why and to help us decide how to proceed, let's use the "How else could this have been said?" heuristic.

Here's an option he could have used:

> I'm so sorry, but I need to reschedule because [some concrete and valid reason]. I'm really disappointed because I was looking forward to our date, and I still very much want to meet! Would you be available [X or Y or Z day/time]?

Do you see how different that is? The option above would have assured her that he definitely wanted to meet and that they just needed to reschedule—no problem. It also would have demonstrated that he had enough emotional intelligence and sensitivity to know that canceling a first date might make someone insecure and took measures to mitigate that insecurity by being kind and reassuring. Those would be major green flags.

He didn't do any of that. But let's pretend we are mediocre men for a second and play devil's advocate; let's assume that he *did* have a legit reason to cancel. Even so, he not only failed to be reassuring or to set up another date, but he assumed and suggested that his cancellation would turn her into a dreaded "angry woman" and burdened her with the emotional labor of having to prove how un-angry she was. She chose to block to burn him, and I think that was the right decision.

Let's go through a more complex example, as seen in a Burned Haystack community member's post:

> Since Burned Haystack talks so much about how things are said and what a person's word choice means . . . I'm genuinely asking if there is a reason I get so upset when someone I'm dating (or trying to date) invites me to do something by saying "You can come if you want." This phrase makes me feel like I was an afterthought or that I'd be just tagging along and that my company isn't truly wanted.
>
> Example: I've been seeing a man, we have some mutual friends. A few days ago he apparently made plans for himself, a friend, and the friend's wife to hang out for happy hour. The next day he invited a mutual friend of ours and the mutual friend's wife

> to join them because those two couples had never met and he thought they'd all get along well. Last night (several days after initial plans were made) he thought to invite me and said, "You can come if you want."
>
> I was very hurt. I spoke up for myself and said so. I shared that I felt like an afterthought, that I felt very left out, and didn't understand why I was the last to be included. The discussion did not go well from there.*
>
> So. Is this the sort of thing we could use CDA or a rhetorical pattern to sort of "explain" why this is so upsetting to me? Or am I making a mountain out of a molehill by being upset by this? Is this phrase off-putting to anyone else?
>
> ---
>
> *I realize if I shared more of what was said six thousand of you would come at me with "girl, B2B!" (and honestly I'd love you for the support), but I'm not really asking if this guy is B2B, I'm really wondering what it is with that particular phrase.

My response to this is that it's a *great* time to use CDA, and specifically the "How else could this have been said?" heuristic.

The reason his message was so upsetting to her is that it's extremely minimizing (perhaps intentionally so). What he offered was not an invitation; it was an expression of tolerance. Now, let's look at this heuristically and ask ourselves, "How else could this be said?"

Here's how: "Hey, I'm not sure if you're available, but I would really love if you could join us. These are good friends, and it would mean a lot to me to be able to introduce you to them." And he should have invited her initially, not waited until after the fact.

One other possibility about this exchange that is worth mentioning here is that this man *may* have been intentionally employing a tactic called "negging." In contemporary dating parlance this is short for "negative feedback" or negating someone intentionally to make them feel insecure. It frequently takes the form of a backhanded compliment, such as "You look pretty good for your age" or "That dress is actually flattering for someone with your body type." The most insidious examples of negging present in such a way that it's impossible to "prove" someone is trying to hurt you, yet it still ends up making you feel insecure. Such as, say, organizing an event and inviting everyone else far in advance of inviting you. Negging is one manipulation strategy of the pickup artist community (PUAs), which employs neurolinguistic programming (NLP; see page 163) to manipulate and exploit women for sex.

NLP outside the context of dating is a practice of using language to effect certain responses and actions in the person it's being used upon (negging for sure, but it goes beyond that). It's been used therapeutically in psychology (not without critique), but when you see it referenced within the context of PUAs it refers to a fairly dangerous group of underground Incels who have real-life conventions and internet groups dedicated to teaching men how to manipulate women for sex. NLP is one of their primary tactics, and they hire linguistics experts to teach it. It's intended to destabilize women and make us insecure in order to render us more pliable, desperate, and ripe for abuse.

The most famous account of this was captured in a book by Neil Strauss titled *The Game: Penetrating the Secret Society of Pickup Artists*. Strauss was a well-established journalist when he went undercover and embedded himself in these groups. He then got totally sucked in, actually *became* one of them, and rose to the top of their ranks. *The Game* is about that experience. He later denounced his involvement in it in a subsequent book titled *The Truth: An Uncomfortable Book About Relationships*. (I've read both books, and the writing is great, but they're *super* disturbing, and Strauss has, admittedly, done some really problematic stuff himself.)

As I've mentioned, most therapists and psychologists now consider NLP to be a pseudoscience, though like a lot of things, it still has its proponents in various niches. Linguistically, it's fascinating in a theoretical way, but I don't consider it a huge factor in contemporary dating.

The group of men systematically practicing NLP in the dating sphere is not large; they get attention because they're so extreme, and I think it's helpful for women to know that this practice exists. However, I don't believe this is what's going on with the vast majority of problematic men, primarily because most men aren't willing to dedicate the amount of time and energy necessary to learn neurolinguistic programming. A significant percentage of men can't even be bothered to read the text of women's dating profiles, so it seems unlikely that they're going to do a deep dive on an esoteric theoretical practice.*

Let's do one last example of the "How else could this have been said?" heuristic:

A Burned Haystack community member shared a screenshot of a man's profile that seemed almost red flag free. For his relationship preference he'd picked only one—monogamy—which is exactly what she wanted too.

The one problem with this guy's profile was that after specifying "monogamy," he added "I don't share."

I fear too many women would gloss over this just because it sometimes seems hard to find men who are truly monogamous and committed to monogamy as a relationship structure. However, the right answer here is simply "Monogamy." *That*'s the preference: Say less!

This man revealed himself fast. He's not monogamous because

---

* Related but unscientific finding: I once polled the Burned Haystack Facebook group about which was the most severe problem related to men on dating apps: cluelessness, aggression, or laziness. I thought the winning answer would be aggression, but a whopping 71 percent of women (from about four thousand polled) said "laziness." This is disappointing for a lot of reasons, but it also suggests that in the big scheme of things there aren't really that many men hunkered down studying neurolinguistic programming.

he has a comfort level with that structure or because it aligns with his faith; he's monogamous because "he doesn't share."

On top of revealing that it's a possession thing and not a love thing for him, he's also revealed that he has no social awareness, he sees women as objects, and he thinks it's okay for him to "lay down the law" with women even in advance of meeting them. Block to burn.

Thin-Slicing

We've talked about this little rhetorical trick previously and how useful it is for analyzing the dating apps; you can easily extract just one line from someone's bio ("NO DRAMA!!!" or "I will never hit you") and know everything you'll ever need to know about him. Here I'll share an example of thin-slicing from an experience that happened to a good friend of mine:

She had recently started dating a man who was showing all green flags. The first time she went over to his house (they'd been on several dates at this point, and she was ready to spend the night with him), he mentioned while giving her the house tour that he'd stocked the guest bathroom (which was spotlessly clean!) with some basic toiletries and a toothbrush for her "just in case." He presented it naturally and casually, and it struck her as thoughtful.

He then served a delicious dinner (which he'd made) and after dinner announced that it was time for her to go brush her teeth with her new toothbrush. She thought he was joking, but he wasn't. This seemed odd. She stayed for a bit longer but decided to leave and go home to her own house that night. Over the next couple of weeks, this guy became increasingly directive, controlling, jealous, and threatening.

The "time to brush your teeth!" mandate might seem harmless, or maybe just quirky, but in this case that "thin slice" predicted a pattern of behavior that intensified to a frightening degree. She found out later from a mutual friend that he had a history of this kind of behavior with women.

"Individual Quirk" (IQ)

An IQ heuristic is one you make up for yourself to determine something specific. An example would be the "Indian food test" mentioned in chapter 1: A woman who lives in the American Midwest shared that she always recommends an Indian restaurant for the first date because it roots out toxic conservative men. In her experience, most men who fit this description (which is the exact opposite of what she wants) prefer "good ol' meat and potatoes" or think that "ethnic food is weird," so casually suggesting Indian food has forced the red-flag revelations early on in a way that saved her wasted time and energy. This is a great example of a heuristic because it meets the criteria of being not perfect, but good enough for the intended purpose.

Another example of an IQ heuristic, this time from a man one of our community members was chatting with. To be fair, I can't be certain that he was acting heuristically in this example, but I'll give him the benefit of the doubt because it's such a good example of a heuristic.

This man said he liked to kick off dating app conversations with these three questions:

> What are your thoughts on aliens? 👽
>
> What brings you the third most joy in your life?
>
> What's the greatest lesson you've learned in life this far?

If he's using these questions as heuristics, here are some benefits to doing so:

> **QUESTION 1:** If a woman answers and simply says, "I don't believe in aliens," then that exhibits a logical, fact-based orientation—a stone-cold realist who requires physical evidence and hard proof to accept something as fact. This might be exactly

what he's looking for. If someone responds with something like "I highly doubt they're little green men like in the movies, but it also seems egotistical to believe that humans are the only intelligent species in the entire universe, most of which we've not yet accessed." That might be the person he's looking for—someone who's reasonable but also willing to make allowances for some mystery. If someone responds and says, "Yes, I see space aliens all the time. Last year I was abducted by some." Well . . . that's a big red flag.

QUESTION 2: Almost everyone's going to answer "family and friends" for their number one and two joy sources, so this could be a way of bypassing the clichés and finding out something more interesting.

QUESTION 3: I can see how hearing about someone's greatest life lesson could be a good "values reveal."

It's entirely possible that these three answers, taken together, could give him an impression of a woman that might be more accurate (and definitely more interesting) than "Describe your perfect Sunday."

One final IQ heuristic that I used to use quite a bit myself on the dating apps (before I started blocking to burn these guys immediately) is called "flipping the script"—intentionally catching someone off guard by responding in a way they don't expect. Their reactions to your unexpected response can be very telling.

A favorite question of both scammers and insecure (and uncreative) men is this: "How's your experience on this app been?"

In the case of scammers, they're trying to find out what you've been upset or disappointed by, so that they can performatively be the opposite of those things, thus setting themselves apart. So, if you say that men haven't been responsive in messaging, they'll be super responsive; if you say you keep meeting poor men with no education, they'll present as Oxford graduates and aeronautical engineers. In the case of insecure men, they're specifically looking for women who are demoralized, disappointed, hopeless, and suffering from low self-esteem; such women seem easy to manipulate and abuse.

So in order to flip the script, I always answered that question this way: "My experience has actually been delightful! I'd heard a lot of horror stories about how awful the dating apps are, but I've met several fascinating men and been taken out on so many lovely dates!"

This flip-of-the-script accomplishes a few things:

1. It positions you as a proactive, in-demand woman; insecure and abusive men are absolutely repelled by such women.
2. It raises the bar if he actually does want to date you; he now knows he'll need to level up.

What I found is that my flipped-script answer got me unmatched 100 percent of the time. Still a success in terms of heuristic application, because it worked to get rid of the scammers and losers, but once it happened enough times, I realized that even sending it was unnecessary. However, if you get that question (all women get that question), then this is an option if you feel compelled to learn more.

• • •

The heuristics we've just discussed are formalized thought experiments and widely applicable. Now let's consider other tactics that will help you bring your intuition and rhetorical knowledge together into a superpower you can rely upon.

TRUST YOUR GUT—AND PRACTICE "NAMING IT"

Here's the kind of comment I get frequently in Burned Haystack social media platforms: "This behavior has always bothered me, but I never knew exactly why. Thank you for giving words to my intuition." My hope is that as you read this book and practice the Burned Haystack method, you'll quite naturally begin giving words to your intuition on your own. This will happen partly through learning the rhetorical patterns and the analytical techniques of critical discourse analysis and the heuristics such as "Translate it to real life" or "How else could this have been said?" I hope it also happens because you begin to trust yourself more, because you start to understand deeply that it was never "just your feelings" or "your trauma" or "your fear" or, my favorite, "the feminist agenda." When I'm talking to women about these types of things, my innate and immediate (and almost always justified) opinion is that all these ways of knowing are legitimate; they're just being minimized and trivialized and twisted and used to gaslight us. We've been socialized to distrust our highly accurate women's intuition.

Knowing why you're feeling put off or fearful or distrusting isn't totally necessary; it just helps to have the words and knowledge to back it up—it gives you more confidence. Even if you're unable to figure out why you're feeling uneasy, though, I would still encourage you to be mindful and proceed with caution.

Here's a personal example of a time I had a feeling that something was just "off" even though it didn't rise to the level of toxicity or clear deceit or any of the Burned Haystack rhetorical patterns:

When I was on the apps during the early stages of the Burned Haystack project, I matched with a man who listed his career as "carpenter." Our conversations were compelling and easy from the very beginning. He was articulate and witty and engaging. We agreed to meet for dinner, and he made reservations at a great restaurant halfway between his town and mine. I was looking forward to the date, and I was thoroughly enjoying messaging with him, but the more we did, the more I felt like something didn't add up. I have never filtered for degree because I don't care, but there was something about this guy's writing that did not square with his profession of carpentry. I don't mean because I wouldn't expect a carpenter to be highly literate or sophisticated—that wouldn't surprise me at all. I taught for a year inside a max-security prison, and most of the men in my class had not graduated from high school, yet many of them wrote literary prose that was among the best I've encountered in my teaching career. I think people who read a lot tend to be strong writers, and at first I assumed this guy was just very well read; he'd alluded to other things that gave me that impression as well. But the more I read his writing the more uneasy I became about who he actually was. His writing sounded not just articulate and literary but *manipulated* in the way that academics manipulate syntax into unnatural rhythms that aren't seen elsewhere. It's possible there are carpenters out there reading literary theory and criticism, but why? I probably wouldn't if I didn't have to. And he hadn't said anything to indicate to me that he read stuff like that.

The day before our date, I called a friend who's an attorney and asked her to check him out (I had his first and last name at that point). She found him immediately: he was *also* an attorney—one who'd been disbarred for bilking vulnerable senior citizens out of tens of thousands of dollars.

So that explained it. At the time, it was "just a feeling," it was "just my intuition," except that it wasn't "just" those things. I'd sensed a disconnect between a fact he shared with me—that his profession was "carpenter"—and his writing, which signaled membership in a discourse community to which a carpenter would not belong, one that was close to my own discourse community, since academia and law share certain tenets. Before I asked my lawyer friend to help research the guy, I hadn't "named" my intuition concretely because I didn't have enough information; all I knew was that something was off. Once I had more facts, I could say, "This man is performing within the norms of a discourse community to which he does not belong, and that indicates deception."

Bottom line, my instincts were correct—and I bet yours almost always are too. Obviously, I blocked to burn him (and also reported him, in this case).

I want to address four more rhetorical terms that will reinforce your ability to trust your gut in the dating sphere. Having a grasp of these concepts will alert you to specific red flags or red-flag-ish things and will empower you to know that those "off" feelings you have are grounded in sneaky rhetorical patterns.

GLITTERING GENERALITIES

These are vague and/or abstract words employed to appeal to people's emotions in a positive way, but that are unsubstantiated by evidence. Glittering generalities are frequently employed in political campaigns, advertising, and propaganda, and they involve words such as "freedom," "holistic," "sustainable," "equitable," "wholesome," and so on. Use of such words is intended to tap into and connect with people's deeply held values, which can create immediate identification in a way that leads to automatic acceptance without questioning. Men's profiles that go on about soulmates and sunsets and loving to laugh and all the other vapid clichés with which the dating apps are littered are guilty of employing glittering generalities. It doesn't necessarily mean they're toxic, but it might mean that they're unoriginal and boring. It also means they're simply spouting off things they've heard that seem vaguely "good," when we'd prefer that people be specific and concrete in their language so that we can actually learn something about who they are.

LOADED WORDS

These are employed to evoke a strong emotional response, either positive or negative, but more frequently negative. Words like "hate," "rape," "lynch," "crazy," "illegal," and so on are considered loaded because of their cultural connotations. More common in everyday life is when people use loaded words in such a subtle way that you either can't figure out why you're reacting negatively to something or you begin to question your own reactions. I've seen men employ loaded words in their dating app profiles to, I assume, elicit some sort of reaction or to "test" in some way the women reading it.

WEASEL WORDS

These are just what they sound like: people weaseling out of things. This can take various forms. For example, forensic linguistics experts look for people to use "qualifying" or "distancing" words when they're lying. When Bill Clinton didn't want to admit that he'd been in contact with his mistress Gennifer Flowers, he said, "She left our state, and for years, I didn't really hear from her and know what she was doing." The qualifying word there is "really." This is a subconscious attempt to "soften" a statement, to build in internal wiggle room so that the speaker can avoid fully reckoning with the lie or evasion. (This happens subconsciously, beneath our radar. With the exception of actual sociopaths, who comprise a very small percentage of the population, people are deeply uncomfortable with lying—it causes a cognitive clash—so sometimes the mind compensates by slipping in these little qualifiers, these little weasel words.) Put more generally, if you feel like someone is trying to weasel out of something—if what they're saying just doesn't makes sense, or they're giving you *way* more irrelevant detail than you asked for, or if their explanation of things is convoluted, then you are most likely hearing weasel words.

THOUGHT-TERMINATING CLICHÉS

As discussed in the previous chapter, these phrases are used to shut down conversation in a way that leaves the upset or complaining person without a path forward to any dialogue. Imagine a woman consumed by stress who is told that "God only gives us the load we can bear," or a man grieving a loved one who is told that "it must have happened for a reason," or a woman rightfully upset by her partner's neglect who is told to "sit with her feelings and question why she is afraid to be alone with herself." These are all thought-terminating clichés. Other examples often used in the dating sphere are: "It is what it is." "I guess we'll just have to agree to disagree." "You're just overthinking this."

If a man on a dating app says something overly suggestive to you and you call him out on it and he responds with "Whoa, seems like someone doesn't have a sense of humor!" then that is a thought-terminating cliché. The actual issue is that he's being sexually aggressive, but by hijacking that discussion to a pronouncement about your lack of humor, he has effectively terminated critical thought.

A NOTE ABOUT INTERNALIZED MISOGYNY

I want to address the concept of internalized misogyny in this chapter because I believe that having a nuanced understanding of how it operates will help you to censor some voices that might be interfering with your success in finding a good man. Too frequently one of those voices is your own, not because you have low self-esteem or poor analytical skills or because you're a bad feminist, but because everyone who is raised in a patriarchy suffers from some degree of internalized misogyny that should be confronted. Once you understand how insidious and pervasive internalized misogyny is—how embedded in the fabric of our society—you'll start seeing it everywhere.

The term refers to the unconscious biases that women absorb; it is complex and multifaceted and emerges as a set of "by-products" of living in a patriarchal system. I want to share a specific example from the Burned Haystack Facebook community. It involves a man named Harold who one of our members matched with (the same "Harold" addressed in the Humor Break on page 266). Harold somehow managed to get his penis past the Bumble filters and included in his primary profile pic. I wrote a humor piece about this, and one of the community members took issue with that. She said that it was "mean" and "shaming" of me to mock this man, and that she "didn't appreciate my tone."

(Sidenote: "Tone policing" is far more frequently leveraged to critique women. When men use a strong tone it's because they're "strong" and "definitive" and "clear"; when women use a strong tone it's because they're "bitchy," and this judgment is frequently a sign of internalized misogyny on its own.)

The red flags of internalized misogyny show up in various ways. Sometimes they manifest as women being distrustful of other women or assuming men can do something better. (And again, this can be entirely subconscious. If every doctor you went to growing up was male, you might assume that men are naturally better equipped to be doctors, even though they just benefited from a social system that privileged men's education over women's—it was always systemic and had nothing to do with gender.) Other times, internalized misogyny looks the other way or makes excuses for toxic male behavior and instead casts the blame on the woman who has suffered from that behavior. This is exactly what we see when people say things like "But what was she wearing?" in the aftermath of a sexual assault.

The woman who was upset about my humor writing was concerned that I was being "mean" to Harold and that he was being "shamed." I *critiqued* him through satire, for sure, but that's different than being shamed. I didn't pick on Harold for his appearance or his age or his height or his dis/ability status or his intellect. Harold was critiqued because he posted a picture of his penis in his Bumble profile, the photo taken explicitly from the perspective a woman would have if she were performing oral sex on him.

Internalized misogyny may have (subconsciously) inspired the message sender to critique my humor writing and to call me "mean" while forgiving or making excuses for Harold's sexual harassment. The problem with this is that it actively works *against* the well-being of other women.

Many scholars believe that internalized misogyny is not just a by-product of the patriarchy but an active agent of it; as long as women are busy going after each other, the patriarchy continues to operate unfettered, repeating and strengthening its dynamics, and women do its work by weakening each other.

Back to Harold: Harold is a sexual harasser. The women who signed up for and paid for Bumble did not consent to behold Harold's penis. They also didn't agree to contend with hundreds of other pictures of hundreds of other men shot from the exact same angle; the photos themselves are aggressive and inappropriate and triggering for many women.

And even if I *were* shaming Harold, some people and some behaviors—the kind that harm others—deserve to be shamed. Harold deserves to be mocked and shamed, and defending or apologizing for his behavior in any way can only come from internalized misogyny. Making its effects explicit can alert us to its power and help us to dismantle it over time so that we're not replicating these insidious structures.

SUCCESS STORY!

Excerpt from the first post:

Hi Burners!
 I'm thirty years old and I live in LA. I have never been a fan of hookup culture. I was so sick and tired of feeling that things were happening *to me* while using the apps and felt there was another way. While I don't have a professional background in rhetoric, I have a science background, I do research, and (as one may assume) I'm incredibly observant. I have a penchant for (consciously and subconsciously) approaching a number of things in my life like research projects.
 My more intentional awareness in patterns of behavior of men both online and offline has resulted in me ending things early many, many times. It made me feel far more empowered and has also yielded me the absolute best results in the caliber of men that I meet as well as keeping me sane. My mindset has been none of "does he like me?" and everything about "do I like him?"
 Somehow some way, I've been dating a man for over a month now who continues to be a walking green flag. We align

in ways that are scarily similar and share very similar values. He was my first third date in years and tomorrow will be our fifth date. No love bombing or flowery language in the way he communicates with me, and yet, it's been incredible so far (I say this as a bleeding-heart romantic lmao). In fact, I would argue that it is far more profound a dating experience when the dynamic itself speaks volumes without needing poetic language to qualify it.

Moral of the story: stick with Burned Haystack!! You're doing the Lord's work, Jennie!

Posted in response to reader questions and comments:

A rule I made for myself as I defined what boundaries look like for me while dating: You don't have to be subject to a man's response after you tell them they are not for you. I stuck to my script, said, "We don't have the compatibility I'm seeking," and so on, and immediately *blocked* their number after.

Rejection can feel hurtful. And I don't have to be a witness to their inability to handle it.

Block to burn even after the "you are not for me" message.

Much-needed disclaimer: The overwhelming majority of the men I interacted with in the dating context were men that confirmed future dates with me but we never met or men that I went on one date with (so, in other words, low emotional, time, and/or energy investment). These were the men that I ended up implementing my rule on. They were not men that, say, I was interested in staying friends with at the very least. They were men where there was absolutely nothing for me and that is precisely why I was comfortable blocking. They could still respond to my last message if they wanted to, but I wouldn't see it.

At the end of the day, honor your boundaries.

Posted in response to additional questions:

Some of the conversations I am seeing here reminded me of a post I made elsewhere several months ago. It detailed how I was navigating dating in the early stages and how I managed to pace myself and lessen the chances of getting prematurely invested. This is what worked for me. Take from it what you will.

1. Being more invested in myself than men. I'm currently in one of the most prosperous seasons in my life. My business is going well. I have flights to Cancún, Chiang Mai, Taipei, and NYC booked, and a trip to San Diego. I've picked up salsa and bachata dancing and enjoy masculine energy in this controlled context of dancing classes and social dancing. I'm revamping my wardrobe. I go the gym often. I'm fostering my close friendships. I'm so into me right now and I love that for me. I have less emotional energy left over for men.

2. Talking to more than one guy at a time. With the leftover energy I do have, it's not solely given to one man. I have also been in situations where a guy and I will hit it off and either they or myself decide to end things rather early (for me, I end things early due to glaring incompatibility). Nowadays, I rarely feel any type of way if I get ghosted, and I think me not putting all my eggs in one basket has a part to play. Exclusivity is earned.

3. Understanding what chemistry is and what it is not. Chemistry is where my charisma and his dance. Nothing more. Chemistry does not tell you someone's character, doesn't tell you if they will care for you if you were sick, doesn't tell you that they are dependable, doesn't tell you if they are worth the investment. Chemistry only tells you that there's an attraction and that you have things in common, but only time (as in months to years) can tell you if the person is worth the investment.

[The next rule I had for myself is arguably beyond the scope of Burned Haystack, but again, this worked for me.]

4. Exercising sexual discipline. Given #3, chemistry is a poor foundation to build trust with someone else when it comes to my body. Since my goal is a long-term relationship and to be sober-minded when looking for it, I have to understand that it is better to have sex later in these situations. I generally have a harder time being objective in my assessment of a guy I date when sex is had early. When it comes to guys, the ones that want sex but are lying by saying they want a relationship won't want to wait. Crisis averted (for the most part). There's no magic number for how long you should wait, but my rule of thumb is to wait long enough that you can notice patterns and trends in behavior and can draw reasonable conclusions from them. It is entirely up to you when you decide to take that plunge. But this is the standard I set for myself.

5. Actions > words. Every single time. This group should be evidence enough that many men lie. Don't take him at his word. Let him show you.

These tips aren't foolproof, but they have helped me a lot.

Posted several months after the original post:

I have said it before and I will say it again that I have been ruthless, less understanding, and less accommodating with dating this time around. And that has been a *good* thing. I am naturally very empathetic and made the error of thinking that my ability to empathize means I can tolerate. Absolutely not. Behaving this way only hurt me emotionally, mentally, and even physically.

The majority of men I dated this year did not make it past the first date. Pertinent questions were asked no later than the first date. Only three made it past the first date, and only one made it past the second. After losing count of how many dates later, that man is now my boyfriend.

Knowing I was ruthless in my selection process makes me appreciate him more. And I can rest easy knowing that I did not waste my time and I protected myself more. Whether single or in a relationship, I can never get away from me, so I oughta do my best to do everything with my best interest in mind.

Burned Haystack forever and ever. Amen.

Posted with a pic of her needle, a year after meeting him:

Just wanted to add some positivity to the group and share myself and my needle during our one-year anniversary dinner.

My first post in the group was over a year ago where I shared how I was essentially using Burned Haystack without knowing what it was. I mentioned being selective, ruthless, and less accommodating. This attitude was also present in my professional life; earlier this year, I quit my job when I didn't think I was earning what I deserved and realized that clients outside of my work were willing to pay more for my services. After being very "others first" for nearly all my life, me putting myself first led to a better life for me. And that just happened to also include my dream guy that I am even more crazy about now than when we first met.

—*Michelle*

HUMOR BREAK

Jolene Actually Did Take My Man, and This Is What Happened: A Retrospective

I begged her not to take him, but she took him anyway.

Having my man taken was the worst thing I could ever imagine, and I knew at that moment that my life was ruined, so I packed up and went to Nashville and signed a contract with a record label. I was crushed.

I stayed up nights wondering what Jolene was doing with my man.

After the record label and dealing with Nashville and everything, I dabbled in acting a bit, kept singing my songs, just tried to keep myself busy. I even wrote a song about you-know-who, and it rocketed up the charts and got nominated for a Grammy. It didn't matter, though, because I was so miserable without my man.

I heard Jolene and my man moved into one side of a duplex together back in Tennessee.

Anyway, I guess I didn't realize how much time and energy I had been spending on my man until Jolene took him because after she did I won eleven Grammys, a Lifetime Achievement Award, ten Country Music Association awards, four People's Choice Awards, and three American Music Awards. Of course all of it paled in comparison to what Jolene had, which was my man.

I tried to not think about Jolene and my man together because the Good Book says that envy rots the bones, but of course it was difficult. To keep my mind off them I got inducted into the Country Music Hall of Fame and the Rock & Roll Hall of Fame, but the only halls I ever really dreamed of were the ones in the house of Jolene and my man.

Turns out it wasn't even a duplex, though, just a studio apartment, so no halls I guess. I heard Jolene and my man had a couple kids, some substance-abuse problems, mild run-ins with the law, that kind of thing, and eventually got evicted. I'm not sure where the kids went.

I didn't have any kids of my own, but I made up something I called the Imagination Library that's now donated 213 million books to children across the planet and actually boosted childhood literacy rates. Eventually a little organization called the United Way got behind it. So I've done some good, I guess, but it's not the same as having eyes of emerald green and flaming locks of auburn hair, to borrow from my now-immortal song.

Which, to be honest, I've always questioned. I've never even seen anyone with emerald eyes. I'm just being petty, though, because Jolene stole my man and my life went south from there.

I also became an actress, a media mogul, an entrepreneur, and a philanthropist. I sold more than one hundred million records worldwide and became a country music legend, and my net worth is $440 million. Everyone loves me, and my career is stronger than ever fifty-seven years out from that fateful night at the bar, but even now all I can think about is Jolene and my man.

They're both dead now.

Not of Covid, though, because I helped cure that. I donated a million dollars out of my own bank account to fund the Moderna vaccine, and then I made a viral video of myself getting it and certainly saved hundreds of thousands of lives.

I just wish Jolene hadn't taken my man. She ruined my life.

8

DATING APP PROFILES THAT LED TO NEEDLES

What Made Them Work?

This chapter is a formal critical discourse analysis of women's dating app profiles that have *worked* and led to successful, committed partnerships with men we could term "needles," according to Burned Haystack. In the same way that CDA can be used to identify toxic and problematic profiles that reveal danger or other undesirable qualities about men, we can similarly use it to identify language and patterns that have led to positive connections. In this chapter, we'll use CDA for these purposes:

- To provide real-life examples (which we might call "artifacts" in an academic setting) for study;
- To identify why the text and images in these profiles worked so well;
- To identify the commonalities across the set of artifacts we're using so that you can apply the same strategies to your own dating app profile.

CAVEATS

I am not a social scientist, and there are no hard-line definitions around "successful, committed partnership." Burned Haystack is relatively new, and no social scientist would consider its short existence an adequate amount of time to establish or even define "successful committed partnership." Therefore, for the purposes of this chapter, we're studying profiles that were developed and managed in accordance with Burned Haystack and that led to exclusive partnerships.

Also, I do **qualitative,** not **quantitative,** research, and this chapter falls under that umbrella. Qualitative research refers to case study–style investigations that focus in depth on a small number of cases and extrapolate meaning and implications inductively/outward. This is opposed to quantitative research, which is more formal, requiring much larger numbers of subjects, implementation of several control factors, and usually legal parameters. That kind of research wouldn't even be possible with a group such as this one (and it also simply hasn't existed long enough for a study like that to be valid).

ABOUT THE SPECIFIC SELECTIONS FOR THIS ANALYSIS

From the Burned Haystack Facebook group, I solicited examples of profiles that have led to good matches, and that's my selection set. There is no way I could analyze every successful profile I've received (though I remain incredibly grateful to every single person who's shared one!). For the sake of clarity and brevity, I decided to limit my selection set to five successful profiles, and I used these criteria to select them:

1. **I LOOKED FOR A VARIETY OF TONES AND PERSONALITY STYLES.**
2. **I LOOKED FOR "TRANSFERABILITY."** I have several excellent profiles that, while successful for the individual, seem highly specific to

that person and thus maybe not as helpful as general examples. The profiles I selected include rhetorical strategies that are identifiable and adaptable to a general audience of profile writers.

I now want to head off a concern that I hear frequently:

> You're doing all this deep-level analysis of these successful profiles, but it doesn't matter because men don't read profiles, and even when they do, they don't interpret them this deeply.

Some men do read profiles, and we are only interested in crafting our dating app profiles for those men. There's nothing we can do about men who don't read profiles anyway, so let's focus on what we can control.

Also, people (including men!) do not have to be analyzing with intention in order to glean important info from text. They don't even need to be aware that they're gleaning any info at all. In the same way that people reveal things they don't intend to reveal, people also *take things in* beneath the level of their consciousness. That's why advertising works. That's why propaganda works. Because "messaging" is real and people absorb and internalize meanings and messages without interrogating those messages or even being aware that they're reading for any particular purpose.

When you create your dating profile, don't worry about the fact that most people aren't going to read it closely, or that most men won't read it at all. People who *do* read end up reading critically without intending to, and there's nothing we can do about people who don't read at all.

METHOD

Here's a refresher on critical discourse analysis. CDA has two primary goals:

1. To read text in a way that reveals things "beneath the text," generally things people don't even intend to reveal. It can be used to cull meanings, clues, and patterns that can be extrapolated to larger implications and to predict future behaviors.
2. To use the knowledge gleaned from the first goal to make the world better. This is the difference between plain old discourse analysis (DA) and *critical* discourse analysis. It's the "critical" element I'm most interested in with Burned Haystack. I believe that carefully conducted and purposefully applied CDA can literally change the world, and I want to change the world of online dating to make it a better place for women.

For the analyses in this chapter, I employed a CDA model closest to the method articulated by linguist James Paul Gee. (See page 43 for more about him, and if you want to learn more about how to conduct your own CDA project, please see the resources in the Haystack Bookstack on page 293.)

For this particular mission—analyzing successful dating app profiles to figure out what makes them work and to draw helpful conclusions for the use of others—I've whittled my analysis down to seven CDA questions.

CDA QUESTIONS USED FOR THIS ANALYSIS

1. **What is the significance of the meanings or messages that can be read between the lines of the profile? Is there language that appears to be coded in some way?** For example, does the profile use a word or phrase that connotes something other than its dictionary definition, in the way that "Netflix and chill" = "Sex," or "support bodily autonomy" signifies political liberalism in the United States.
2. **What is the significance of the figured world(s) suggested by the profile?** Refer to page 43 for the definition of "figured world," but to

share a quick relevant example, here's a description of a profile I remember encountering myself: In his main profile pic, he was sitting in the driver's seat of his two-seater Harley all decked out in leather and fringe. The other seat was empty. *All* his profile pics featured his motorcycle in one way or the other. He used the phrases "ride or die," "partner in crime," and "looking for a daredevil gal to make my life complete." This is what I might term a "biker babe"–figured world, in which the "babe" in question would clearly be a sidekick and accessory to him. I suppose if that were my thing this might have been great, but since it's decidedly not my thing, it was helpful for me to immediately identify the figured world as one in which I definitely did not want to live.

3. **What is the significance of references to other texts/artifacts in the profile?** Such as the Bible, or the Declaration of Independence, or the "cool girl" monologue in *Gone Girl*. The texts and artifacts people reference—whether they're documents of faith, folk-song lyrics, governmental policies, or white nationalist emblems—reveal *a lot* about the person who invokes them, so this is all worth paying attention to.

4. **What is the significance of the discourse communities invoked in the profile?** Remember that "discourse community" refers to a group of people who talk to each other in similar ways, such as a group of attorneys or engineers or roller derby skaters. If someone's dating app profile indicates that they attend many Democratic rallies or demonstrations, they are telling you that this is an important discourse community for them. Having that information gives you considerable insight into their value system, as you can assume it aligns closely with the values of the Democratic Party.

5. **What sort of activities are implied by the subtext or references in the profile?** For example, if a person's dating app profile is full of passionate statements about the great outdoors and pictures of mountains, you can conclude that this is not someone who wants to

stay inside and stream a lot of shows. If their profile refers to interests such as art and museums and books, you can assume this person enjoys intellectual and artistic activities. If someone is wearing a different kind of athletic jersey in every pic, you will know they enjoy sports.

6. **What identities are implied by the subtext, figured worlds, or references in the profile?** An identity might be something like "public servant," "gym rat," or "corporate exec." These are important things for potential matches to glean about someone.
7. **What sort of relationships/connections are implied by the subtext, figured worlds, or references in the profile?** This one is easy to gloss over, but the kinds of connections people forge can tell you a great deal about them. Do they seem to lean toward loud, large-group activities such as attending NFL games? Or do they appear to prefer one-on-one quiet time browsing art galleries and sitting in coffee shops? Do they seem like a "joiner" who wants to go on group hikes and church retreats, or does their profile scream strong introvert?

OTHER CONSIDERATIONS

Recall our discussion in chapter 3 of rhetoric forms other than textual (visual, material, embodied, and semiotics). That is, basically anything *other* than language that signals relevant information about a potential match. In that chapter, we applied it to men on the apps, and how we've all been turned off by the bathroom mirror selfies whose backgrounds feature dirty towels and toilet seats in the "up" position, the dreaded "pillow pics" guys who are clearly lounging on dirty sheets covering ratty mattresses on the floor, the Confederate flags and mounted deer heads and crushed beer cans and too much video game paraphernalia for a childless man in his forties. Viewing a dating app through these lenses is a powerful practice of applied rhetoric.

We should apply those same lenses and employ the same level of discernment before we publish our *own* profiles. I'll use myself as an example here. I'm a generally tidy person who has almost zero tolerance for clutter, so if I choose to share a pic of myself inside my home, I'm going to be sure the background that day reflects my typical orientation toward neatness. I might also intentionally choose to include the grammar comics poster I have hanging on my wall (yes, I have a grammar poster on the wall of my home!) because I want to signal that writing is important to me. I also have a framed poster of a McSweeney's piece I cowrote with my son because it's special to me and because I love the cover art the editor chose. (McSweeney's is a snarky, uber-liberal internet satire site; I honestly cannot imagine myself even having coffee with a man unfamiliar with it, so including it in my bio, even incidentally like this in the background without talking about it, could serve to forge a meaningful connection for me.)

Essentially, you want to think of your dating app profile as a media presentation, something that portrays a cohesive narrative or tapestry of who you are.

RESULTS

This next section includes a detailed critical discourse analysis of five successful dating profiles. For each profile, I will apply the seven CDA questions listed above. I think you'll begin to see meanings, implications, and ideas emerge that you might not have at first glance. Slowing down and answering analytical questions such as these doesn't so much "teach" you anything you didn't know as much as bring to the surface of your consciousness what you've already intuitively sensed.

I would bet that the men who were attracted to these profiles were attracted because they perceived the same things my CDA questions reveal, but they probably didn't recognize exactly *why* they were so attracted. But that doesn't matter. The recognition of something or attraction to it can happen just as powerfully without the perceiver intentionally interrogating what they encounter. They might just think, *I like this*, or *I want to know more*, or *This feels familiar.*

The point of reading analyses like the ones you're about to encounter is that it can help you to slow down and be very intentional and very *specific* and *concrete* when crafting your own profile. It can help you to think about the story you want to tell about yourself and the ways in which you can craft it. I'm not referring to willful manipulation or any kind of "sales pitch." Rather, I'm suggesting that first impressions are incredibly important and always a one-shot deal, so it makes sense to put your best foot forward in a way that's still honest and authentic—just as you would in real life.

ANALYSIS OF EFFECTIVE PROFILE #1: RACHEL

My greatest strength

No bunny ears filters

Also—

Not a yoga teacher/"life coach"

Not/don't have a "crazy ex"

Don't care about your Monday

Will eat "Sunday roast"

Epitome of "passionate"

Not a stepdad hunter

You should *not* go out with me if

You:

Demand I be "no drama"/other code words

Are 50 and not sure you want kids

Tell me your love language (it's physical touch)

Are in bed

Post bike/paddleboard pics—I'm familiar with all modes of transport

I geek out on

Absurd humor

Modern art

All the music (Fugazi? Cat Power? NWA? Yes!)

The sea

A good rave

Intersectionality

Creativity

True love

Living alone

Hugs

Buying books I don't read

Kids (50% timeshare)

Red shiny shoes

What is the significance of the meanings or messages that can be read between the lines of the profile? Is there language that appears to be coded in some way?

The brilliant thing about this profile is that the writer took all the coded words that already exist in online dating and recruited them to craft her own profile. Invoking terms like "passionate," "stepdad hunter," "no drama," "physical touch," and so on, *and* doing it with humor, essentially communicates this message: "I'm already onto every trick there is. I'm also funny about it rather than angry, though, so I'd probably be fun to hang out with. But you can't fool me." Think about what a powerful and appealing stance that is from which to kick off a relationship.

What is the significance of the figured world(s) suggested by the profile?

There's an implied figured world here of "caricature of a toxic dating app man," which the profile writer explicitly mocks and rejects. She also recruits the figured world of a "cool girl" and says clearly, "Yeah, I'm not that." Invoking both these figured worlds serves as a shortcut because, by referring to cultural archetypes, she saves time and text by not having to explain too much. Essentially, she says, "I'm not going to play the 'cool girl,' and I'm not going to engage with 'toxic dating app dude.'"

What is the significance of references to other texts/artifacts in the profile?

This profile also works on two levels here. She's nodding to all the dating app clichés and essentially dispatching the men who play into them, thus precluding wasting her time with any of them. She's also alluding to interests such as modern art (suggests creativity and a certain level of intellectual engagement); specific music (which could forge connection with someone who likes the same); cultural themes such as intersectionality (suggests "educated and liberal"); true love (suggests romanticism, which is important in this profile since she's also effectively saying "but I'm not dealing with any bullshit," and bringing "true love" back into the discussion balances that out and restores the tone to romantic hope, which is appealing to most people on a dating app); living alone (which suggests emotional security, financial security, independence, and confidence); and red shoes, which ends the list with lighthearted fun.

What is the significance of the discourse communities invoked in the profile?

The major discourse communities invoked are "dating app talk" (which she's *clearly* fluent in) and social progressivism (which will help her attract same if that's what she wants, and I'm assuming it is).

What sort of activities are implied by the subtext or references in the profile?

Intellectual activities, creative activities, family-oriented activities, romantic activities—all of these are strong "pro-date" activities. Even the ones she rules out, like the line that says "don't go out with me if you've got bike or paddleboard pics because I'm already familiar with all the modes of transport," which actually creates *more* opportunities for connection, not fewer, and here's why: This profile writer has done such a good job crafting a tone of humor and directness in her profile that the right guy—one who can match that humor and directness—could easily write to her and say something like "You sound like an amazing person. Just removed all my bike and paddleboard pics so you'll talk to me."

What identities are implied by the subtext, figured world(s), or references in the profile?

Identity of a strong, funny, independent woman, yet one who is open to love.

What sort of relationships/connections are implied by the subtext, figured world(s), or references in the profile?

Egalitarian, humorous, transparent, hopeful.

ANALYSIS OF EFFECTIVE PROFILE #2: SHANNON

> I'm an extroverted, independent plant geek. I'm very optimistic and laid back and have a career that I love. I'm pretty nerdy, I prefer reading or games over TV and visit the library often. I love iced coffee of all kinds, festivals and music too.
>
> I'm a solar-powered early bird who loves to laugh and I have a positive, nonjudgmental attitude. Pro-choice and proud LGBTQ2 ally here!
>
> I love to try new things—especially if it involves people, plants, food, and/or sunshine. I can often be found dancing while I cook, talking to strangers, or singing badly in the car.
>
> I have a great relationship with my ex and I am not seeking a stepparent for my son.
>
> I am looking to meet people here and see where it goes. My free time can be somewhat limited but I will prioritize someone with similar energy and values.
>
> Do I sound like someone you want to get to know? Let's meet for a coffee and discuss our favorite things. Thanks for reading!

What is the significance of the meanings or messages that can be read between the lines of the profile?

Writer conveys intelligence and creativity with a humorous twist. This is someone who knows exactly who she is and states it clearly and directly with no tonal problems or limitations set upon the reader.

Foregrounding "pro-choice and proud LGBTQ2 ally" makes her political orientation crystal clear, and this too is stated declaratively but not provocatively (as in it doesn't bait anyone or invite fighting).

What is the significance of the figured world(s) suggested by the profile?

Interdependent, progressive, hipster creative people hanging out.

What is the significance of references to other texts/ artifacts in the profile?

Clearly signaling liberalism, creativity, and adventurousness.

What is the significance of the discourse communities invoked in the profile?

Career unclear, but the fact that the writer states she loves it suggests a professional orientation (also use of the word "career" as opposed to "job").

What sort of activities are implied by the subtext or references in the profile?

Interactive activities, outgoing personality, high energy ("solar-powered early bird").

What identities are implied by the subtext, figured world(s), or references in the profile?

Independent, self-assured, happy, quirky, open-minded, cooperative, articulate, creative, and energetic.

What sort of relationships/connections are implied by the subtext, figured world(s), or references in the profile?

Equitable, equal, balanced, supportive, open-minded, and accepting.

ANALYSIS OF EFFECTIVE PROFILE #3: MICHELLE

> About me
> Your neighborhood private academic test prep tutor/mentor, neuroscience researcher, musician, and wannabe gym rat. Lived in 3 countries before the age of 8. Nonreligious. Loves to dance. No kids. Never been married. Seeing if this app can offer quality the same way Bumble BFF did for me.
>
> Don't judge a book by its cover, but my cover says
> Some folks think that my "cover" says that I'm not a huge nerd. But that could not be further from the truth. #NerdGang

What is the significance of the meanings or messages that can be read between the lines of the profile?

The message I'm getting is this: "I'm super smart, but I'm also funny and fun." Including the word "neuroscience researcher" at the top of the profile is an attention-getter because it's so unusual. It's also concrete in a way that's visualizable and economical. She could have written: "I'm an intellectual person who takes academic work seriously but also knows how to have a good time. I take good care of myself, and I'm funny and fun to be around." That's vague, a little cheesy, and not something people can visualize. Putting together the phrases "neuroscience researcher," "musician," and "wannabe gym rat" is concrete and specific and memorable, while still taking less time/fewer words to say than my other option above. The combo of "concreteness and specificity" is a secret weapon of successful dating app profile text.

What is the significance of the figured world(s) suggested by the profile?

"Hot Nerd Girl." I don't mean this in any kind of derogatory way at all. This is a pop culture trope that people are familiar with (and easy enough to google, if not), and crafting this persona will resonate with the right kind of matches. Tapping into archetypes or well-known personas such as Hot Nerd Girl is an economical way to quickly give potential matches an image of who you are, provided the one you choose is attractive to the kind of person you want to meet. For example, stepping into the archetype of "Tomboy" will work for some sets of men but not others; same with the archetype of "Type A Businesswoman" or "Earthy Hippie Chick." This is a good thing: You don't *want* to match with everyone, you want to match with people who want to match with *you*.

What is the significance of references to other texts/ artifacts in the profile?

Standardized test prep tutor/mentor: This does a few things. For anyone who knows about this profession, it's an immediate flag that this is a super-sharp person, because the test prep companies only hire people who themselves have scored extremely high on tests like the SAT or ACT. So referring to that provides a credential that for the right match does all the informative work on its own. The act of teaching/ mentoring also conveys authority, kindness, patience, and perhaps even maternal instincts, all of which could be highly appealing. Additionally, being a "neuroscience researcher" locates this person within the halls of academia and intellectual communities, as discussed above. Nodding toward the gym establishes the writer as someone who is active and health-oriented and takes good care of herself.

What is the significance of the discourse communities invoked in the profile?

The primary discourse community is an intellectual one, yet the writer makes clear that she functions just as well outside that community. She specifically excludes herself from religious discourse communities. This too is very smart, as it prevents wasting time with matches for whom belonging to a faith community is important.

What sort of activities are implied by the subtext or preferences in the profile?

Intellectual activities, physical activities, nurturing activities with others, and general fun as she loves to dance.

What identities are implied by the subtext, figured worlds, or references in the profile?

Strong, confident, intelligent, fun, clear, and intentional.

What sort of relationships/connections are implied by the subtext, figured worlds, or references in the profile?

This profile communicates a woman who knows what she wants and isn't afraid to say it: "I'm seeking intentional connections. If we match, tell me why." This does a lot to preclude men who haven't read her profile. I find this interesting too: she mentions that she's already successfully used Bumble BFF to find friends. This tells potential matches that she put friendship in front of romance, which suggests confidence and someone who's intentionally building a holistic and supportive community around herself, as opposed to someone with single-track vision to "find a man."

ANALYSIS OF EFFECTIVE PROFILE #4: ROBIN PLETT

About me
I love to hike, really even just to walk. Anywhere. Something about the body/mind meditation when I'm doing it alone, and it's my favorite way to visit with a friend. I appreciate wit and banter. I like words. You start the conversation, but you don't have to hold it up by yourself.

Aspirations
Getting my 1962 Shasta Airflyte on the road. Planning trips and play time for the upcoming year.

I could probably beat you at
Scrabble, bananagrams, word games in general

My golden rule
I have a couple. The only person's behavior I can control is my own. Everyone is on their own path. Happiness is a choice.

I value
People. I value friends and family, most people do, but I value people. I find them fascinating.

The last show I binged
Endeavour! So good. I also really enjoyed *The Last of Us* and *Ted Lasso*.

A perfect day
A long hard hike with a friend. A long hot shower. A meal prepared and enjoyed with family and friends.

The last time I was embarrassed
Happens all the time. I just fall on my sword and move on.

What I'm actually looking for
I am so new to this! I'm learning and exploring. For now, I'm enjoying meeting new people and seeing who is out there. Keeping it light.

The single most important thing in politics today
The threat that the conservative right poses to our democracy.

I'm Pro-Choice

Woman | Straight | Monogamous (single)

She/Her

5 ft 5 in | Average build | doesn't smoke, doesn't drink, vegan

---

What is the significance of the meanings or messages that can be read between the lines of the profile?

This profile is written declaratively and transparently so that reading between the lines isn't necessary. It features crystal-clear statements such as "pro-choice," and "doesn't smoke, doesn't drink, vegan." Political liberalism is foregrounded and presented neutrally, yet clearly as a nonnegotiable. Instead of "coding" language around this topic, this writer has chosen to state it definitively, knowing that this will help her weed out matches that won't work for her. (Note: You should also be aware that many men will simply lie about political orientation so as not to be "disqualified." For this reason, some women choose to not "give anything away" in their profiles so as not to bias/tip off men about how to interact with them. I think there are benefits/drawbacks to both signaling and masking political orientation, and I think to identify or not in this way has to be an individual call. In the case of this profile, it paid off for her.)

What is the significance of the figured world(s) suggested by the profile?

I can't identify a specific figured world, but notes toward "sincere, nature-loving, healthy person."

What is the significance of references to other texts/artifacts in the profile?

She has many allusions to political liberalism in her profile, as discussed above. Invoking "the threat that the conservative right poses to our democracy" reads not only as liberal but as "informed and able to articulate position clearly." References to three specific shows she loves give potential matches an idea of whether they might be compatible in an economical way—three is a good number of examples as it doesn't overwhelm the reader. Let me explain how this might work using *Ted Lasso*. For anyone who's watched the show, this is what loving *Ted Lasso* communicates: "I have a sense of humor, I'm fascinated by people's idiosyncrasies, and I value human kindness, decency, and strength of character. I can balance sincerity and emotion with humor and a bit of irreverence." But see how much faster it is to say "I loved *Ted Lasso*"? This is how nodding to other texts and artifacts works in dating profiles. If you read the profile holistically, everything she says supports the important elements of *Ted Lasso*: "Everyone is on their own path. Happiness is a choice. I value people. I find them fascinating." Crafting a cohesive picture of who you are by lining up what you say about yourself with what you like communicates an authentic and honest person who is trustworthy.

What is the significance of the discourse communities invoked in the profile?

Primary discourse communities: outdoors lover and political liberalism. Both say a lot about who this writer is and what's important to her.

What sort of activities are implied by the subtext or references in the profile?

Hiking and natural activities and social activism.

What identities are implied by the subtext, figured world(s), or references in the profile?

Sincere, kind, direct but not fighty, growing as a person, healthy, straight arrow. Specifically: See her response to the prompt "the last time I was embarrassed." That response conveys humility, lightheartedness, and resilience—all super appealing to most people.

What sort of relationships/connections are implied by the subtext, figured world(s), or references in the profile?

This writer is transparent that she's new at this and still finding her place in the dating world, which will appeal to the right matches because it's honest and open and nonexclusionary.

ANALYSIS OF EFFECTIVE PROFILE #5: JILL

> About me
> I'm a writer, and I love hiking, coffee shops, reading, small towns, lakes, and mountains. I haven't traveled much internationally but want to.
>
> My opening move questions
>
> 1. If you could immediately change one thing about America, what would it be?
> 2. If AI really does usher in the apocalypse, what skills or abilities do you have that might be helpful?

What is the significance of the meanings or messages that can be read between the lines of the profile?

This analysis is going to differ from the first four in that the writer intentionally stripped her profile of anything that could indicate political leaning. She is liberal but kept meeting conservative men who misrepresented themselves on the apps and ended up wasting her time. Her theory was that if the men she matched with had no clue where she stood, they would just be truthful because they wouldn't know what to lie about.

The result of this is that there's very little "reveal" here in terms of meanings or messages to be culled from between the lines. All we can really get is that she is literate and at least moderately active and able and willing to travel.

What is the significance of the figured world(s) suggested by the profile?

Perhaps we could identify a figured world of "Hallmark movie small-town writer," since these are common characters/themes in Hallmark movies. We can also probably speculate that this is a person who enjoys quieter activities as opposed to "big-city party" types of activities. The mention of "not traveled much internationally but want to" adds to this "small-town girl in a Hallmark movie" figured world; she's curious but not terribly worldly or experienced. In terms of significance of this figured world, there's nothing clearly political to discern, which was the profile writer's intention.

What is the significance of references to other texts/artifacts in the profile?

Another way in which this profile differs from the first four is that we are able to read the profile writer's "opening move" questions (on some apps these function simply as ice-breaker prompts; on others they require responses in order for the other person to initiate a match or messaging exchange).

In this case, the profile writer used these two questions to elicit specific information. The first, which asks about changing one thing in America, was intended to reveal political position (or apathy), and according to the profile writer, it did that almost every time. Men responded with answers such as "Get the Pledge of Allegiance back in the schools" (strong conservative) or "Initiate true tax reform that redistributes wealth and opportunity in this nation" (strong liberal) or, in one case, "I can't think of anything." She pressed him on this, asking if he truly believed America was perfect in 2025, and he stopped answering.

The second question was intended to "bait" men who couldn't resist making things immediately sexual so that they could be quickly blocked to burn. The profile writer reports that it worked even better (or worse, depending upon how you look at it!) than she expected. The first man who answered that question said, "I can def go down." She also got several good answers in which men identified actual skills that truly would be useful in an apocalypse, both practical and emotional.

What is the significance of the discourse communities invoked in the profile?

Again, intentionally deleted from this profile. In addition to being a writer, she is a teacher but decided to omit that part of her profession since it generally codes liberal.

What sort of activities are implied by the subtext or references in the profile?

Noted above in "Small town girl/Hallmark movie" discussion.

What identities are implied by the subtext, figured worlds, or references in the profile?

Purposefully neutral on most identity factors.

What sort of relationships/connections are implied by the subtext, figured worlds, or references in the profile?

Not much to go on here either, again intentionally.

A final note on this one: Rhetorically, this profile exemplifies a shift from **productive** to **receptive rhetoric**. The first four profiles we analyzed were intended to repel or attract men based on information shared. We call this productive rhetoric because the profile writers intentionally produced rhetorical effects to do certain things (scare off conservative men; make transparent some aspect of their lives that might not be a good fit for some men; convey a sense of humor; establish a concrete list of likes or dislikes in order to determine compatibility; demonstrate savvy and a lack of gullibility, and so forth). A careful application of productive rhetoric, as we've seen since the first four led to needles, can be highly effective and prevent wasted time.

This fifth profile writer decided to employ an almost completely receptive rhetorical mode. She crafted a neutral profile intended to draw in a large percentage of men (she lives in a somewhat rural area, so this makes sense), and she decided that she would do all the rhetorical work herself in vetting matches. There are benefits and drawbacks to this. She risked wasting a lot of time combing through profiles of men who wouldn't be a good fit, and she potentially risked missing out on good men who were looking for more concrete and revealing information in women's profiles. She was aware of this but decided to take a gamble, and it worked and led her to a needle.

DISCUSSION

As you read through the above analyses, you probably began to detect some commonalities across all of them, regardless of specific approach or tone. Here is how I would articulate those commonalities (e.g., *this is what's working*):

1. **CLARITY:** Set your boundaries (which you can do clearly, politely, and even appealingly; every single one of these successful profiles sets clear boundaries without defaulting to offensive tones). It's also worth noting here that in advance of (or perhaps instead of) overtly stating your boundaries, you need to be crystal clear on them with yourself. Most important, you have to trust yourself enough to act upon them. If one of your core boundaries is violated, you must be prepared to block to burn and move on without further deliberation.
2. **DIRECTNESS:** Don't try to appeal to everyone, and don't play the "cool girl" or the "pick-me girl." You are an adult woman who knows what you want, and it's perfectly fine for you to state that clearly; you can do it matter-of-factly and without coming across as either apologetic or argumentative.
3. **INTENTIONAL CRAFTING OF APPEALING TONE (IN A VARIETY OF WAYS):** Delete anger from your profile. (It's fine to *be* angry; there's a *lot* to be angry about. But it doesn't work in dating app profiles.) Ditto for an "instructive" tone. Having someone "lay down the law" or getting "lectured" at by a stranger from their dating app profile is off-putting to everyone of all genders; all women I know hate it, and I assume most datable men do as well. Do not tell men what to do or how to behave or how to treat you or who to be. Tell them who *you* are. Another consideration with tone: Allow yourself to write the way that you speak in terms of formality, vocabulary, using specific expressions, and so on. The more closely your dating app profile replicates your personality, the more effective it will be

in brokering a connection with someone who appreciates you for who you are. Definitely don't try to conform: too many dating app profiles already sound exactly alike—it's far more powerful to be the individual you actually are.
4. **SPECIFICITY AND CONCRETENESS:** Nix the clichés—no "living life to the fullest," no "love to laugh." Get specific and concrete.
5. **BREVITY:** Economy of language is super important in writing your dating app profile. For one thing, many apps limit the number of characters you get anyway. More important, though, it's presumptuous to go on and on about yourself with someone you don't even know yet. Share what's relevant and appropriate for a first introduction to someone, and save the rest so that you can let it unfold naturally over time if your connection turns into a relationship.

You can use the seven questions we used in the analyses above, perhaps with slight alterations to accommodate for context, for all kinds of analyses. CDA, practiced over time and in different applications, will become something you do naturally, intuitively, automatically, and accurately. It's a true superpower. Sinking into and thinking about words on this granular level will sharpen not only your analytical skills but your writing skills as well. In other words, doing so will make you both a better reader *and* a better writer of dating app profiles/messages (and of everything else!).

WHAT *NOT* TO DO IN YOUR DATING APP PROFILE

This section is not a formal study or a comprehensive list, but there are a few things I see women doing repeatedly that I'm certain are working against them, even and perhaps especially with men who would make good long-term partners.

The first mistake is being too directive or exclusive in your language. In current dating discourses (on social media, in popular books, from dating coaches, and so on), there is a lot of talk about transparency and about clearly stating needs and expectations. This messaging flies in the face of old-school dating tips about playing hard to get or appearing "fun" in order to get the guy.

Thankfully, we've mostly moved away from framing love as a game as well as from assuming that an exclusively traditional-male conception of relationships is so baffling that it must be superior, that it must be some crafty code deserving of being cracked and hacked and emulated by women. Many previous bestsellers have betrayed this assumption, especially the ones authored by men. The titles include phrases such as "Get the Guy: Learn Secrets of the Male Mind," "get the guy, keep him interested," "The 7 Irresistible Qualities Men Want in a Woman," and "Think Like a Man." Do you see what the message is in all this language? If you want to be partnered with a man, you have to abandon your own orientations and inclinations and figure men out, learn how they work, literally crawl inside their heads so that you can *be* like them, and then they will want you. Essentially, these guys are telling women that the entire key to healthy partnership is self-negation and the embodiment of maleness, or at least the performance of it. This thinking is akin to a problem that I (and many others) had with Sheryl Sandberg's book *Lean In*, which was groundbreaking and insightful and yet: There was something that didn't sit quite right. And then the *New York Times* ran an opinion piece titled "Enough Leaning In. Let's Tell Men to Lean Out," with the subtitle: "The assertiveness movement has taken a male-defined value system and sold it back to us as feminism." I remember how struck I was by that title because it was exactly true; she'd isolated the problem. We've seen this same effect with dating advice given by male authors and influencers; they weren't telling us how to pursue our own happiness or dreams—they were telling us how to appeal to *male* happiness and dreams. They were telling us how to succeed in a world defined entirely by men, as though that had to be the "right" world, the "best" world.

Today, there are a lot of really smart voices calling bullshit on that misogyny and talking directly to women about how to speak confidently for ourselves. These more progressive counselors, coaches, and influencers are telling women that it's not only okay to have feelings and needs and expectations, but that it's empowering to state them clearly and explicitly.

Within the context of an established relationship, I agree with all of this. However, in my work with women on the dating apps, I'm seeing a particular application of this messaging that I know for a fact is working against women.

Here's an example of what this looks like. This is a dating app profile text shared with me by an early member of the Burned Haystack Facebook group:

> I'm a successful, independent woman who is dating very intentionally; my time is valuable, and I expect clear date plans (not just coffee or drinks), punctuality, and respect. I need a partner who has excellent communication skills, who is always working toward self-improvement, and who has a secure attachment style.

There's nothing wrong here with what she *wants*; this is what a lot of people want. The language, though, is going to work against her, and I'll explain why in a minute. First, let's look at one more real-life example, this one of an early dating app messaging convo (in advance of the first date).

> **Man:** Would you want to meet up for coffee or a drink?
> **Woman:** Sure! When and where?
> **Man:** How about I drive to you for the first date? [They live an hour away from each other.]
> **Woman:** Sounds great! Just let me know when you've got everything set up.
> **Man:** Okay, but is there anywhere you like in your neighborhood?

> **Woman:** I am sure you'll figure something out! One of my expectations is that men engage in the emotional and actual labor of date planning! 😊

Okay, let's break this down. I get what she's doing, and it intersects with Rule 9 of Burned Haystack ("No men who can't plan the date," page 69). The point of that rule is to balance the labor in a way that women aren't doing *all* the planning *all* the time, which is a huge problem in hetero relationships. The woman in the messaging convo above, though, is misapplying that rule. Here's why:

This guy doesn't actually seem like he's trying to shift all the labor to her. For one thing, he asked her out clearly and then offered to do all the driving so that the date would be super convenient for her. At that point, simply asking her which places she likes in her own neighborhood is a great way to cocreate Date #1. I don't see that as a display of male laziness. His final message (picking up where we left off above), was this:

> **Man:** You know, on second thought, I'm not sure this is going to be a good match. I do wish you all the best, and I've enjoyed chatting with you!

I can't blame him for this, and I think this serves as a great example of how the "clearly state your needs and expectations" advice tends to go south when it's applied too early (and when it needs to be applied constantly, regardless of the relationship timeline; more on that below).

I think there are three primary reasons overstating your needs and expectations ends up a rhetorical "fail":

1. If you're on a dating app, either browsing matches or engaging in early messaging convos, then you don't know each other yet. You're strangers. If a man I'd just matched with on a dating app started immediately holding forth with me about his needs and expectations,

I would probably laugh so hard it might take me an extra second or two to block him. Language similar to the examples above is off-putting because it's inappropriate to demand things of strangers and because it suggests this whole relationship is going to be about *me, me, me.*

2. You're simply handing someone the playbook. Anyone can be on time for a few dates and pretend to be engaged in self-improvement and engrossed in pop psychology books. That's a matter of just straight-up following instructions. But you don't want to know if someone can follow instructions; you want to know that he *doesn't need* the instructions, that he's a mature and emotionally intelligent person in his own right. Giving over the playbook, in addition to facilitating a lot of wasted time, also renders the owner of the playbook highly vulnerable. If you're dealing with a skilled manipulator, he could keep the whole façade going long enough to do real damage.

3. This third problem with stating needs and expectations applies at *any* stage of a relationship, not just the earliest: If you find yourself saying "I need you to" or "I expect you to" *constantly*, then (a) you might have too many needs and expectations; or (b) it's probably already over, because they simply don't care—they would be doing those things already, or at least asking you about them so that you're not constantly having to issue these mandates. Yes, there's a learning curve in new relationships, that's normal. But if the person you're dating isn't initiating approximately 50 percent of the questions in that negotiation, then I don't have much hope for the future of the relationship. And that's their right; people have a right not to care what you need and not to meet your expectations. And you have a right—and a responsibility to yourself—to recognize that and to remove yourself.

And finally, to end this chapter, I want to share what I call the Seven Deadly Syn(drome)s of Dating App Profiles:

1. **INSTRUCTION SYNDROME:** These tend to be written in "second person" (using "you"), and I've never read one that sounded appealing. When men write these profiles, they usually sound like this: "You need to be equally comfortable in jeans or a cocktail dress," or "You need to be affectionate, fit, and open-minded." When women do, they tend to sound like this: "You need to be funny, financially secure, and respectful." None of this is appealing to anyone. To be clear: You *should* have criteria in mind, and you should honor whatever your criteria are. But there are two dangers associated with Instruction Syndrome: The first is that you simply turn people away. The second is that you're basically telling someone how to *present* to you, not how to *be*. People already are who they are. If someone is disrespectful, all you're doing is tipping him off about what you want so that he can pretend to be that thing (for a while; it'll break down fast, but not until after he's wasted your time). If he is already a respectful person, then there's no need to tell him to be respectful.

2. **PICTURE-FRAME PERSON SYNDROME:** You know how when you buy a picture frame there's a photograph of a person or a couple or a family in it that's so generic you wouldn't recognize them if they were in front of you two minutes later? They're pleasant-looking, sure, but not memorable or appealing in any kind of sustainable way. This is how that translates to dating app text: "I like sunsets, happiness, good food, and friendship." *Everyone* likes those things. It's fine to include a list of your likes, but it needs to be concrete and specific in order to do anything for you.

3. **HOSTILITY SYNDROME:** Self-explanatory, but a pervasive problem. With men it tends to allude to women who've cheated on or left them (as though you're being punished for someone else's sins before you even meet them). With women it tends to sound like "Don't even think about swiping right on me if you're [xyz]," or "I will not tolerate disrespect, sexual come-ons, or men who don't make at least $100K a year." Again, you can have and uphold all these criteria, but this kind of language doesn't belong in any dating profile.

4. **FANTASY GIRL SYNDROME:** Don't pretend to be a frivolous, down-for-anything, 100 percent uncomplaining fun sort of two-dimensional fairy-tale woman (unless you are, but I'm assuming you're not). It will attract men you don't want, it wastes everyone's time, and it's dishonest. Here's how it sounds in dating profiles: "Not looking for anything serious, just wanna have some fun," or "I'm easygoing, laid back, down for whatever, and fun to be with." Again, if these things are all true, then go ahead, but if they're not, then you're just misrepresenting yourself.

5. **PRESUMPTIVE PLANNING SYNDROME:** I see this a lot in profiles, and it sounds like this: "We'll go for walks in the sunset and then cap off the evening with dinner under the stars before falling into each other's arms." I think most people find this either off-putting or just boring.

6. **THIRD-PERSON SYNDROME:** You don't want your dating profile to sound disembodied or like a newspaper personals ad from 1983. Here's third-person syndrome: "Likes dining out and cats. Easy to laugh, easy to please, hard to ruffle." I'm not saying you can *never* use the third person—it can be an economical way to write, and a lot of the apps really limit your word allowance. However, you want to sound like you're introducing yourself as a human, not writing an ad pitch for a product.

7. **DISSERTATION SYNDROME:** Self-explanatory, and a lot of the apps have taken this decision out of people's hands. If you *are* using an app that gives you tons of space, I still recommend limiting your profile text to about two hundred words maximum. People don't like to encounter a long wall of text, and you don't want to give people the impression that dating you would be like attending a lecture. Save some of it for the actual dates.

SUCCESS STORY!

Hi Jennie!

I recently posted that I met a standout who was definitely a needle. The big question was whether or not he was "my" needle, and I am happy to say that he is!

I entered into dating life a bit broken still and completely naive; I had quite a difficult time of it, but early on, I stumbled on Burned Haystack and dove into the community and really started applying the principles and rules to my strategy (uh . . . actually, this was the start of having a strategy at all). Additionally, I set out to really conceptualize in great detail who I was looking for. What ended up happening was something I hear repeatedly from women who follow this dating method and have succeeded: I began to gain confidence. I began to heal. I adopted an abundance mindset. And most of all, I became very datable myself because I was secure in who I am and felt worthy of everything I desired. I *became* the level of partner I was looking for: calm, curious, discerning, *intentional*. I became empowered.

And one day a man came across my feed. His profile was not something that jumped out at me either way. It wasn't negative but it wasn't necessarily exciting to me. He wasn't normally my type, but hey, where did that get me so far, right? So I liked one of his comments (on Hinge) and he responded with something funny albeit a little awkward. But he recovered and after some (respectful and curious) small talk, he began to plan a date to meet. We met at a local, busy greenway/walking trail with my yellow Lab and talked a blue streak the whole way. We hit it off so much, we went for street tacos on a restaurant patio with my doggo and that was the beginning. It was so easy.

My "needle" is kind, emotionally intelligent (and available), financially stable, a good listener, and a feminist, and we are beyond compatible. We've discovered so many little similarities between us that it's gotten a little surreal a few times. He's my new best friend, and get this . . . he lives three miles from me, quite a rarity in Metro Atlanta! Thank you, Jennie, for changing the landscape of online dating for me and so many people. I look forward to seeing where all this takes you!

—Julie

9

BURNED HAYSTACK BEYOND THE APPS

Date-Me Docs, Speed Dating, and Meeting in the Wild (AKA "Haystack Hacks")

When I was a first-year teacher, I taught eleventh-grade English in a last-ditch public high school (an "alternative" school) in an impoverished area of the rural Midwest. It was a rough gig, and I was constantly in my principal's office railing against something or other—the System, the in-my-opinion-pathological rule structures of the System, the limitations on creativity imposed by the System, and on and on and on. Finally, one day when his patience with everything (including me) had been pushed to the limit, he looked me square in the eye and said, "Look, Jennie. You're right. We work in a shitty, shitty system. And we can spend all our time focusing on that and fighting it. We can churn so much energy into those battles that we'll end up sacrificing our students, our efficacy, and our dignity. *Or*, we can exploit this very shitty system that we're trapped in and wring out whatever little advantages we're able to wring out and try to do whatever good we can do."

I've never forgotten that. Idealism as a life philosophy is appealing, but pragmatism is more effective, and this conversation with my principal was my first true introduction to that fact. A pragmatic approach informs the Burned Haystack method, and this chapter will lean heavily into that orientation.

Here's the hard truth about the dating apps: They're horrific. They're commodified, exploitative, and ineffectual if you use them the way the app companies want you to. Dating apps are built upon misogyny, fake algorithms, and corporate greed. There's exactly one good thing about them, and it's inescapable: They're still where the people are. This is changing as people, especially women, become increasingly disillusioned and leave the apps, but I'm not convinced they're going away anytime soon, because what they *do* offer is too indispensable to modern life: accessibility and convenience.

So my very first suggestion for dating "beyond the apps" is to stay *on* the apps, but to exploit them right back: to capitalize on their offerings (lots of people) and then hijack the processes and mechanisms to get better results. The dating app algorithms don't work; nobody thinks they do. And the companies behind the dating apps don't care; they just want to hook people into the scrolling and swiping to ensure continual paid subscriptions and advertisements.

How do we effect this exploit-and-hijack plan? (*Doesn't it sound subversive??? Don't you love it already? I hope you do.*) Here's one idea, and it's one I can't take credit for, but I think it's brilliant.

AUDREY'S STORY

Please let me introduce you to Audrey. She's an undergraduate student in North Carolina who happens to be the cousin of one of my former "Rhetoric of Dating and Intimacy" students in Wisconsin. That's how we got connected.

Audrey, a climatology major, engineered her own unorthodox way of using the dating apps ("I'm a STEM girlie; I love experiments!"). She shared her method on YouTube, which I posted in the Burned Haystack group on Facebook, and we were *fascinated*. I've been in awe of her since. Audrey named her method DASE, which stands for Dating App Survey Experiment, and she ran it twice, at the end of 2023 and the beginning of 2024. She intended for each run to last twelve weeks, and the first one did; keep reading to find out what happened in the second run. She committed to run the experiment for one full year, until she found a partner, or until she got sick of dating—whichever came first.

This is how Audrey conducted her DASE:

1. She set up dating profiles on Tinder, Bumble, and Hinge.
2. She created a Google survey with eleven questions for prospective matches to answer.
3. She linked to the survey from her profile (not all apps enable active links, but people could still copy and paste; if anyone had trouble with that, Audrey just messaged them the link).
4. She kept *detailed* color-coded spreadsheets, pie charts, and notes about each person who completed her survey. ("Buckle up, because this is some incredible data," Audrey quips in the YouTube video that documents this journey—spoken like a true STEM major!) She also created slide deck presentations for each quarter's experiment. This helped her do an excellent job of assessing the responses she was getting and enabled her to share her process with friends and followers. (The Burned Haystack community on Facebook benefited from all this, and I also have to remark here that Audrey, who was twenty-one years old at the time, exhibited the patience of a *saint* explaining to women up to eighty years old what Google surveys are and how they work! DASE became a true public-service-and-scholarship project of its own, which is of course the perfect fit for the Burned Haystack community!)
5. She went out on dates with the very few men who "made it through," and she kept detailed notes of that as well. (This amounted to 5 out

of 155 survey takers in the first run of DASE, 6 out of 263 in the second run.)

As a young college student who'd had one previous relationship (which lasted three years and ended badly), Audrey realized that she "had never dated in the adult world." She first went into the apps somewhat uninformed and spent a "miserable six months having horrible experiences." She then gave up and deleted everything for a month. *(Does this sound familiar to anyone??? I had done the exact same thing myself pre–Burned Haystack, multiple times.)*

During this month, she learned about Burned Haystack from her cousin in my class in Green Bay. She began practicing the method because it "doesn't take any crap from men, which is very much what I was into at this point," but she also recognized that it was heavily geared toward trying to find "the one," and because of her age and circumstances she wasn't sure she wanted that right now. She recalled briefly matching with a man on Hinge who was using a survey. (Sidenote: This is not a common practice; I'd never even heard of it before I learned of what Audrey was doing.) She decided to combine his survey idea with some principles from Burned Haystack to customize her own dating method, which brought her to DASE.

Her goal for the first run of DASE was to learn more about her own preferences and what she might eventually want long term, and to meet, in the meantime, "not terrible people." Her ultimate goal was "meaningful connections," since her first six months on the apps had been characterized by interactions that were either completely surface level or overtly negative, and Audrey "didn't want to waste any more of my precious time when I could be studying for Calc 3."

Whatever the final outcome might be with any men she met, she did have a list of things she knew were important to her:

- Similar politics, values, and life plans (e.g., she knew she wanted a family someday).

- Physical attributes she found attractive and a healthy sexual dynamic.
- An organized profile; she wasn't interested in meeting any "swipe to find out" dudes.
- Effortful answers; she was looking for full sentences, responses to the actual question, and sophisticated sentence structures. "If you can't put it in a bio, I don't want you."
- Excellent grammar; this was very important to her.
- Willingness and enthusiasm to participate in the survey; Audrey considered this a sign of compatibility. She wrote the survey with humor and personality intentionally embedded throughout, and she knew that anyone who would be a good match for her would enjoy it and take it seriously.

Okay, let's go through Audrey's questions taken from her DASE Google survey, with comments from me following each one.

Dating App Survey

The most efficient way to not have small talk for four days and then ghost each other (this does not collect your email or any information beyond what you provide).

[This shows you how Audrey inserted humor, clarity, and sensitivity from the get-go. Rhetorically, this is supersmart; it shows any survey taker that they're now in the vicinity of someone who is funny, direct, and respectful of boundaries (assuring them the survey would not share their email).]

Name/age, pronouns, number/socials, what app are you from:

[Audrey said the pronoun question was telling, and I'm not surprised. The very mention of pronouns in the United States

right now sends a certain percentage of conservative men right around the bend, and what better way to weed them out?!]

What are you looking for? (be fr)
- ○ Hookup/fuckbuddy
- ○ Hanging out (friends)
- ○ Hanging out (intention of situationship/fwb/ eventual dating)
- ○ Casual dating
- ○ Serious dating
- ○ I just wanted to see the survey (lame)

[Even though hookups weren't Audrey's goal, she wanted to know how the people she might date were conducting themselves. (She also didn't automatically rule out hookups, since at this point she was leaving her own long-term goals open.)

There were many men who'd listed "long term" in their dating app bio but then picked "hookup" in her survey: This was an auto B2B for her because it conveyed dishonesty and disingenuousness.]

Hookups: answer all of the following: Have you been std tested? What is your ideal pre-hookup activity (or no activity at all)? Do you use birth control?

[The range of responses Audrey received to this one was wide: some were offensive, others were great. Some men answered with no defensiveness and immediately offered to take responsibility for birth control. This question was as much about judging character as it was about the actual content, and she said what she was looking for specifically were men who answered with "maturity, grace, and completeness."]

Please pick one of the following topics and elaborate: favorite childhood memory, biggest flex, a random paragraph in a language you know that isn't English, attempt to guess my whole life story, trauma dump about your ex, or your favorite comedian:

[This question was intended to show personality, passion, and humor, though many seemed not to understand the question. "Favorite comedian" was the most common response, and Audrey said she actually was introduced to a lot of great comedians via this question.]

Which of the following is a deal-breaker for you?
- ○ I enjoy eating weird food combinations, such as chocolate cake with BBQ sauce.
- ○ I've seen my favorite TV show eleven times over and I'm going to make you watch it too.
- ○ I have weird thumbs.
- ○ Other:

[The majority chose "Other."]

What is your ideal first date activity?
- ○ Art museum and Anguish: We harshly judge every piece of art and then buy a postcard
- ○ Bakery Brigade: We visit three or more doughnut places and rank them
- ○ Grocery Games: We each pick three random snacks
- ○ Movie Madness: We watch each other's favorite movies but we're allowed to talk the whole time to analyze them
- ○ Other:

[The majority went with "Movie Madness."]

In twelve words or less, why did you "like" me?

> *[This question was intended to reveal whether the survey takers had read Audrey's profile and if they were thoughtful. She reports, "Some did well, some talked about themselves, some left it blank, and a disturbing number answered 'big ol' titties.'"]*

In two sentences, tell me why I should go out with you.

> *[Many failed the "two sentences" rule. "I get it; we're not all good test takers," Audrey quips on her YouTube review.]*

What is your job/school? What do you do/study? What do you like about it?

> *[This question was written to gauge passion and motivation; Audrey was looking for positivity and drive and passion. She wanted people who had long-term plans that they could articulate.]*

Comments, questions, recipes?

> *[This one was fun: Some left recipes for something like "garlic butter," whose ingredients were garlic and butter; some complimented the survey; some wrote random weirdness ("I tried to get a vasectomy once"); one proposed marriage; one wanted her opinion on* Star Wars; *one just wrote "Meow!"]*

Do you vape? (I am allergic to vapes, not against them.)

> *[Audrey added this last question because someone kissed her after vaping. She also noted that she truly is "against vaping" but didn't want to prejudice people's answers.]*

RESULTS OF DASE I

PERSON 1: FROM BUMBLE. Went to her school. Twenty-one years old, six foot two, mustache and long hair, excellent grammar, honest and respectful answers, zero commenting on her body. Became FWB. She loves him as a friend and is happy she met him.

PERSON 2: FROM TINDER. Said six foot but lied; maybe five foot ten. Also had a mustache. He picked "casual dating" but attempted to unzip her pants the first (and only!) time they met. He lied on most of his answers. His politics were wrong for her. This was the worst experience of DASE I.

PERSON 3: FROM HINGE. Said casual dating and meant it. Nineteen years old with a mustache and long hair, six foot five. They went kayaking for their first date, which was lovely. Date two featured dinner and a drive and a kiss under the stars. They talked for a month, and then he ghosted. He kept the container from some cookies she made. "Just, why did you keep my container?" Audrey muses on YouTube. Overall, "It was a good experience—he was very nice. But there were lifestyle differences, and ghosting is annoying."

PERSON 4: FROM BUMBLE. This guy was twenty-five, the oldest one she met. Six foot one and had a mustache ("I'm realizing I have a type!" This is something she intentionally wanted to determine from her experiment). He picked "casual dating" on her survey but made it clear that kinky sex was a must for him (a red flag for Audrey). He was otherwise respectful, paid for everything, and took her to brunch on her birthday, but she felt uncomfortable with his sexual preferences. Also, he took a patriarchal attitude and mansplained climate change to her. "I was done," Audrey says. "We slow-ghosted each other. I hated the mansplaining politics thing."

PERSON 5: FROM BUMBLE. Twenty-one years old, six foot one, mustache and "very cool hair." He picked "hookup" but she gave him a shot because his answers and profile were "super intriguing"—she'd seen him many times on apps prior to this. It ended up being an awesome experience. They went out twice, the first date to a coffee shop where they hung out for nine hours straight. He paid. They talked a ton and had great conversations, and Audrey adored his personality. He was interested in DASE. For date two they went to his apartment and hung out for eight hours. Though it ultimately didn't last, Audrey characterizes her time with Person 5 as a "freaking amazing seventeen hours total—great personality, beautiful experience, really really nice." He was also the last person she dated in DASE I, and she was feeling burned out on dating at that point. She did miss Person 5 when it ended, though, and this made her realize that she wanted to do more "relationship things" and work more toward a long-term relationship rather than a series of first dates.

Overall results of DASE I

- She now knew her physical type (tall, mustache, cool hair).
- Bumble delivered better results for her than Tinder or Hinge.
- She enjoyed meeting and learning about new people.
- She had no regrets.
- Her faith that there are good people out there was restored.

She took a brief break to recharge and focus on school and then began DASE II.

RESULTS OF DASE II

Audrey met six people from this run of the experiment, and the first five dates included visiting a pregnant stingray, hanging out at Barnes and Noble for two hours ("Okay, but no vibe. Friendly at best. He was willing to spend two hours in a bookstore without even getting a kiss, but sorry, I don't owe anybody anything, nobody owes anybody anything."), and finally, one man who genuinely believed the earth is flat. "Obviously a deal-breaker."

Person 6 turned out to have taken the survey during DASE I, but they hadn't ended up meeting. Audrey had liked his answers, but he'd selected "hookup," and by that point in the experiment she wasn't into it. They matched again this time, though, and she decided to meet him. He was twenty-two years old, six feet tall, with a mustache and curly hair, and he had just graduated from her university with a degree in music, which was appealing to Audrey. They were already connected on Instagram. This time he did not pick hookup, and she noticed that he referred to all their get-togethers as "dates." He liked the survey and showed incredible communication skills right off the bat. He was super honest and able to talk about feelings, in addition to being kind and smart; they also had compatible senses of humor, similar values and future goals, and he cared about the environment. They both wanted kids.

They became exclusive after the third date, so Audrey ended DASE II. She ends her YouTube review of the experiment by saying, "I'm actually at his place right now making this video while he's at work. I'm so, so happy. I'm glad I stuck this out and found somebody. I learned a lot about what I wanted for my future, I'm definitely one hundred percent ready to be doing this, and I'm so happy to be able to say that I deleted the apps in under six months. It was rough for a while; it was feeling like it was taking too long. It's so hard to find people who are honest and up front about their values. I'm looking forward to finally putting my emotional and physical energy into a relationship and cultivating a future with this person instead of staring at survey data. And I'm so happy to say that I found a boyfriend! And he's awesome! And I really, really like him!"

Risks and Drawbacks to Audrey's Method

- Some additional work up front.
- Requires some level of technological savvy, though honestly not much.
- Two different modalities to navigate: the app itself plus the survey.
- Once you leave the app, you've lost the app's ability to screen anything out, such as profanity and unsolicited pics. However, as any woman who's spent a lot of time on the dating apps knows, men can be pretty creative about finding their way around filters or even extremely aggressive or toxic while remaining within them.
- No one to "report" bad behavior to.

Personally, I think the benefits outweigh the drawbacks here. Using a survey gives you way more control over the questions and removes the word limits imposed by the apps (and thus offers much more opportunity for rich engagement and a more complex data set of initial information).

In terms of privacy, you can choose not to reveal your own email that's attached to the survey, and you can always go back to the app for messaging, where you're protected by what the app has to offer there.

I believe the additional work in setup and technology management is certainly offset by the much smaller number of interactions you'll receive; most men simply won't take the time to complete the survey, which is actually a *great* haystack burner. You don't want to date a man who doesn't care enough to fill out an easy survey (that's mostly about himself!). I would rather spend more time reviewing fewer surveys than scrolling through hundreds of "Hey gorgeous" messages.

KARLA'S STORY

A few years ago my friend Karla Brooks, a busy marketing professional, got tired of being single, and she was ready to meet the love of her life but didn't want to use the apps. She posted this status on Facebook (you'll see my name here, but this was pre–Burned Haystack, so I was cheering her on simply as a friend at this time):

> FRIENDS OF FRIENDS I had an idea years ago when I read a book about finding love again. It said one third of new relationships began with an introduction from a friend, family member, or acquaintance. Well, I've been single for a bit and ready to meet the love of my life. With the encouragement of my friends Tami Sargin Wessley and Jennie Young, I put together my profile. Message me with your email address if you're interested in receiving my bio sheet and making introductions—or if you're just curious 😊

Karla
Seeking men 50–60 for a long-term relationship

About me

Relationship Status: Divorced

Children: Son and daughter-in-law

Education: Bachelor's degree, Business & Marketing

Body Type: Average

Height: 5'6"

Faith: Spiritual with Christian roots and open to all beliefs, although I'm not compatible with fundamentalists or atheists

Politics: Not a fan

Pets: A special kitty

Occupation: Sales and marketing career and a side gig best described as Life Is Good meets Tony Robbins

Assessments: ENFP; StrengthsFinder: Activator, Strategic, Woo, Maximizer, Command; Enneagram: Seven

In my own words

I'LL GIVE YOU COMPANIONSHIP, AFFECTION, AND YOUR OWN SPACE. Let's *do* things together. I love a Friday night fish fry, walking or bike riding in the park, and catching up at the end of a long day. I can also spend hours writing or creating something new and respect that you may want to play fantasy football or love fishing. So, let's share a life that allows us to have our own space, *and* we come together to create something even better as a couple.

ENGAGE WITH ME IN STIMULATING CONVERSATION AND LAUGHTER. Let's go deep in conversation; exploring all of life's possibilities. I also like to have fun, screw off, and laugh—stupid movies like *Office Space* are a great distraction. I'm an extrovert and can talk to anyone yet crave one-on-one time with that special someone with whom the problems of the day seem to fade away.

I'LL SUPPORT YOUR DREAMS AND EXPECT YOU'LL LISTEN TO MY STORIES AND GRAND VISIONS. I'm always full of ideas and act on them, which has led to some amazing adventures both close to home and around the world. I never have to make anything up because I've lived it, and now want to create something together with you!

ACCEPT ME THE WAY I AM, AS I ACCEPT YOU. You be you and I'll be me. We might not always agree, yet we can sort through our differences and respect each other's opinions. Here's how my son described me a few years ago.

Q: What makes this individual unique?
A: Very passionate about things she likes. Also, very caring and interested in what other people have to say.

Q: What do you enjoy about this individual?
A: Always finds a way to cheer me up even though I may be grumpy.

Q: What are the strong characteristics of this individual?
A: Always wants to get stuff done and completed.

Q: What are this individual's gifts and talents?
A: One talent is having a strong connection to children.

BE ENTHUSIASTIC AND SPONTANEOUS WITH ME. Grab your passport and let's take advantage of a last-minute travel deal or take an impromptu road trip to an eighties icon's concert in the city. It's always fun to invite family and friends over for a backyard barbecue and chill out around the campfire.

LET'S "SAVOR" THE PRESENT MOMENT TOGETHER. I'm a free spirit and happy on my own, yet prefer not to be alone long term. Together, we're lit up and inspired by one another, grateful for having found each other, and *never* take it for granted.

Karla also included a professional headshot and five other captioned pics of herself doing fun things that she enjoys; her photo set mirrored what most people would include on a dating app. The bio sheet was in PDF form—full color and very professionally formatted—like a brochure or advertising flyer.

A former colleague of Karla's asked for the bio sheet and shared it with a college friend of hers, whose name is Mark.

Here's Karla's post one year later:

> **UPDATE FRIENDS OF FRIENDS: TRUE STORY**
>
> Today is the one-year anniversary of meeting the love of my life. Last year I planned to spend the month of February in Italy. That trip got canceled and the day I was supposed to arrive in Florence, Italy, I was introduced to my man . . . and he's Italian. Next month we're heading to Florence together. This happened because of the post (attached) I put out last year after my trip was canceled asking Facebook friends for introductions.
>
> FRIENDS OF FRIENDS. So grateful for the introduction. Yes, I boldly put myself out there and there's no shame in asking. There's power in intention.

And two years later:

> **TODAY IS OUR TWO-YEAR ANNIVERSARY** and now Mark and I are married. It keeps getting better!

Did Karla get wildly lucky? Maybe, but the dating apps involve an element of luck too, as does meeting anyone anywhere. What Karla did was find a way to make social media replicate the way people generally found their partners generations ago—through family and friend connections.

I share Karla's story less as a directive blueprint and more as a way of saying, *We can get creative with this mission.* I can even see ways to combine what Audrey did and what Karla did: You could make a Google survey and write a social media post similar to Karla's and then just share the survey link.

These sound like outlier chances, and to be fair, they are, but aren't all shots at love outlier chances in some way? As people become increasingly disenchanted with dating apps, we're beginning to see these sorts of creative attempts to connect in the public sphere as well.

Jenny Gross and Livia Albeck-Ripka, in a 2023 *New York Times* article, describe the emergence of "Date-Me Docs": shareable online documents meant to expand one's dating pool. They write, "'Date-me docs' are both an emerging dating trend and a relic of a past era, more akin to newspaper personal ads than any bio posted on an algorithm-driven, swipe-based app." This movement skews young right now, probably because users must have some level of technological capability and also be comfortable sharing this kind of thing on the open internet (status quo for digital natives who grew up on Instagram, but perhaps not as comfortable for Gen X and older).

In form, Date-Me Docs range from plain-text documents with basic demographic info to polished résumé-type formats to highly professional multitabbed websites that are multimodal and interactive. There are various "hosts" of these documents, but there's currently not a well-known central clearinghouse or commercial site, which is part of what makes them less accessible and has compromised their popularity.

Even more old-school and grassroots is a brick wall in New York City that the *New York Post* referred to in a 2024 headline as the "Hottest Pick-Up Spot in Brooklyn." Here's how it works: Hopeful singles show up and, for a cost of twenty-five dollars, have two Polaroids taken. You take one pic home and stick the other on the brick wall, along with a card that contains only the most vital info—name, age, gender, and just a few words about who you are and the kind of partner you hope to meet. If you see someone's pic whom you'd like to connect with, you just tell one of the organizers and they handle making the first reach-out.

I love this idea. It feels as safe as or safer than online dating with far less risk from scammers and bots.

This type of grassroots, analog approach probably wouldn't work outside of population-dense major metro areas, but it does speak to people's collective app fatigue and willingness to try other methods of finding love. I think we're going to see more and more of these creative attempts in coming years, both through innovative dating app concepts and methods that depart from the apps. There's no way to know yet how the whole thing will shake out. I assume that the ways in which people seek and find love will just be a changing and evolving phenomenon for as long as human beings walk the earth; history suggests as much.

What I do feel confident about is that the analytical skills we use in Burned Haystack will benefit you regardless of how you seek connection and love.

SPEED DATING AND MEETING IN THE WILD

I'm conflating these two categories since speed dating replicates most features of meeting organically, only with more planning and a clearer purpose. The biggest challenge of speed dating is the "speed" part, and though it's a different modality than dating apps, I believe that time spent practicing Burned Haystack on the apps could be a huge boon in speed dating. One benefit of the apps, since they begin with written, not-happening-in-real-time communication, is that you can take the time to sit there and analyze, to connect people's words and images to rhetorical patterns, to solidify the intuition you felt immediately by identifying that bad gut feeling as "weaponized spirituality" or "conditional decency" or "disciplinary/directive." The other benefit of spending time on the apps is that it's such a concentration of horror and nonsense that you'll have plenty of material with which to practice. In speed dating, that time advantage is removed and the pressure is on—but if you've already honed your analytical skills and internalized the rhetorical patterns, you'll be a much sharper and savvier speed dater.

This is all true in every other "in the wild" scenario as well. When your coworker you've had a crush on starts gaslighting you with thought-terminating clichés in a meeting, you might want to rethink that attraction. When the cute guy who tends bar at the pub down the street keeps delivering real-life "tests and apologies," you might want to question what lies beneath his flirtatiousness. When the financial planner your aunt wants to set you up with seems to have a super-hard time scheduling the first date because he's "such a busy man," you may want to decide that *you're* too busy for *him*.

RULES TRANSLATION TO IRL

Not every single rule of Burned Haystack translates to real life, but most of them do. Let's go through the rules in chapter 4 again one by one and discuss how you can apply them for dating decisions beyond the apps.

Rule 1: The app is a tool; it's not a place to live, and it's not a game or somewhere to hang out and kill time.

The takeaway from this rule, translated to real life, is hard to abide by when you very badly want to find love, but I think it's important: Don't make dating and looking for love the sole focus of your life. That doesn't mean you need to give up on it, and I'm definitely not feeding you the "it'll come when you're not looking for it" cliché. I think the key here is to find a balance that feels healthy for you, a balance between looking for love and conducting your life with other activities and people and pursuits that bring you comfort and joy.

Rule 2: Focus on messaging over scrolling/swiping. Messaging is where you'll find the info you really need.

The closest translation here is to social media and other forms of self-representation versus organic, IRL interactions. The way someone presents on Instagram or Facebook or LinkedIn is a created artifact; it is not an authentic representation of who they actually are. It's a good starting place, just like a dating app; and also just like a dating app, you can use social media to quickly and effectively rule people *out*; but you don't want to use it to rule them *in*. For that, you need in-real-time, in-real-life interactions.

Rule 3: No notifications.

On the apps, the intention behind "no notifications" is that you prioritize your own life over the demands of a piece of technology and of strangers on the internet. In real life, this means that you don't sacrifice your own time and energy to be at men's beck and call, to be available for last-minute, hastily planned get-togethers. It means that when your coworker texts you at midnight because he's bored and wants some woman to off-load upon, you simply don't respond. It means that you do not need to drop your own work projects, plans with friends, or family obligations when a man you're attracted to suddenly has time to interact with you. In a patriarchy, women are socialized to be accommodating, and too frequently that is messaged (and then internalized) as "be available and flexible," which by extension means it's women who are expected to be responsive, to be present, to be "ready to drop everything," because that's what a good woman does. We need to correct this imbalance, and metaphorically "saying no to notifications" is one way to do that.

Rule 4: Block to burn.

This one absolutely translates, with very few alterations. Walk away, hang up, block him on your phone, change your locks, go to HR, call the police, whatever it takes (obviously there's a much wider spectrum of what "block to burn" means once we depart from the apps; you must employ it in a way that's appropriate to the situation). The important thing is that you use it. The fact that some guy spewing "sexual non sequiturs" is sitting across the table from you *does* make it harder and more uncomfortable to block to burn; I know that's true. Personally, I would *love* to see in-person block to burns normalized. At the point some guy on a first date violates a boundary, the woman across the table from him would say, "That's inappropriate, and now I'm turned off by you," and stand up and walk away. (And that's the effective language, by the way. Men who are boundary violators actually get off on transgressions and making women uncomfortable or scared; they hate it when women say it's a sexual turnoff.)

I realize that walking out of a date in process might feel too socially uncomfortable. In those cases, I would advise you to do whatever works for you. If the guy says something low-key and nonthreatening, maybe it's easiest to just finish the date and decline any future offers. If it's really bad, I would advise you to get up to use the restroom and simply walk right out the door (the back door, if there is one, and it should go without saying that you must have your own transportation or access to public transit on all first dates with strangers). Or make something up: I once faked a sudden realization that I was supposed to have online office hours with my students so that I could end a dinner date early. He wasn't doing anything toxic, unless you consider lecturing me about the nuanced details of structural engineering toxic, which I did. I do not feel bad about this.

Rule 5: No fighting with men.

This one also translates directly. In a real-life scenario, "no fighting" does not mean you need to avoid all conflict or refrain from engaging in a healthy intellectual debate; it means that you should not waste a second of your precious time explaining to a man why you don't love his sexual aggression or appreciate his insults. Simply be gone.

Rule 6: Don't be a pen pal.

Keeping women as pen pals is a form of breadcrumbing, and it happens in real life constantly as well. If the guy you want to date in real life interprets "being in a relationship" as texting you every four days and inviting you over late at night when he runs out of other things to do, it's time to block to burn.

Rule 7: Set your geography, but don't share your location.

There's not as direct a translation to real life here, but I would still caution you against moving too quickly with someone who's just in town for a wedding or a business meeting. People do meet in these ways and end up in legitimate relationships, but until you know that a legitimate relationship is also the goal of the other person, I would not recommend engaging romantically with people who are just passing through. This is not any kind of moral judgment; if you're not looking for a long-term monogamous relationship and your cousin just introduced you to a man she knows who seems like he'd be a lot of fun for one night, then by all means have at it, but since Burned Haystack operates on the premise that its practitioners are looking for long-term monogamy, I am framing these rule translations in keeping with that premise.

Rule 8: No "ludic looping" and no "attractions of deprivation."

The ludic loop danger does not loom beyond the apps, but the attractions of deprivation danger definitely does, and it's something you'll want to mindfully avoid. Refer back to page 66 for a refresher.

Rule 9: No men who can't plan the date.

This rule has a direct translation to real life as well. On an app, men will frequently say something like, "We should meet up in person!" and then just leave it at that—wait for you to handle all the logistics, all the emotional and actual labor it requires to plan a date. On an app, I would advise a woman to simply respond and say, "That sounds great!" and then go from there (if he drops it at that point, he was never serious). I think in real life it happens similarly: maybe you're leaving the office on a Friday evening and a coworker says, "We should hang out sometime!" If that's something you'd like to do, and if he seems like he's someone who shares your goals, I would say something similar to the above: "I'd like that!" and then say *nothing* else. You've now answered affirmatively to validate his suggestion, and the ball is back in his court. Any man worth dating will come back to you with an actual plan that involves a time, a place, and an activity (and the activity will not be "hanging out"). Just as in the app-based rule, this doesn't mean that he needs to "take charge" and plan every element of the date or that he needs to plan every date forever; it means that he needs to demonstrate early on that he is a person capable of modern partnership in the modern world, and that means sharing domestic and emotional labor.

Rule 10: Treat the process of online dating as a job search, not a take-out order.

This rule is probably the least translatable to real life because it refers to the fact that too many people tend to see the dating apps as human-ordering (or sex-ordering) devices. In real life, it always makes sense not to dive in too quickly, that there are both emotional and practical reasons for holding the initial interactions to a pace that's comfortable and natural and nonpressurizing.

• • •

There are an infinite number of ways to meet people. I teach with a couple who met because she moved to the United States from Spain for graduate school and sublet his apartment while he went to Germany to study. (They had never met in person; this was strictly a real estate situation.) She loved the apartment and asked if she could just stay after he came back, and he said yes. (He still had not met her in person.) They fell in love and have been together since. She told me she liked him before they met because he had a collection of records, books, and films that showed excellent taste; that was the pre–dating app version of a compelling profile. Now they're married with two adult children, and they cochair the Modern Languages Department at my university.

No matter how or whom you meet, though, your goals should remain the same: Take your time, read the signs, identify the patterns and the flags, keep your boundaries intact, and make decisions based upon character as much as chemistry. Regardless of the situation or modality, apply the rules of Burned Haystack however they are applicable so that you can identify the needles no matter what kind of haystack you encounter.

SUCCESS STORY!

I'm a forty-nine-year-old woman living in a large city on the West Coast; I got divorced seven years ago (after an eighteen-year-long relationship/marriage). During my first foray into dating at age forty-three, I subscribed to the "it's a numbers game" strategy (the exact opposite of Burned Haystack), going on thirty-plus dates over eight months (mostly disappointing). I eventually met someone in real life, but when that relationship broke up, I went back on the apps and found a partner relatively quickly. However, after three years I recognized it was unlikely to lead to the long-term open and communicative relationship I wanted, as he wasn't emotionally available (and I had also held back from asking for what I needed and wanted).

I took six months off dating to work on myself and redefine my relationship goals, went to therapy, listened to Jillian Turecki's podcast, and read *Attached, The Origins of You,* and *How to Not Die Alone* [see the Haystack Bookstack on pages 293–294].

I embarked on dating for the third time since getting divorced, and this time I used Burned Haystack. I was on Match and Hinge and was looking for men forty-five to fifty-nine, divorced/widowed, any children to be older than sixteen. I specifically wanted someone who had a similar sense of humor as mine—laughing together was important—as well as being financially solvent, enjoying all types of food, travel, and having a relationship with open and honest communication.

During the first eight weeks, I burned close to 350 guys. I had just two first dates during that time and the men were nice, but they didn't make me laugh. I found a freedom in block to burn, as previously I would have likely gone on multiple dates to "give them a chance."

As my three-month trial period on Match was about to finish, I connected with a guy, let's call him Connor. His first message referenced multiple points from my profile, and his message showed interest and was amusing. Due to our schedules we were unable to meet for two weeks, so we messaged back and forth every few days asking each other questions and sharing little pieces of information.

On the first date, conversation was incredibly easy; we met at six o'clock and closed the bar down at midnight and still had more to talk about. I was uncertain if there was a spark, but was following the advice from Logan Ury to try a second date and ask her "Post-Date Eight" questions. I also reread her "F**k the Spark" chapter.

On the second date, conversation flowed again, I shared that I was doing Burned Haystack and that he was one of the few men to get past the burning. I was also up front about the fact I planned to date casually for the summer before making any commitments (my previous pattern was to attach myself to the first person who seemed okay and then try to make it work).

We met up one to two times per week for the next six weeks. Eventually, Connor said he really liked me and asked if I was just looking for a friend, saying I was hard to read and he didn't know if I liked him in a romantic kind of way. I wasn't sure if there was sexual attraction there; however, from a personality, humor, and communication point of view, Connor was everything I had been looking for. I had taken him to a friend's birthday party and all my friends loved him. He wasn't my usual type physically, and I was unsure about how to proceed.

Eventually Connor, with the clear and open communication style I wanted, said that he would like us to try to have an exclusive relationship; he was worried he was starting to have deeper feelings for me and needed some kind of clarity on what we were doing. He wanted to kiss me for a start (I had been fairly standoffish), and wanted to make our relationship official.

I was still hung up on whether I was attracted to him; he was an attractive man but very different from my usual type. Some soul-searching and more therapy helped me to realize I was potentially self-sabotaging and nitpicking about incredibly minor things. He turned out to be an excellent kisser!

We have now been together for six months and have met each other's friends and family. This is the most myself I have ever been in a relationship. He pushes me to be more open and communicative (I realize you often want things that you don't have yourself!), the physical aspect of our relationship is excellent and has surprised me in a very positive way, we laugh together all the time, and will be spending Thanksgiving with his family and Christmas with mine.

—Anne

HUMOR BREAK

The photo to which this piece refers is an actual profile pic on Bumble, provided by a Burned Haystack community member. You may remember our discussion of Harold from the internalized misogyny section on page 196. He's the one who managed to include his penis in the frame of his Bumble profile, the photograph taken from the vantage point of a woman performing oral sex on him. While most men are less successful in beating the app filters, "pillow pics" images taken from this angle are common. This satire was originally published on my Substack featuring a (cropped!!!) version of Harold's actual profile pic.

An Open Letter to the Pillow Pics Men on Dating Apps

Dear Harold et al.,

First, you can thank me for scratching out your face, which you may assume I did to protect your identity but which I actually did to protect the internet from the contents of your nostrils.

Secondly, I know this profile isn't working for you, but I suspect you don't know why, so let me explain.

You seem to be offering up this debacle of an image as some kind of thirst trap. And it's not that we don't *get* the implications of this exact vantage point—we definitely *get* it. We just hate it.

In addition to our concerns about how icky you are, we have additional concerns about your critical thinking skills or appalling lack thereof.

You must be under the impression that what you're displaying here is appealing to women, and this suggests a fundamental misunderstanding of *How Things Work.*

Do you believe, Harold, that the dating apps are full of middle-aged women combing through Bumble in hopes of finding a lazy man who would like a blow job?

That is actually not difficult to find, Harold. That is like finding a golden retriever who would like a steak.

We are sorry to pick on you specifically, Harold, but you chose such a horrifying picture that you deserve it. We know you're not alone. We know you have thousands upon thousands of brothers on pillows—reclining upon the unwashed sheets of your mattresses on the floor.

We know you're going to stumble out of that mattress and wander into your dirty bathroom to take a mirror selfie and then hop on your sweet motorcycle to go catch a fish or shoot a deer or pose with women who would clearly never date you.

And then at the end of the day you'll fall back into this pose, take another snapshot from the perspective of your own sad penis, and curse the unfairness of it all and the women who are depriving you of what you feel you deserve.

You'll drift off to sleep comforted only by the constancy of your own unwavering and self-referential confidence, the one true and loyal companion of mediocre men on the dating apps.

Good night, Harold. We're going to report you.

10

BURNED HAYSTACK BEYOND DATING

Rhetoric in Real Life

When I started using and sharing this method, I did not envision it beyond dating. It wasn't until other women started pointing out the nondating ways in which they'd been using it that I realized I had been applying it in other ways in my own life as well. Every now and then, a group member would note that she was a therapist and using it in her practice, or someone would mention she volunteered in a domestic violence shelter and the staff was using it there, or someone in treatment herself would share that she was in an abuse-recovery support group and the facilitator was using it. This piqued my curiosity, and I queried the Facebook group about whether there were others using the Burned Haystack method clinically and/or therapeutically.

I was blown away by the responses, which were immediate and numerous and included comments such as "I'm a psychologist/therapist in the UK and use your methods in my own dating as well as with my clients. The theories behind Burned Haystack fit brilliantly with cognitive analytic therapy, which focuses on the roles and patterns that we get into in a relationship." I had never heard of cognitive analytic therapy; however, any practice or methodology grounded in analysis shares certain features, so I can see how there could be parallels. Other therapists mentioned working with patients recovering from PTSD. One woman reported that her clients are working to overcome "relational trauma [and] working on healthy connections [and] need to see that they *do* know what a red flag is and that they *can* respond in a way that honors who they are"; she said they were using the examples in the Facebook group to provide "tidbits of what respectful discourse is."

Others mentioned using Burned Haystack methodology in trauma-informed care frameworks, and specifically for those healing from narcissistic abuse. I believe many of the problematic rhetorical patterns we see in male profiles can in some way be attributed to narcissism—not necessarily because these men have a diagnosable personality disorder, but because in any patriarchal structure there's an inherent level of narcissism that tends to reside within whoever sits at the top of the hierarchy. In America, that's white men, and the more economic power and aesthetic power (physical attractiveness) they possess, the more the narcissism is reaffirmed. A commenter on Instagram calls this out more explicitly: "I'm learning so much from this group. It's fascinating how the patriarchy threads itself into so many rhetorical patterns. I so needed these lenses and now I see so much everywhere!"

People sometimes ask me what has been to me the biggest surprise about Burned Haystack. In addition to "everything," because I never could have foreseen a fraction of what this community has become, I usually end up talking about its other real-world applications. I do not think that dating is a fluffy or inconsequential endeavor; I think it's quite literally of life-and-death importance and should be viewed as such. That said, if the methodology can be recruited to help women stay safe and empowered in their families and workplaces, if it can be employed therapeutically to help women heal, then I see that as equally if not more important, and I want to consider these vital applications in my future work.

All these intersections—between dating and clinical practice, between academic rhetorical analysis and therapeutic intervention—are fascinating from an intellectual perspective, but they also require unpacking and articulation so that those new to Burned Haystack can begin to translate what they're learning about dating to other aspects of their lives. Many long-term Burned Haystack community members are now so fluent in applying the methodology that they have become experts at intuitively translating it and articulating the ways in which it can work across different domains.

For example, a group member who is a licensed mental health counselor and found her own needle using Burned Haystack now uses the methodology to train other counselors in professional practice. Another community member notes that she uses it with clients navigating workplace frictions, teaching people that the rhetorical patterns "give you a lot of info about [people] so you can stop wondering what's wrong with you, and you can B2B in your mind. You just set up that mental boundary in your mind and move on with your life . . . and maybe start looking for a new job."

Many women mentioned using Burned Haystack at work, noting that they used it for both clients and employees and are "so happy that women are setting these boundaries around *all types* of bad male behavior."

Some pointed out specific rhetorical patterns that emerge in the workplace: "I've worked in so many professional environments where the man's perspective of 'I'm the prize' is a position I feel required to support and even celebrate in order to maintain good standing professionally. It always feels like self-betrayal, and the worst part is it's a pattern I fall into constantly regardless of the context—of keeping the man happy and his 'prize' status intact, because I learned a long time ago that doing so equals safety."

One member garnered collective cheering from the Burned Haystack community when she shared, "I left my previous job last year after I B2B'd my toxic male boss who exhibited all the Burned

Haystack rhetorical patterns. Now my former boss is unemployed, and I am up for promotion in my new job after just six months! Burned Haystack really does apply to all aspects of life."

As the Facebook group continued to expand and evolve, I caught comments about extensions of the methodology into more avenues of life. One group member stated this quite poetically, noting that she has "found the Burned Haystack principles to be something that spreads, like ripples in a pond." I love this. I can't think of a better manifestation of Burned Haystack than for it to be sort of naturally absorbed and intuitively applied across multiple planes of existence.

One member noted that she "used the method with a handyman who tried to scam me recently. He sent me so many text messages after I told him I no longer needed his services. I had a comeback for every one of his BS, gaslighting, and manipulative messages, but I simply blocked him. Here's to saving our emotional energy for people who deserve it!" Another shared that she was "definitely applying it outside of dating. I just had an interaction yesterday at work with a man, not a coworker but a guest in our building. He clearly assumed he could treat me like his secretary. I clearly didn't act like his secretary."

Others drew connections to how the methodology could be recruited to help neurodivergent people navigate the world: "Jennie's work is so insightful for understanding everyday interactions. I am high-functioning autistic and struggle with human social communication . . . and critical discourse analysis is like a key that unlocks some of the subtle (and not so subtle) aspects of human communications." As a neurotypical person who has always analyzed language quite intuitively, I had never considered this benefit, but it makes tons of sense within the context of CDA; the whole theory of CDA is premised upon making the vague concrete, the sensed nameable, and the implied overt.

A comment that made my theoretical researcher's heart sing stated, "I've been combining Burned Haystack with the 'Let Them' theory, and it's really been working for me in all areas of my life as well!" This woman is doing the scholarly work of theorizing—of taking two conceptual frameworks and conflating them in a way that is useful to her. This is very literally how some academics articulate the theoretical foundations of their dissertations and/or their research initiatives.

That's been another huge surprise of the evolution of Burned Haystack: I was told, repeatedly, that "the internet has no attention span. Keep it simple and surface level if you want anyone to pay attention to you." Well . . . that's not the case in the Burned Haystack community. I don't know how to do anything simple and surface level, nor do I see the point. If it were that simple, then why would I even need to do all this? Instead, I've made multiple series of eight-minute-long Instagram reels in which I agonizingly deconstruct every word of men's profiles, explaining how those words intersect to form toxic rhetorical patterns and then offering real-life examples of each pattern. And women have been decidedly "here for it." Women have sensed all along that they're being duped and manipulated by men on dating apps; what Burned Haystack did was teach everyone how to decode that nonsense and, because it resonated intuitively, people paid attention. And once women realized there was a way to dismantle and defuse the toxic nonsense, they started doing it in all kinds of other ways beyond the apps.

Followers on all platforms make clear how intuitively this can be done once one has internalized its patterns. One woman went so far as to say, "Amen and hallelujah to the *Burned Haystack Lifestyle!!!* Jennie and this sisterhood not only snapped my vision clear on datable and undatable men, it helped me release this self-imposed guilt that I *should* be dating, when I really didn't feel compelled to wade through the effluent waters. *And* it helped me *fix* the additional unreciprocated labor I was constantly investing on behalf of my male work colleagues to compensate for their lesser effort and reliance on my 'help.' Nope! Burned Haystack cured me of the 'Razzle Dazzle' show to demonstrate my great value. Now I match energy and wait until it is returned. Cannot put in words how much *energy* this has returned to my life. And it is *my* life!"

There have been *many* mentions in the group of using Burned Haystack to overcome the lingering trauma of growing up with difficult fathers. One member says, "A lot of us have been subconsciously conditioned into tolerating toxic patterns by our fathers. We're breaking through transgenerational trauma collectively. It's exciting."

Some women have found peace through blocking to burn harmful relatives, while others have used the method to chart healthier patterns of interaction: One woman shared the following anecdote: "I've noticed that I dissect language from all the people around me, women included. Noticing patterns has allowed me to safely narrow my circle, find my needle, and find more peace. I too have a rough relationship with my father; the difference is that he recognized his own toxicity with his granddaughters and made some changes. This has allowed the two of us to start to develop a better understanding of one another. All of this to say: I am grateful for this group, and for the power of words, and of change."

Another "difficult father" story was shared by group member Becca, and the response was overwhelming (and overwhelmingly resonant and supportive):

> Dear Jennie,
>
> I just wanted to share that the Burned Haystack method has undoubtedly raised my standards for the type of behavior I will accept from men, and up until last week, I didn't realize how the method could be applied to my relationship with my father as well.
>
> It's obviously a bit different in that I did respond to accusations and toxicity that I wouldn't have responded to from a random man, because he's my father and I put a bit more effort into trying to preserve that relationship than I would from a man I'm interested (or not) in dating, but I found myself reflecting on our latest argument via the framework of your method. I won't bore you with the details, but my father and I have always had a difficult relationship.

He's a misogynist, racist, homophobic, transphobic bigot, quite honestly. If I could have chosen a different father, I would have. But, alas, that's out of my control. And after he spewed toxicity at me that I would *never* accept from another man, I asked myself why I'm accepting it from him, and the answer is familial ties. That's it. I've absolutely accepted that I'll never have a good relationship with him, and I've accepted the inevitability of not having a relationship with him at all.

And it's partially due to the way we discuss men's behavior in the group. And the (maybe) weird part about it is that I'm not sad. . . . Because my self-worth is so high that I no longer pine for and long for relationships with people (re: men) who treat me poorly. Why would I want a man like that in my life, sucking the energy right out of me with his negativity and toxicity? I've got no time for it anymore, and I feel empowered by the community you've created because I can see other women who are also absolutely done putting up with shit behavior and being "ruthless" (to quote them) with cutting off access to poorly behaved men.

I'm probably the most passionate feminist in my friend group, and have highly prioritized decentering men, so sometimes my friends don't see what I see because they're just not quite there yet. (But one of them is in the group! So I'm hoping she becomes as ruthless as me one day!)

All that word vomit to say that who knows, maybe without Burned Haystack I would have still been making excuses for the way my father behaves both toward the world and to me. Maybe I wouldn't be able to see the roots of his toxicity as straight-up misogyny and unacknowledged straight white male privilege. Maybe I'd still be trying to make the relationship work because he's my dad and that somehow gives him a pass that other men in my life don't get. Idk.

But I *can* say that I am where I am in my refusal to tolerate poor behavior from men in part because of you and your work.

> So *thank you* for helping me feel empowered and firm in my expectation of mutual respect and human decency, particularly from men. You're doin' the Lord's work, Jennie!!!!

Facebook group member Lauren Scylla shared how she used the method to finally end a toxic relationship with a male friend:

> Going to try to summarize ten years of toxic sludge, but thanks to your method I had very little emotional trigger (not none, but significantly better than the last time five years ago when it last arose) when I cut off communication with an old "friend."
>
> He's one of those men who claims to be my friend, but is just waiting around for me to sleep with him. I've completely cut off communication with him several times (literally blocking him via any method of communication) and like "whack-a-mole" he waits a few years and turns back up somehow. He just recently *flew across the country unannounced out of the blue*, using his teenager visiting a college as a cover (gross), to test the waters with me yet again, despite my shutting it down five years ago. I realize my engaging with him at all is at fault. I won't again. I swore that five years ago and sometimes have caved due to our long friendship/shared history.
>
> He's a funny, bantering friend who has a good heart. He's a liberal, master's degree, people-helping business creator, who lives in a liberal city, is on the board of a woman's health org—a "do-gooder." He's been in therapy his whole life, fancies himself a feminist and incapable of seeing where he's a Gen X testerical bro, and he's also *really effing toxic in intimate relationships with women*. I didn't rearrange my schedule at all but I met him for dinner after my professional and personal obligations were attended to.
>
> This time, armed with your rhetorical patterns and super crystal clear I didn't have romantic interest in this person unless a treasure trove of revelatory work had been done on his part (it

wasn't! not surprised), I was able to document the abusive/toxic rhetorical patterns he uses (and no, they haven't changed in five years since I last experienced them).

Within five hours he used:

My kids come first
I'm a very busy man
Test and apologize (on repeat)
Objectification
Fluent in sarcasm
Are you my mother?
Weaponized . . . therapy (not spirituality)
I'm the prize
I dare you!

and also just plain gaslighting, plausible deniability, insulting and lashing out at me that I didn't want a romantic relationship.

I 100 percent considered just ignoring him—end of story. The version of block to burn but in person/via text with someone I knew vs. a stranger on the app.

We've been friends for thirty years, so my sentimentality and values to treat someone with respect/not dismissively had me write a text to firmly say: We don't have the same values around communication; *I don't want to teach you about my values, which is not saying you aren't capable of learning on your own*; I am not interested in an intimate relationship with you.

A choice I was aware would possibly harm me to even engage, but because he's said before I just opt out without reason and "normal healthy relationships navigate this together," I elaborated why: I work really hard to not communicate in toxic ways and have spent fifteen years studying this issue and cannot abide the ways he communicates.

This brought about a toxic manchild temper tantrum lashing, laden with plausible deniability/gaslighting tsunami, as you would expect.

> My response: "I don't allow anyone in my life to be cruel like that to me and being friends for thirty years doesn't give you a pass to treat me like that."
>
> And now I'm done. I will say goodbye to fond memories/laughs and never engage again.
>
> The win here is that your information helped me *name* the abuse that I've experienced from him and others in my past. Last time I suffered it with him five years ago, I partially (although I knew better and my therapist affirmed it wasn't me) internalized that maybe I *had* communicated unskillfully. I now know I communicated kindly and skillfully then, and I did so again now.
>
> His tactics are to manipulate, not take no for an answer, and then insult people when he doesn't get what he wants.
>
> I can reserve my compassion for him from afar, without subjecting myself to the patterns again.
>
> Thank you!

This, too, resonated with many Burned Haystack community members. The "Oh my god, *me too*," comments poured forth.

Yet another subculture I admit I was somewhat ignorant of, having grown up in a secular family, was the subset of women recovering from religious abuse and weaponized spirituality (one of our rhetorical patterns; it's frequently employed on the apps by men, but also apparently a salient feature of far too many people's childhoods). The methodology can be used to decode and unravel that messaging as well (all forms of toxic manipulation share rhetorical features, which is why dating patterns are so similar to abusive-father patterns, which are so similar to exploitative indoctrination patterns).

An Instagram follower commented, in response to my "weaponized spirituality" rhetorical pattern reel, that she was "not sure if you realize how powerful the work you are doing is to all of us! I'm a PK (pastor's kid), was married to a deacon for twenty years, participated in purity culture and everything. This type of messaging is deeply rooted in most Christian churches, coming out you literally have to reprogram yourself. I've never felt so free and happy since my divorce. I love how your face tries to hide the thought of how much patriarchal bulls*** this is. I'll say it for you! I should start decoding your post in sistah girl terms."

Another follower on that same reel notes, "This is just the same old religious patriarchy telling women to submit and we're not buying it anymore," and a third comments, "Yes! Time we speak up and get out of these kinds of marriages (they will not change), then tell others how not to get into them. I'm still figuring out what a relationship looks like that isn't all of this, but I'll get there with the Burned Haystack method (which I randomly found, or it found me!)"

So there are all these potential applications beyond dating: recovering from/preventing trauma and abuse; finding empowerment at work; building healthier family dynamics; identifying spiritual violence. I don't know where it all goes from here, but in thinking about it I posted this note for the Facebook group recently:

> Good morning, Friends. I just scrolled through and read the comments on the last post from yesterday from the OP who used Burned Haystack to extract herself from a toxic relationship from her father.
>
> Reading all your comments was deeply affecting and heart-touching, and I'm so grateful for these words. I wanted to respond to a couple of specific things:
>
> Because of things so many of you have said over the past two years, and because of the ways people are now applying the methodology (i.e., in clinical counseling and in facilitating support groups for women escaping domestic violence), I've come to understand that not only is dating not the only use for this method, it's not the most important use for it.
>
> Your words from last night affirm that belief, and I just want you to know that I'm reading and listening and using your

> experiences to carve the best path forward for this community and this method. I don't know what it is yet, but I know two things:
>
> 1. The method is bigger than dating.
>
> 2. The community is bigger than the method.
>
> That's the most succinct way I can say it right now. I feel like these two points have to drive how we carry the Burned Haystack movement forward. I love this group, and the work we're doing here has become the central focus of my life. Thank you thank you thank you for being part of it.

And that's where I remain right now: The method is bigger than dating. The community is bigger than the method. A recent comment from a Facebook group member expresses this: "You are changing so many lives. This has become a feminist movement in no time and gaining momentum day by day. I came here to become more efficient at dating, and now I don't care about dating at all. Burned Haystack is so incredibly empowering that I now feel complete on my own, and for the time being really can't be bothered going on the apps. The community is amazing, and I check in here every single day and get a love and power boost from this group."

Ironically, not being overly invested in dating or giving it outsize importance in your life is the best way to position yourself for a healthy relationship (not that that should even remain a goal for anyone who's decided she's perfectly happy on her own!). Finding a method for dating that makes you feel so good you're not staking your happiness on dating is the best possible outcome no matter *what* the outcome is.

We see comments like this constantly—women crediting the community itself with providing love and support and empowerment and with changing their lives.

There is so much potential, so much opportunity, and so much work to do. Burned Haystack has become a social feminist movement in the most organic way possible. It happened because it's *necessary*. The patriarchy is not going to fix itself, because why would it? Nobody wants to relinquish power and privilege. And nobody wants to engage in labor that benefits others more than themselves.

But here's the thing: Women's collective voices, once they become united across hundreds of thousands of individuals, cannot be ignored.

A few weeks prior to the time of this writing, the Burned Haystack community (we call ourselves Haystacktivists when we do stuff like this) took to social media to call out a major dating app (that rhymes with "Fumble") for not honoring women's "blocks"—for continuing to match us with men whom we had clearly said no to and wanted to "burn." Our collective anger spread like wildfire (pun intended) across the internet, crossing over from social media to mainstream media, and culminated in me speaking on a D.C.-based morning radio show, talking about what our group was up to, all the way from my couch in Wisconsin. The dating app finally issued a statement that they would honor our blocks.

Do I think this happened because the app cares about its users? Of course not. This happened because women's collective voices and women's righteous anger became, at least for a few days, big enough and loud enough to affect their bottom line and make them listen. I have no respect for American capitalism as a governing structure of society, it's pure evil, but if we're stuck with it, we might as well exploit it to do good, even in small ways.

I've now turned this chapter from idealism back to pragmatism, which is very much in alignment with Burned Haystack methodology. We want meaningful and symbolic action, but we also want to *fix things*, lots of things, and as long as there are enough of us working together, we can.

As I've said a million times, and apparently I feel compelled to say it one more time at the end of this book: Toxic men are *not* going to be one of the things we fix. Men have to fix themselves or their improvement means nothing. However, if we keep refusing to engage with the nonsense and the abuse and the exploitation and the manipulation—whether it's coming from Random Dude on an app or your toxic boss or your gaslighting uncle or whoever—if enough of us refuse to engage then things have to change, because men want to keep dating, workplaces need to stay open, and your uncle needs someone to visit him in the nursing home (I'm being snarky now, obviously, but there's some truth in this as well).

So, I end this final chapter with these goals for myself, and I'm inviting everyone else to join:

1. Remain clear-eyed and aware of what's going on. See things as they are.
2. Keep doing the work we've been doing. This is no time to scale it back.
3. Be creative and open to what else we can do. I think there's a lot.

ABOUT THE SUCCESS STORIES

What do all the Burned Haystack Success Stories in the book have in common? I've boiled them down to these five consistent messages from women:

1. I blocked men ruthlessly.
2. I blocked any man who kicked off messaging with a comment about my appearance.
3. At the first hint or mention of anything sexual in early messaging, I blocked immediately without any response.
4. I became keenly attuned to "test and apologize" and other rhetorical patterns, and I blocked without a single word at the first sign of those patterns.
5. I decided whom to connect with based on words and behavior, not appearance or chemistry.

And finally, because the first Success Story shared in this book was a little unorthodox, I want to share one more that also has a bit of a twist. Burned Haystack community member Danielle Thomasson had written previously to tell me that she'd found a needle. And then a few months later she wrote again. Here are the words of her second email:

> Good morning, Jennie!
> I wanted to offer more data for you. The needle I found wasn't my needle. We made it about a year and decided we wanted different things. But I think an oft-missed important point about the needle mythology is that even though he wasn't my needle, I came out of the relationship feeling healthy. I was sad and I do miss him, but I'm not traumatized or questioning my self-worth. As we were breaking up, he even took a moment to make sure I knew that it wasn't because I was "too much" (my ongoing concern that I shared with him periodically as a result of being a strong, independent woman in a patriarchal society).
>
> I just wanted to tell you how much I continue to appreciate this method and how it has supported my growth as a stronger, complex, and whole woman.

I still consider Danielle's story a "success story" because it's a success *for her*. Finding a needle who turns into a life partner is a wonderful thing, and I'm delighted every time it happens. But Danielle's email hit me on a deeper note because I recognize that what she's saying is ultimately more important. Partners pass into and out of our lives for myriad reasons across the span of our lives. Sometimes those transitions are our own choices, sometimes they happen against our wishes, and sometimes the universe throws everyone involved a chaotic curveball that nobody could have anticipated. That's just life, and we're never going to control the whole show. The only constant in any of our lives is that we must always live with ourselves. If using Burned Haystack and being a member of the beautiful community it's become can render women healthier, stronger, and more whole *regardless* of partner status, then that's actually a more meaningful outcome than my original intentions.

I thought it was about finding good men, and that's frequently a happy by-product. But I get it now, in ways I never could have predicted: It's about *us*—it was always about us.

A LOVE LETTER FROM ME

To the Burned Haystack community,

And especially to those of you who've been here since the beginning—*WOW*, right? Who knew? I did not know. And neither did you, and that did not stop you from showing up to talk about feminist applied rhetoric—*on Facebook*—with strangers. But we didn't feel like strangers, did we? Even now, even as the number of members has skyrocketed, the Burned Haystack community still feels tight-knit to me; it feels like a group of sisters and friends. I realize that sounds cheesy.

I'm not a sentimental person, and I have no tolerance for false intimacy or fake friends (I've built this entire method on those facts about myself), so I can only believe that the reason this community feels so right and so real is because it is, in fact, right and real.

This book would not exist if it weren't for you. There would not have been a book to write because there would not have been a story to tell. There might have been "a method," yes, and it might have been mildly interesting to other rhetoricians to read about an unorthodox application of critical discourse analysis in some articles published in dusty journals somewhere, but that's not a story.

We are the story. We're a group of women initially unknown to one another who came together with a clear and sober recognition of a societal problem that was getting almost zero productive attention. Public scholarship has been a thing for a while: academics sharing their expertise beyond the walls of the academy, people accessing platforms such as Instagram and TikTok to learn from them. That's wonderful, but the Burned Haystack community has taken it up several notches.

It's one thing to seek new knowledge and be open to its implications. It's another thing altogether to dedicate the time and effort to learning something like critical discourse analysis—an obscure, graduate-level subdiscipline of academic rhetoric—so well that you can literally teach it to other people, to strangers. Many of you have been doing that for quite a while now. And it's not only brilliant to be able to do that—it's generous, and generative, and *kind*. It's an act not only of intelligence and patience and curiosity, but of love.

This is what I witness daily in the Burned Haystack community:

- Unfailing generosity—of spirit, of knowledge, of collaboration.
- *Lots* of laughter. This community is razor sharp intellectually, but it's also knee-slapping hilarious. I built humor into Burned Haystack intentionally; it then continued to happen organically because this group is so funny in the way that only a group of women who've been through some serious shit can be.
- Tenacity. When we found out "Fumble" was continuing to send men whom we'd blocked to our profiles, you didn't just get angry; you took it to social media right alongside me and didn't relent until we got a public apology from the dating app and ended up in *Rolling Stone*. That is super badass.

And finally: Thank you. Thank you for being willing to listen and talk about all this, thank you for being patient with me while I figured out how to be a social media person, thank you for helping me and guiding me when I needed help and guidance, and thank you for buying and reading this book. The Burned Haystack project is now a social-feminist movement that's taken on a life and an energy of its own. I'm so excited for all of us to see what happens next.

Love, Jennie

ACKNOWLEDGMENTS

First, an unquantifiable thank-you goes to the OG "needles," my parents, Jane and Stephen Young. Two kids in love with zero plan who proceeded to make the whole thing work—really well—for our entire family, beginning when they met at fourteen and sixteen years old. When I was a baby, the three of us lived in a dorm room because they were dorm directors in college. They tell me it was wonderful because there were babysitters everywhere. So thank you, also, to any random college students from the 1970s who babysat me as an infant. You know who you are (joking). In seriousness: These two people are the epitome of love, commitment, consistency, mutual respect, resilience, and a joint killer sense of humor that has carried all of us through a lot of stuff. There is no way to adequately say thank you, but *thank you*, Mom and Dad, for everything.

To my son, Gray. He has been behind this project and this mission from day one and served not only as emotional support but as editor, sounding board, Gen Z consultant, tech support, and humor writer. He also deserves special accolades for not once balking when his middle-aged, Midwestern mother decided to become a "dating influencer," which is undeniably "cringe." To his girlfriend, Alice, a brilliant young feminist who has similarly been an insightful resource, a satirical critic of systemic misogyny, and a supportive Burned Haystack community member.

To my brother, Brad, and his wife, Libby, and their children,

Cooper, Caitlyn, and Ella, for sharing time, friendship, and support over the years and for always making all of us laugh.

To my inner-circle girlfriends who have endured my dating disasters, been the nonconsensual recipients of texts that contain horrifying male profiles, heard *way* more than they (or anyone) has ever wanted to about Critical Discourse Analysis, and still want to be my besties.

To my friend and colleague Ryan Martin, who saw what I was doing and said, "You need to be sharing this on Instagram. If you put Reels of this stuff up, people will pay attention." He then patiently taught me how to make and post said Reels, and even though I only went along with the whole thing to appease him, it turned out he was right. He has also served as de facto social media consultant and strategist, having already experienced viral success in his own discipline, and because we work in the same office, he could not escape my constant questions and pleas for tech help. His generosity and patience are admirable.

To my feminist literature and rhetoric students at University of Wisconsin–Green Bay, who have been an evolving source of information, insight, sensitivity, humor, and creativity. I wish everyone reading this book could meet them. They have shared their frustrations, fears, experiences, and dreams in a way that's informed this book and the Burned Haystack mission in general.

To Noah Michelson, the director of HuffPost Personal, who saw the value in Burned Haystack before the social media numbers suggested it would turn into anything at all. Noah not only accepted an article about an obscure dating method created by a complete unknown that was grounded in esoteric academic theories, he saw the social-movement potential it contained and nudged me to articulate it in a way that informs the revolution to this day. I will be forever grateful.

To my agent, Alison Fargis of Stonesong Literary Agency, who reached out to me while I was still trying to summon the courage to start begging agents to talk to me. Alison "got it" immediately—she saw a future for Burned Haystack that I didn't at that point, and she expertly shepherded me through the entire journey, from our initial call during which we just "clicked" all the way through to the final book. Her vision and guidance have informed the method, the mission, and the book you are now holding in your hands.

To Cassie Jones, SVP/Executive Editor at William Morrow/HarperCollins. Alison and I had exactly one meeting with publishers for *Burn the Haystack,* because after talking with Cassie and her team, we canceled all the other meetings. That first Zoom—all women in the Zoom room who not only already knew the method but understood its necessity and its potential—felt to me like a meeting of minds established years prior. Every day going forward working with Cassie and everyone else at HarperCollins has been a dream, and I am not a writer who ever writes phrases such as "has been a dream." But it has been, every step of the way.

To editorial assistant Nicole Braun, who was tasked with the highly unpleasant job of transcribing men's dating app profiles, complete with typos, misspellings, shocking degrees of toxicity, and horrifying images. Apologies to Nicole for any lingering trauma she may have sustained, and may her labor help pave the way toward a future where fewer young women must encounter such nonsense.

To William Morrow publicist Tess Day, who met her needle using Burned Haystack well before we met. Our delightful first in-person meeting happened the week they got engaged!

To Melissa Esner and the marketing team at William Morrow, whose skills and creativity helped share the Burned Haystack message with a much larger audience and in much cooler ways than I would have ever imagined.

And obviously, to every single member of the Burned Haystack community. There are not enough words. Thank you.

APPENDIX
THE TOXIC RHETORICAL PATTERNS

Are You My Mother?, 94
At His Earliest Convenience, 145
Blue Ribbon for Bare Minimum, 142
Bombastic Syntax (or, Simply, BS), 106
Bored Toddler, 130
Conditional Decency, 129
Crazy-Making Communication, 119
Cult Leader Lingo, 116
Designing My AI Girlfriend, 113
Disciplinary/Directive, 96
Final Piece of the Puzzle, 148
Fluent in Sarcasm, 109
The Greek Tragedy of Funny Guys on the Apps, 123
I'm a Very Busy Man!, 95
I'm the Prize, 132
Let's Be Cuddle Bears, 112
Looking for a Tradwife, 114
MANic Pixie Dreamer, 101
Man's Planning, 102
My Kids Come First, 103
Ontology of Fitness Bros, 126

Opposite-Impossible Woman, 105
Peace Seekers, 138
Performative Sensitivity Gone Horribly Wrong, 143
Pet Namers, 125
Problematic Prompts, 150
Receptacles for Randomness, 120
Rescue Pups and Eeyores, 115
Sexual Non Sequitur, 141
Six Flags or Red Flags?, 109
Test and Apologize, 93
Weaponized Spirituality, 131
"Were You at the Capitol on January 6?," 107

HAYSTACK BOOKSTACK

Recommendations for Further Reading

Since the beginning of the Burned Haystack project, I've published a series of posts in the Facebook group that I call "Haystack Bookstack." Because it's been a popular series and because the texts listed either inform or embody the ethos of the method, I wanted to include it in this book as well.

The nonfiction books are ones I think anyone in the dating pool would benefit from reading.

The novels are mostly taken from the reading lists I use in the feminist literature courses I teach at the university (the course topic is "Gritty Chick Lit"). These books are not directly related to Burned Haystack or dating, but they've been well received and generated excellent discussions when I've recommended and reviewed them in the Facebook group.

NONFICTION

Bolick, Kate. *Spinster: Making a Life of One's Own.* Crown Publishing Group, 2015.

Gee, James Paul. *An Introduction to Discourse Analysis: Theory and Method,* 4th ed. Routledge, 2025.

Levine, Amir and Rachel Heller. *Attached: The New Science of Adult Attachment and How It Can Help You Find—and Keep—Love.* Tarcher/Perigee, 2010.

Turecki, Jillian. *It Begins with You: The 9 Hard Truths About Love that Will Change Your Life*. HarperOne, 2025.

Ury, Logan. *How to Not Die Alone: The Surprising Science That Will Help You Find Love*. Simon & Schuster, 2021.

FICTION

Alderman, Naomi. *The Power*. Little, Brown and Company, 2016.
Audrain, Ashley. *The Push*. Pamela Dorman Books, 2021.
Braithwaite, Oyinkan. *My Sister, the Serial Killer*. Doubleday, 2018.
Broder, Melissa. *Milk Fed*. Scribner, 2021.
———. *The Pisces*. Hogarth, 2018.
Emezi, Akwaeke. *Freshwater*. Grove Press, 2018.
———. *The Death of Vivek Oji*. Riverhead Books, 2020.
Erdrich, Louise. *The Mighty Red*. Harper, 2024.
———. *The Round House*. Harper, 2012.
Flynn, Gillian. *Gone Girl*. Ballantine Books, 2012.
Giddings, Megan. *The Women Could Fly*. Amistad, 2022.
Gunty, Tess. *The Rabbit Hutch*. Alfred A. Knopf, 2022.
Honeyman, Gail. *Eleanor Oliphant Is Completely Fine*. Pamela Dorman Books, 2017.
Ivey, Eowyn. *The Snow Child*. Reagan Arthur Books, 2012.
July, Miranda. *The First Bad Man*. Scribner, 2015.
Kukafka, Danya. *Notes on an Execution*. William Morrow, 2022.
Leilani, Raven. *Luster*. Farrar, Straus and Giroux, 2020.
Mandel, Emily St. John. *Station Eleven*. Alfred A. Knopf, 2014.
McKinney, Kelsey. *God Spare the Girls*. William Morrow, 2021.
Moshfegh, Ottessa. *My Year of Rest and Relaxation*. Penguin Books, 2018.
Penner, Sarah. *The Lost Apothecary*. Park Row Books, 2021.
Reid, Kiley. *Such a Fun Age*. G. P. Putnam's Sons, 2019.
Stein, Leigh. *Self Care*. Penguin Books, 2020.
Williams, Katie. *My Murder*. Riverhead Books, 2023.
Zevin, Gabrielle. *Young Jane Young*. Algonquin Books, 2017.

INDEX

The 5 Love Languages (Chapman), 56–57, 163–64

abuse
   applying the Burned Haystack rules to heal from, 269, 273–75
   boundary violations, 94
age
   Gen X women, 2–3
   senior dating app experiences (Sheila), 175–77
Albeck-Ripka, Livia, 254–55
All Things Considered (radio show), 67
amusement parks metaphor in dating profiles, 109–11
applied rhetoric, xv–xvi, 37
archetypes, 220
arguing with men, 64
arrogance, 124
Attached (Levine and Heller), 170
attachment theory, 170–71
attractions of deprivation, 67–69
attractions of inspiration, 68
Audrey (exploiting the dating apps), 240–50

behavior standards for men and women, 89, 171

Blink: The Power of Thinking Without Thinking (Gladwell), 19
block-to-burn (B2B) technique, 4, 52–54, 62–64, 200, 258–59, 280
boundary violations, 94
breadcrumbing, 92
Bumble, 52–54, 196–98, 247–48, 266–67, 280
the Burned Haystack community, 4–5, 278–80, 285–86
Burned Haystack dating method
   accessibility of, xvi–xvii, 272
   ageless nature of, 2–3
   applying the rules at work, 270–71
   applying the rules to heal from trauma or abuse, 268–70
   applying the rules to real-life dating situations, 257–61
   being pragmatic about the, 88–89, 153–54, 239–40
   block-to-burn (B2B) technique, 4, 52–54, 62–64, 200, 258–59, 280
   Frequently Asked Questions (FAQs), 77–89
   intuitive nature of, 173–74
   media coverage of, xi–xiii, 5
   origin story, xiii–xvii
   primary metaphor level, 49, 63

Burned Haystack dating method (*cont.*)
  rules, 59–74, 257–61
  shared tips and tricks, 3–4
  support for, 7–10, 268–72

Chapman, Gary, 56–57, 163–64
chemistry, 201
Clinton, Bill, 195
coaches, dating
  benefits of qualified, 174
  common phrases and advice, 165–72
  "fraudulent five" phrases used by, 162–65
  strategies of, 172–73
  toxic coach example, 160–61
coffee dates, 170
communication. *See also* language, decoding
  nonsense statements and responses, 119–20
  random pictures or messages, 120–22
  thought-terminating clichés, 165–66, 167, 195–96
the complexity of all human beings, 168–69
control, 118–19
critical discourse analysis (CDA)
  applications of, 34, 206
  compared to discourse analysis (DA), 40–41, 209
  of dating profiles, 49–51, 206, 207–13
  goal of, 43, 171, 208–09
  use by neurodivergent people, 271
"cuddle" ("snuggle") in dating profiles, 112
Cultish: The Language of Fanaticism (Montell), 118

"Date-Me Docs," 254–55
dates, planning, 69–72, 102–03, 170

dating apps
  Audrey's experiences exploiting, 240–50
  author's "bitchy profile," 27–29
  author's experiences with, xiii–xv, 6, 18–23, 74, 90–92, 135–37, 145–48, 192–93
  beating the algorithms, 59, 62–63, 240
  coded meanings of common terms, 25–26
  financial incentives for, 21, 33
  heuristics, 179–91
  Karla's experiences using Facebook instead of, 251–54
  messaging hierarchy graphic, 61
  old-school alternatives to, 254–56
  problematic prompts, 150–52
  proportion of men to women on, 58
  resuscitating dating app conversations, 88
  selecting, 64
  stimulus-response pattern of, 67–69
  talking to more than one man at a time, 201
  using block to burn (B2B), 4, 52–54, 62–64, 200, 280
  using filters, 63–64, 65–66, 84–85
Dating App Survey Experiment (DASE), 240–50
dating coaches. *See* coaches, dating
dating experience, 169
dating "in the wild," 256–57
dating profiles. *See* profiles, dating
Deeper Dating: How to Drop the Games of Seduction and Discover the Power of Intimacy (Page), 67–68
Devil Guy dating profile, 18–21
discourse
  compared to critical discourse analysis (CDA), 40–41
  defined, 40

discourse analysis (DA), 40, 209
discourse communities, 121, 210
discourse norms, 121–22, 126
discursive practices, 42
naturalized, 43
dopamine releases, 67

education and degree status, 84, 139
embodied knowledge ("gut reactions"), 46
embodied rhetoric, 36–37
emotions
  pathos, 38–39
  performative sensitivity, 143–45
Enneagram personality typing system, 164
ethos, 38–39

Fairclough, Norman, 41, 43
family issues, 273–75
fathers, difficult, 273–75
"feminine energy/masculine energy,"
  162–63
"figured worlds," 43–45, 209–10
filters, using, 63–64, 65–66, 84–85
"final piece of the puzzle" primary
  metaphor, 148–49
"flipping the script," 190–91
Frequently Asked Questions (FAQs)
  avoiding giving men communications
    tips, 87–88
  being pragmatic about the vetting
    process, 88–89
  dating app conversations, resuscitating,
    88
  expectations of men *vs.* women, 89
  judging potential dates, 78–79
  making the first move, 79–80
  "needle behavior" examples, 80–83
  seeking strictly long-term
    relationships, 84
  sexuality, 85–87
  strictness of the Burned Haystack
    dating method, 77–78
  using filters, 84–85
friendships, ending toxic male, 275–77

*The Game: Penetrating the Secret Society of
  Pickup Artists* (Strauss), 186
gaslighting, 20
Gavin (peace seeker) dating profile,
  138–41
Gee, James Paul, 43–44, 45–46, 209
gender issues
  behavior standards for men and women,
    89, 171
  datable men *vs.* datable woman,
    number of, 166–67
  "feminine energy/masculine energy,"
    162–63
  men as the sun/women as the moon
    primary metaphor, 149–50
  misogynist message of "thinking like a
    man," 167–68
  planning dates, 69–72
  proportion of men to women on dating
    apps, 58
  smile requests from men to women,
    41–42, 43
  the tradwife phenomenon, 114–15
  women helping women, 2, 5, 7
generational issues
  Gen X women, 2–3
  social reproduction, 43
geographical considerations, 63–64,
  65–66, 145–48, 260
Gladwell, Malcolm, 19
grace, granting, 165
Gross, Jenny, 254–55

Haydock, Leah, 17
Heller, Rachel, 170

heuristics
  defined, 179
  "flipping the script," 190–91
  "How else could this have been said?", 183–88
  "individual quirk" (IQ), 189–91
  thin-slicing, 19–23, 86, 188
  "translate it to real life," 179–83
hierarchical ranking, 162, 163
"high-value man/woman," 162
Hinge, 135–36, 247
"Hottest Pick-Up Spot in Brooklyn" (article), 255
How to Not Die Alone (Ury), 24–25
hubris, 124
humor
  Greek tragedy patterns, 123–25
  Harold's inappropriate Bumble profile picture, 196–98, 266–67
  Jolene, 204–05
  sarcasm, 109
  sex-positive women, 158–59
  as a tool, 16–17
hygiene, 142–43

"ideas" primary metaphor, 47–48
If Books Could Kill (podcast), 164
"I'm the prize" tactics, 132–38
Incel groups, 164, 186
"individual quirk" (IQ) heuristic, 189–91
internalized misogyny, 196–98
intuition, 20, 35, 79, 173–74, 191–94
investing in yourself, 201
IRL applications of the Burned Haystack rules, 257–61

Jeff (long-distance) dating profile, 145–48
Jill (successful dating profile), 225–28
Johnson, Mark, 46–48
Johnstone, Barbara, 42, 43

Karla (Facebook post instead of dating apps), 251–54
kids
  "my kids come first" rhetorical pattern, 103–05
"king/queen" labels, 163

Lakoff, George, 46–48
language, decoding. *See also* communication
  coded meanings of common terms, 25–26
  connotation *vs.* denotation, 112
  "cuddle" ("snuggle"), 112
  cult leader lingo, 116–19
  "feminine energy/masculine energy," 162–63
  glittering generalities, 194
  "high-value man/woman," 162
  "king/queen" labels, 163
  loaded words, 194–95
  "loyalty," 24–26
  "peace," 138–41, 168
  within profiles, 21–23
  semantics, lexicon, and syntax, 107
  "take a chance," 100
  text, subtext, and context, 23–24, 103–05
  thought-terminating clichés, 165–66, 167, 195–96
  weasel words, 195
language, figurative
  primary metaphors, 45–49, 149–50
language used by toxic dating coaches
  common phrases and advice, 165–72
  "fraudulent five" phrases, 162–65
Levine, Amir, 170
location. *See* geographical considerations
logos, 39

INDEX

love languages
    misinformed nature of, 163–64
    "physical touch" as a euphemism for sex, 151
    physical touch love language profile, 56–57
"love" primary metaphor, 48
"loyalty" in dating profiles, 24–26
ludic looping, 66–69

material rhetoric, 36–37, 211
meeting in real life, 64–65
mental illness, 119
Merzenich, Michael, 67
messaging within dating apps
    content, 60
    hierarchy graphic, 61
    notifications, 62
    responding in kind, 59–60
Metaphors We Live By (Lakoff and Johnson), 46
Michelle (successful dating profile), 219–22
misogyny
    internalized, 196–98
    "think like a man" directive, 167–68
monogamy, long-term, 11, 84
Montell, Amanda, 118

narcissism, 269
"needle behavior," 80–83
needs and expectations, 232–34
negging (negative feedback), 185–86
the neurodivergent community, 271
neurolinguistic programming (NLP), 164, 186–87

objectification, 85–86, 113–14

Page, Ken, 67–68
pathos, 38–39

pet names, 125–26
photos
    Harold's inappropriate Bumble profile picture, 196–98, 266–67
    ontology of fitness bros, 126–29
    random, 120–22
physical affection. *See* sexuality
pickup artist community (PUAs), 186
planning dates, 69–72, 102–03, 170
primary metaphors
    of the Burned Haystack dating method, 49, 63
    compared to semantic metaphors, 45
    "final piece of the puzzle" example, 148–49
    "ideas" example, 47–48
    identifying, 45–46, 48–49
    "love" example, 48
    men as the sun/women as the moon, 149–50
    "up is good" example, 46
productive rhetoric, 228
profiles, dating. *See also* successful dating profiles
    amusement parks metaphor in, 109–11
    analysis of successful, 209–13
    author's "bitchy profile," 27–29
    critical discourse analysis (CDA) examples, 49–51, 213–28
    Devil Guy, 18–21
    Gavin (peace seeker), 138–41
    glittering generalities, 194
    humorous male profile written by a woman, 17
    Jeff (long-distance), 145–48
    lackluster but not toxic profiles, 80–81
    loaded words, 194–95
    mistakes women make when writing their, 230–38

profiles, dating (*cont.*)
   physical touch love language profile, 56–57, 151
   political orientation, 223
   Seven Deadly Syn(dromes) of Dating App Profiles, 234–36
   stating your needs and expectations, 232–34
   weasel words, 195
pseudoscience, 163–64

qualitative *vs.* quantitative research, 207

Rachel (successful dating profile), 213–17
receptive rhetoric, 228
recommended resources, 293–94
red flags. *See* rhetorical patterns
red herrings, 165–66
religion
   granting grace, 165
   the tradwife phenomenon, 114–15
   weaponized spirituality, 131–32, 165, 277–78
rhetoric
   applied, xv–xvi, 37
   author's early career experiences with, 37–38
   defined, 35
   embodied, 36–37
   material, 36–37, 211
   productive, 228
   receptive, 228
   satire, 16
   semiotics, 36
   subcategories, 35–37
   visual, 35–36, 126–29
rhetorical appeals
   ethos, 38–39
   logos, 39
   pathos, 38–39

rhetorical patterns
   author's experiences and advice regarding, 90–91, 93, 153–54
   appendix of, 291–92
   are you my mother?, 94–95
   blue ribbon for bare minimum, 142–43
   bombastic syntax (BS), 106–07
   bored toddler, 130
   breadcrumbing, 92
   conditional decency, 129–30, 152
   crazy-making communication, 119–20
   cult leader lingo, 116–19
   designing my AI girlfriend, 113–14
   disciplinary/directive, 96–101, 134
   final piece of the puzzle, 148–50
   fluent in sarcasm, 109
   the Greek tragedy of funny guys on the apps, 123–25
   at his earliest convenience, 145–48
   I'm a very busy man!, 95–96
   I'm the prize, 132–38
   let's be cuddle bears, 112
   looking for a tradwife, 114–15
   MANic Pixie Dreamer, 101–02
   Man's Planning, 102–03
   my kids come first, 103–05
   ontology of fitness bros, 126–29
   opposite-impossible woman, 105–06
   peace seekers, 138–41, 168
   performative sensitivity gone horribly wrong, 143–45
   pet namers, 125–26
   problematic prompts, 150–52
   receptacles for randomness, 120–22
   rescue pups and Eeyores, 115–16
   sexual non sequitur, 141–42, 181
   Six Flags or red flags?, 109–11
   test and apologize, 93–94

weaponized spirituality, 131–32, 165, 277–78
"Were you at the Capitol on January 6?", 107–09
Robin Plett (successful dating profile), 222–25
romantic relationships
  chemistry, 201
  as the foundation of society, xii
  long-term monogamy, 11, 84
rules for using dating apps
  1—limiting time spent on dating apps, 59, 257
  2—messaging appropriately, 59–61, 257
  3—disabling notifications, 62, 258
  4—using block to burn (B2B), 62–64, 258–59
  5—refusing to argue with men, 64, 259
  6—meeting in real life, 64–65, 259
  7—setting your geography, 65–66, 260
  8—avoiding ludic looping and attractions of deprivation, 66–69, 260
  9—planning the date, 69–72, 260–61
  10—waiting for the right response, 73, 261

scams, 39–40
scarcity mindset, 165–66
Schüll, Natasha, 66–67
Scylla, Lauren, 275–77
semantics, lexicon, and syntax, 107
semiotics, 36
sensitivity, performative, 143–45
Seven Deadly Syn(dromes) of Dating App Profiles
  1—Instruction Syndrome, 235
  2—Picture-Frame Person Syndrome, 235
  3—Hostility Syndrome, 235
  4—Fantasy Girl Syndrome, 236
  5—Presumptive Planning Syndrome, 236
  6—Third-Person Syndrome, 236
  7—Dissertation Syndrome, 236
sexuality, 85–87, 105, 112, 141–42, 158–59, 180, 202
Shannon (successful dating profile), 217–19
social media. *See also* specific platforms
  author's initial private Facebook group, 1–4
  development of Burned Haystack groups, 4–5, 278–80, 285–86
  Karla (Facebook post instead of dating apps), 251–54
speed dating, 256
Strauss, Neil, 186
successful dating profiles. *See also* profiles, dating
  commonalities among, 229–30
  Jill, 225–28
  Michelle, 219–22
  Rachel, 213–17
  Robin Plett, 222–25
  Shannon, 217–19
success stories
  Bumble experiences with B2B (Lisa), 52–54
  coming out of a needle relationship (Danielle Thomasson), 283–84
  commonalities among, 283
  confidence gained from Burned Haystack principles (Julie), 237–38
  effectiveness of the Burned Haystack dating method (Kim), 30–31
  mother's story about her confident daughter, 14–15, 43
  no initial "spark" (Wendy), 155–56

success stories (*cont.*)
   putting yourself first (Michelle), 203
   questioning attraction (Anne), 263–65
   senior dating app experiences (Sheila), 175–77
   taking things slowly (Mangala Holland), 75–76
surveys. *See* Dating App Survey Experiment (DASE)

"take a chance" in dating profiles, 100
Ted Lasso (TV show), 224
text, subtext, and context, 23–24, 103–05
thin-slicing heuristic, 19–23, 86, 188
Thomasson, Danielle, 283–84
thought-terminating clichés, 165–66, 167, 195–96
timing
   waiting for the right response, 73
Tinder, 44–45, 67, 247
toxicity
   blaming women for male toxicity, 169–70
   ending toxic male friendships, 275–77
   language used by toxic dating coaches, 162–72

   requiring men to fix themselves, 280–81
   rhetorical patterning examples of, 96–101
   toxic dating coach example, 160–61
the tradwife phenomenon, 114–15
"translate it to real life" heuristic, 179–83
trust, 118
trusting your gut, 20, 35, 79, 173–74, 191–94
The Truth: An Uncomfortable Book About Relationships (Strauss), 186

"up is good" primary metaphor, 46
Ury, Logan, 24–25

visual rhetoric, 35–36, 126–29

"Want to Meet Decent Men Online? Write a Bitchy Profile" (article), 27–29
wealthy and high-status men, 135
weaponized spirituality, 131–32, 165, 277–78
White, Anwar, 180
working on yourself, 167
workplace issues, 270–71